Equatoria

No, the weight of all the museums in the world will never tip the
scales of knowledge as much as a single spark of human empathy.
—Aimé Césaire, *Discours sur le colonialisme*

So much would have to be said that has no possible interest:
insipid details, incidents of no significance. . . . And yet here I am,
all set to tell the story of my expeditions.
—Claude Lévi-Strauss, *Tristes tropiques*

Equa

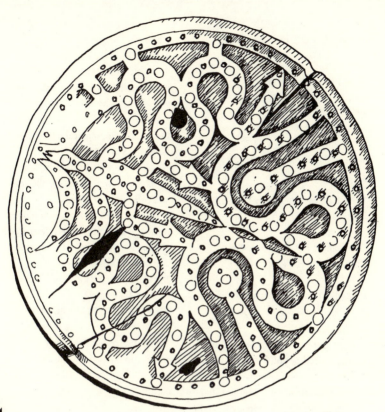

toria

RICHARD PRICE &

SALLY PRICE

with *sketches* by Sally Price

ROUTLEDGE New York · London

Published in 1992 by

Routledge
An imprint of Routledge,
Chapman and Hall, Inc.
29 West 35th Street
New York, NY 10001

Published in Great Britain by

Routledge
11 New Fetter Lane
London EC4P 4EE

Copyright © 1992 by Routledge,
Chapman and Hall, Inc.

Printed in the United States of America

Library of Congress Cataloging
in Publication Data
Price, Richard, 1941
Equatoria/Richard Price & Sally Price,
with sketches by Sally Price.
    p. cm.
Includes bibliographical references.
ISBN 0-415-90610-5 (cloth)
1. Maroons—Museums—Suriname.
2. Maroons—Antiquities—Collectors
and collecting—Suriname.
3. Maroons—History. 4. Ethnological
museums and collections—Suriname—
History. 5. Suriname—Description
and travel.
I. Price, Sally   II. Title
F2431.N3P72   1992
988.3′00496—dc20   91-46851
                    CIP
British Library cataloguing in
publication data also available

Richard and Sally Price have been learning and writing about Afro-Caribbean life for thirty years. RP's most recent books include *First-Time* and *Alabi's World*; SP's include *Co-wives and Calabashes* and *Primitive Art in Civilized Places*; together they have written *Afro-American Arts of the Suriname Rain Forest*, *Two Evenings in Saramaka*, and *Stedman's Surinam*. They have taught at Yale, Johns Hopkins, Minnesota, Stanford, Princeton, and the University of Paris, and now live in rural Martinique.

The authors wish to thank Roger Abrahams, Ken Bilby, Leah Price, Niko Price, Peter Redfield, Dan Rose, Gary Schwartz, and Baj Strobel for very helpful comments on a draft of this manuscript. Thanks also to Mimi Chicha for generous advice on the artwork.

All objects illustrated in this book (with the exception of the village founder's stool from Asisi) now form part of the permanent collection of the Musée Régional de Guyane, Cayenne. In those cases when the artist's name is not mentioned in text or caption, it was not known to the Maroons with whom we discussed the object's history.

What to Wear

Travel guides often include practical suggestions—a light wrap for cool tropical evenings, a sundress or two for the city, a pair of comfortable walking shoes, some sunblock. The voyager through Equatoria need be equipped with only a minimum of special baggage, a few printed souvenirs from previous forays into the region.

The English word *maroon* derives from Spanish *cimarrón*, a term with Arawakan [Native American] roots that by the early 1500s had come to be used in plantation colonies throughout the Americas to designate slaves who successfully escaped from captivity. . . . The Saramaka, today some 22,000 people, are one of six Maroon (or "Bush Negro") groups in Suriname and French Guiana [the others are the Ndjuka, the Matawai, the Paramaka, the Kwinti, and the Aluku]. Their ancestors were among those Africans sold into slavery in the late seventeenth and early eighteenth centuries to work Suriname's sugar plantations. They soon escaped into the dense rain forest . . . where for nearly one hundred years they fought a war of liberation [against the Dutch]. (R. Price, *Alabi's World* [1990], p. xiii)

In 1760 and 1762, the two largest groups of Maroons (the Ndjuka and the Saramaka) had won their independence by treaty. But the succeeding decade witnessed unexpected and lively hostilities involving newer maroon groups that lived just beyond the borders of the flourishing plantations. . . . About 1765, the thirty-five-year-old Boni, together with his senior, Aluku, became joint leaders of the largest of these new rebel groups. ("Editors' Introduction and Notes," in John Gabriel Stedman, *Narrative* [1790/1988], pp. xxi–xxii, 641–42)

The Boni [the French name for the present-day Alukus, a group of some 2000 Maroons] . . . remained practically free of any direct Western influence [into the late 1950s], and their way of life centered largely on subsistence. Unfortunately the situation has greatly changed since then. Arbitrarily declared French citizens in 1970, subject to compulsory schooling and social security, and receiving government allowances, the Boni have been profoundly disrupted. (Jean Hurault, "Analyse comparative" [1980], p. 123)

In July 1986 an armed struggle began between the national army of Suriname and a group of rebels, the "Jungle Commandos," under the leadership of Ronnie Brunswijk [a young Ndjuka Maroon]. The fighting began in eastern Suriname and the first victim of the civil war was a [Maroon] child shot dead by the army near the Maroni River. Soon the fighting spread. . . . (Thomas Polimé, "Berichten van de Vluchtelingen" [1988], p. 33)

With its economy shot and its politics in turmoil, Suriname now languishes. The military has not budged. . . . The country's insurgencies and drug trafficking continue, while nearly 10,000 Maroon refugees remain in French Guiana, uncertain of their status and fearful to repatriate until a relocation policy is defined and their safety guaranteed. What will happen next is unclear. (Gary Brana-Shute, "Suriname Tries Again" [1991], p. 35)

Equatoria

There are probably few areas of the world where one finds a more problematic fit between "ethnic identity" and "nationality" than in French Guiana. . . . To say that one is "French" often amounts to little more than a statement of legal status and economic rights in this overseas department, where a portion of the French citizenry speaks no French and has not the slightest idea where metropolitan France is. At the same time, no single ethnic group constitutes an overwhelming majority. . . . French Guiana has become a society thoroughly preoccupied with the question of identity.
  — Kenneth M. Bilby, *The Remaking of the Aluku* (1990), pp. 93–94

The debate [about development] is not exclusively economic. It concerns a cultural dimension as well, for development needs to be questioned if it means the loss of the soul. . . . Undergirding this approach to culture is the axiomatic of Identity.

  — Mimeographed paper handed out to participants at the 1989 Cayenne conference on "*Identité, Culture et Développement.*" (All translations in this book are our own, unless otherwise indicated.)

1

Mariposa House, the Stanford Humanities Center. A rambling Victorian structure in a setting of academic privilege. As visiting scholars, we were installed in commodious offices overlooking well-watered lawns, bright-eyed students, earnest professors, and the campus bike shop. On this spring morning, we'd extracted from the bank of mailboxes in the downstairs library a letter from French Guiana (Guyane), and were facing the fact that we'd have to make a decision.

Just a year earlier, at a conference in Cayenne probing the characteristically Guyanais package of "Identity, Culture, and Development," we had been approached by several persons of standing in the former French colony's ruling bourgeoisie who had been granted generous amounts of government money first to plan and then to put into execution a regional anthropology museum: the Musée de l'Homme Guyanais. (We recalled our involvement, as guest curators, with Santo Domingo's Museo del Hombre Dominicano in the early 1980s. "Is that," our colleague SWM had queried archly, "the Dominican Museum of Man or the Museum of Dominican Man?") Clearly, if we were going to get involved in this thing we'd need to argue for a new name, but that could come later. The question now at hand was whether we wanted to play any part in the new museum at all. Our earlier solution to ambivalent feelings had

3

been a decision simply not (yet) to say no; now we were being asked to commit ourselves to a definite yes. Would we agree to supervise the part of the museum that would be devoted to Maroon life and material culture?

The earliest statement we had seen about the projected museum (then being referred to as the Musée des Arts et Traditions Populaires de Guyane) was dated September 1988 and ran on for 102 pages. Amidst the outlines, diagrams, schedules, financial projections, sketches of the building and parking areas, endless texts of ordinances, decrees, and other fixtures of the legal armature upon which it rested, xeroxes of brochures from kindred projects already in place on French soil, and letters from officials in the Departments of Education and Culture, we found a statement of purpose. It expressed a tone of alarm.

The decision of the Conseil Régional *to initiate speedily* the realization of a Museum of Traditional and Popular Art emerges from an awareness of the CULTURAL STAKES.

At the present time Guyane is a land of profound economic, social, and cultural change. For this reason, traditional ways of life are faced, here as elsewhere, but perhaps faster here than in other places, with the prospect of something resembling deterioration or denaturation—in short, outright oblivion and disappearance.

The transformation of ways of life is without a single doubt disastrous, and it would be futile to deny its presence for virtually any of Guyane's ethnic groups. It is taking place before our very eyes. What saves it from disaster is the fact that this evolution is being understood, overcome, and taken in hand; it is the management of this evolution. In this sense, the knowledge and understanding of traditional cultures is not a backward-looking endeavor.

On the contrary, it allows modern man to situate himself in

[The Boni] live from the fruit of their hunting, fishing and locally-grown crops. Hammocks are their beds (and are extremely comfortable, once you find the right position). You will be won over by their kindness, their spontaneous hospitality, and their simple lifestyle. The visitor must, however, respect their customs and their privacy, never considering them like strange animals or firing away at them with cameras.

  — Air France in-flight magazine (1990)

Working with Island Carib materials, Peter Hulme has reflected on portrayals of "the encounter with the 'last survivors' of an 'almost extinct race'," quoting an early 20th-century account of "the Caribs of the old days, their fine physique, their heroism in battle and their engaging cannibalistic habits" who had degenerated into "distressingly dull and prosaic" Indians, "clad" in ill-fitting, "dilapidated" Western clothing. "The trope of the 'vanishing race' " turns out to be as resilient and long-lived as the races whose disappearance it forecasts; in the 18th century the Caribs were said to be "hastening to extinction"; a century later they were being "swept into oblivion"; in 1902 they were "almost at the last gasp" and a "dying remnant"; in 1938 they were pronounced "condemned to disappear"; in 1963, they were to "vanish within a couple of generations"; and in the 1980s they were "a doomed race lingering on the shores of extinction." Hulme observes that the OED definition of "to linger" is "to stay on or hang about in a place beyond the proper or usual time" and points out the irony of wars of extermination over a period of 300 years, followed by an expression of concern "for the preservation of the remnants of what has so successfully been decimated."

  — See Peter Hulme, "The Rhetoric of Description" (1990), pp. 43–45

his historical context, in his geographical region, in the context of his origins and his roots. It thus allows him to participate actively in evolution without cultural impoverishment, expanding his range of possibilities and thus his freedom.

Modern man has, for example, much to learn from the way in which Amerindians or Bonis have intimate knowledge of the forest. . . .

In Guyane, however, the situation is URGENT. The cultural goal of the museum demands rapid attention. The traditional cultures are in peril. Lifestyles, ways of speaking, languages, everyday technology, musical instruments etc., etc. . . . are on the road to oblivion. To meet the challenge, it is therefore necessary to *go fast* and *do everything at once*. (SEMAGU, "Programme Technique Détaillé," September 1988, pp. 5–7)

During our 1989 visit to Cayenne, there had been a meeting of potential participants in the project, which was clearly intended to be in many ways the model of a modern (yet in many ways traditional) ethnological museum. The director of the future museum was a well-born Guyanaise who had recently completed a doctorate in folklore at a French university and had just been put in charge of the Bureau du Patrimoine Ethnologique (BPE), the museum's institutional precursor. Pierre and Françoise Grenand, French anthropologists, were to supervise the Amerindian portion of the museum. There were also members of some of the ethnic groups to be represented (Carib Indians, Aluku Maroons, and Creoles, among others). And then us.

A diverse set of topics filled the agenda, but the one that now stuck in our minds concerned the *fiches*—mini-questionnaires that had been designed to receive all pertinent information about each object as it passed from native owner to ethnographic collector, and were intended ultimately for storage in the future museum's computers. There were, in fact, four types of *fiches*, dealing respectively

In addition to all the various documents and notes that the collector can assemble, there should be affixed to each object a *fiche descriptive*, filled out in two copies. For this, one will use a notebook known as *manifold*, or an ordinary block-pad (for which we recommend 13.5 cm. by 19.5 cm. as particularly convenient) between each two sheets of which one slips a sheet of carbon paper before writing, *in pencil*. One of these copies will be detached from the block-pad and sent by mail to the Musée Ethnographique; the other will remain in the collector's archives.

The descriptive *fiche* should be based on the following model:

At the top, to the left:

number corresponding to
the inventory list

1. Place of origin
2. Designation and name
3. Description
4. Complementary notes
5. Ethnic information
6. By whom and when the object was collected
7. Conditions of its expedition to the museum (to be filled out by the museum)
8. Iconographic references
9. Bibliography

> — *Instructions sommaires* (Mission Scientifique Dakar-Djibouti, 1931), pp. 23–24

with the collection of the object, the materials used to make the object, the place of the object in the society in question, and the aesthetic/stylistic characteristics of the object. Each was two pages long, typed out in multiple columns, with dotted lines upon which the information was to be entered. We translate just one:

Catalogue number; ethnic group (full name, abbreviation); place collected; name of the object in the native language (in the native alphabet, in phonetic symbols); etymology of that name; French translation of the name; names of the object (in Guyanais Creole, in Sranan-tongo, in Amazonian Portuguese, in other relevant languages); brief description of the object; dimensions; whether object was new or old (age, even if only an estimate); condition upon acquisition (good? bad? all parts present? list of parts missing); condition on arrival in the museum; whether acquisition was a gift (name and address of donor) or purchase (price in money or, if traded, nature of goods exchanged); iconographic documentation (drawing? sketch? diagram? photo? — of whole object? part of object? object under construction? object already completed? object in use? film of manufacture [complete process? incomplete process?], film of utilization [complete? incomplete?]); iconographic documentation of a similar object; place of that documentation; by whom object was collected (name, institutional affiliation); destination of the object; identity of the artisan (name, sex, age, address); place of manufacture; time taken for manufacture (all at once? in separate sessions?); tools employed; materials utilized: "Refer to specialized fiche for details"; one or multiple materials; which ones; animal, vegetable, or mineral; identity of the materials (names in vernacular language; names in French; scientific names — Use extra space if necessary); whether use of these materials is customary; provenance of the materials (and is this customary? unusual?); whether the artisan was the one to gather the materials; preparation of

I'd felt like a fool, but at least I'd learned something: it's not enough just to think about how you can execute your project; you've also got to think about your investment in the project and evaluate how that investment may be ordering the way you're looking at the things of this world. Faustus went all the way, but we're making deals with our devils too. I don't know if we ever really win, but I do know that if we're not aware of the compromises, the negotiations, of the battle to achieve some vision that goes beyond our own interests, we're sure to lose. Or betray.

— Bruce Jackson, "The Perfect Informant" (1990), pp. 411–12

the materials before they were employed; whether the preparation was done by the artisan; whether the object, when collected, was in use (regular use? occasional use?); who was using it; for what purpose.

This was the "Collection *Fiche*"; we had quickly concluded that it would be more than sufficient for our purposes, were we to join the team; the other three were even more discursive and less in line with Maroon conceptualizations of what material culture was all about. (But then, as Toni Morrison's *Beloved* reminds us, in a scene between a slave and a white man, "Definitions belong to the definers, not to the defined.") It seemed to us that this one *fiche* was, in itself, quite capable of structuring a half-hour interview for each purchase, thus testing whatever rapport we would have built with the individuals who were to provide the contents of this museum's storerooms. In presenting our point of view at that early meeting in Cayenne, we took pains not to question the use of the *fiches* for Amerindian objects, since the Grenands were intending to employ the full set. After some deliberation around the table, it was agreed that the Maroon objects would be documented only via the "Collection *Fiche*."

Now, back in Stanford, where the moist spring air wafted Eucalyptus scents through the open windows, we tried to envision ourselves as Ethnographic Collectors, against a lurid backdrop of the crumbling prison buildings of the French Guiana penal colony, the modernistic Ariane satellite-launching station, and the bustling outdoor markets where Parisians, Hmong, and Haitians are as much in evidence as Carib Indians, Suriname Maroons, and Brazilians from the Amazon. The question of whether to involve ourselves brought a rush of memories. The musty, dusty air of the storage rooms in the Musée de l'Homme. Seminars on slavery and resistance in New Haven, Baltimore, and Minneapolis. Lectures about calabash carving to feminists in San Juan. Images of Griaule in 1930s Africa via

The earliest European account of the Canarians was originally written by a Genoese merchant, Niccoloso da Recco, in 1341. . . . Two ships supplied by the King of Portugal and with men from Florence, Genoa, Catalonia and various parts of Spain on board set sail from Lisbon "carrying with them horses, arms, the machines of war, to destroy cities and castles" (Boccaccio 1960:202). . . . The houses [they found] "were made of dressed stone, marvelously constructed" (203). . . . [But] the doors were locked . . . so they knocked down the doors with stones. The Canarians, gathered at a distance, "angry at what they saw, let out great cries" (Ibid.) . . . There follows the extraordinary detail of a small temple "where there was no painting or ornament other than a stone statue of a naked man with a ball in his hand, his shame covered with branches of palm, according to the customs of the country. They stole the statue, loaded it on ship and took it to Lisbon" (204).

— Peter Hulme, "Tales of Distinction" (1990), pp. 32–33

6 September [1931]

[In a small structure housing sacred relics, we find] on the left, hanging from the ceiling amidst a bunch of calabashes, an unidentified bundle, covered with the feathers of different birds, and containing, thinks Griaule after palpating it, a mask. Irritated by the foot-dragging of the people [who have been making an annoying string of demands for a sacrificial offering], our decision is made quickly: Griaule picks up two flutes and slips them into his boots, we put things back in place, and we leave.

[Following further irritating discussion about the sacrificial offering,] Griaule then decrees . . . that since it's clear that people are making fun of us, it will be necessary for them, in recompense, to surrender the *Kono* to us in exchange for 10 francs, and that otherwise the police hiding (he claimed) in the truck would have to take the chief and the village dignitaries into custody and drive them to San, where they could explain their behavior to the Administration. Dreadful blackmail!

. . . The chief of the village is devastated. The chief of the *Kono* has announced that, under the circumstances, we would be allowed to carry off the fetish. . . . With a dramatic flourish, I give the [sacrificial] chicken back to the chief, and . . . we order the men to go inside and get the *Kono*. After they all refuse, we go in ourselves, wrap up the holy object in the tarpaulin, and emerge like thieves, as the agitated chief runs off and, some distance away, chases his wife and children [who are not allowed to lay eyes on this sacred object] into the house, beating them with a stick.

. . . The 10 francs are given to the chief and, amidst a general confusion,

Leiris, and then Leiris in Africa via Clifford. Classes on creolization for Antillian students at the University of Paris. Childhood visits to the Big Canoe on Central Park West. Once-vibrant Maroon textiles, bleached pale, hanging in the equatorial sun of the Suriname Museum. Paul Rabinow's Paris seminars on norms and forms in French colonial architecture. Our 1986 expulsion from Paramaribo, being driven across moonlit savannahs by military police and deposited at the border with French Guiana. An ongoing project on travel journalism, focused on books such as *Malaria Dreams*, *The Rainy Season*, and *Running the Amazon*. Hunting forays along a silent creek off the Suriname River in the 1960s. Martiniquans' stories about a "mad" local artist, exiled to the French Guiana penal colony in the 1930s. Lonely nights in the Dángogó menstrual hut. Talks on connoisseurship to the cultural elite of Santo Domingo.

Maroons, French colonialism, the Guianas, art and material culture, fieldwork, history and slavery, and museums — every aspect of this project evoked things we had cared and thought about over the previous twenty-five years. Perhaps participating in this strangely anachronistic enterprise would help us understand better what Anthropology had once been about — and what it might someday become. In sum, it seemed a risky endeavor; we would have to walk a very thin ethical and epistemological line.

The idea that had been proposed in Cayenne was for us to oversee the whole Maroon portion of the museum. In terms of collecting, we would be starting from scratch, responsible for the Central groups (notably the Saramaka) on our own, but enlisting the cooperation of two other anthropologists for the Eastern Maroons: Ken Bilby, who had just completed a rich and imaginative dissertation on the Aluku, and Diane Vernon, a long-time student of the Ndjuka. Both Ken and Diane were potentially interested; it was our own uncertainty about whether non-violent (non-hegemonic) collecting was an oxymoron that was holding us back. A long phone call to our friend and colleague Bill Sturtevant at the Smithsonian

we take off in haste like unusually powerful and daring bastards, bathed in a demonic glow. . . .

12 November

Yesterday people refused, horrified, our request for several rain-producing statuettes as well as a figure with raised arms that had been found in another sanctuary. If we took away these objects, it would be the life of their land that we would be taking away, explained a boy who . . . nearly wept at the idea of the misfortunes that our impious act would cause to happen. . . . Hearts of pirates: while saying an affectionate farewell to the elders. . . , we keep watch over the green umbrella that is ordinarily opened up in order to shade us but today is carefully tied shut with string. Swollen with a strange tumor that makes it resemble the beak of a pelican, it now holds the famous statuette with raised arms, which I myself stole from the base of the conical mound that serves as an altar for this statue and others like it. I first hid it under my shirt. . . . Then I put it in the umbrella . . . pretending that I was urinating in order to turn away people's attention. . . .

14 November

. . . the abductions continue. . . . Sanctuaries and trenches where old masks are thrown are systematically explored. . . .

15 November

. . . The sneakiness continues and I sometimes feel like breaking everything, or else just going back to Paris. But what would I do in Paris?

— Michel Leiris, *L'Afrique fantôme* (1981 [1934])

Griaule's writings are unusual in their sharp awareness of a structural power differential and a substratum of violence underlying all relations between whites and blacks in a colonial situation. For example, in *Les flambeurs d'hommes*, an adventure story Griaule called "an objective description of certain episodes from my first trip to Abyssinia" . . . he cooly notes a "given" of colonial life: the members of his caravan having shown themselves reluctant to attempt a tricky fording of the Nile, "there followed blows, given by the White Man and not returned; for a White is always a man of the government, and if you touch him complications ensue." . . . A revealing stylistic device is employed here, as elsewhere in Griaule's accounts of fieldwork . . . : a use of the passive voice and of generic terms for himself — "the White Man," "the European." . . . The story of the beatings suggests an automatic series of events to which all parties acquiesce. A European in Africa cannot, should not, avoid the pasts [parts?] reserved for him. Griaule does not think of eluding the privileges and constraints

allowed some of the relevant issues to be hashed out, but failed to produce a clear decision. We temporized by taking the time to write out, helter-skelter, our thoughts at that point in our deliberations, thinking particularly about next summer's proposed collecting expedition, slated to be among the Aluku:

Assuming (as seems probable) that there is only slight overlap between any "modern" Alukus who might, for political reasons, wish to contribute to the Aluku section of a Guyanais "national" museum, and those Alukus who own, say, "collectible" woodcarvings or textiles, then only some kind of cajoling (a combination of moral and financial suasion) could cause objects to change hands. So, unless all or many Alukus really believe that a museum would be to their personal or collective benefit (which we don't imagine they do believe—nor do we imagine that it's necessarily true, either), our collecting would have to be in some sense "violent." In which case we would become ameliorators, participants in some kind of as-benign-as-possible colonial (hegemonic) enterprise. Of course, we can always reflect upon it and write about it, and hope, through that act, to give it some other kind of value. In fact, the present act of writing (more precisely, composing on the computer) might constitute the beginnings of such an enterprise, since there is already an authorial voice, a tone of discourse, and an imagined potential audience taking shape.

This collecting project brings out our personal distaste for an approach to knowledge we've often encountered in France— at once Cartesian, normalizing, authoritarian, centralist, and bureaucratic. We're being invited to participate in an unproblematized, old-fashioned collecting project, not—at least not yet—being asked how we might conceptualize an exhibit about Maroons for a museum in Cayenne in the 1990s. The *fiches scientifiques* that we would have to complete "*soigneusement*" run strongly

of his ascribed status—a dream that obsesses, and to a degree paralyzes, Michel Leiris, his colleague of the Mission Dakar-Djibouti.

. . . one watches with discomfort and with growing anger as the ethnographer [Griaule] bullies, cajoles, and manipulates those whose resistance interferes with his inquiry, natives who do not wish to see their ancestral remains collected in the interests of a foreign science.

— James Clifford, *The Predicament of Culture* (1988), pp. 76, 78

It is often difficult to collect recent human skulls and bones, but every effort should be made to do so.

— Royal Anthropological Institute, *Notes and Queries* (1954 [1874]), p. 364

The move to repatriate Aboriginal relics from the UK is reviewed in the *Financial Times* (8/12/90). . . . In June the Pitt-Rivers Museum returned five skulls and a penis.

— *Anthropology Today* (February 1991), p. 22

A good proportion (perhaps as much as 25 per cent) of the Hunt Kwakiutl collection at the American Museum, and especially the oldest pieces, was gathered from caves. . . . Evidently it was the Kwakiutl practice to inter family heirlooms along with the deceased in isolated caves. . . . Also, as Hunt noted, digging in caves was cheaper than buying from the Indians.

— Ira Jacknis, "George Hunt, collector of Indian specimens" (1991), pp. 193, 202

A *New York Times* article (August 13, 1990) . . . describes Zuni cultural rights to control the use of their religious art. The Zuni have succeeded in reclaiming masks and images of gods from collections and museums in order to allow them to decay outdoors, returning to the earth, as they were intended to do.

During a 1989 NEH-funded summer institute in Austin, similar native traditions in Mexico were described as justification for questionable practices in the collection of Mexican masks. . . . The collector . . . pays poor village farmers. . . . The masks in the distant fields are "collected." When asked about the ethics of such collecting, the reply [from the collector] was, "Oh, they are just put out there to rot. No one places any value on them. If we didn't rescue them, these beautiful masks would simply be allowed to disintegrate."

"Why are they put out there?" I asked.

against our latter-day Boasian, cultural-relativist grain. We remember someone intoning, during that meeting in Cayenne, the factors that were to be used in determining an object's value: "The value of an object is determined by (a) the difficulty of its fabrication (b) its rareness and (c) its age." Meanwhile, our own judgment as ethnographers (who might be thought to know something of how value is conceptualized in the society being represented) is apparently irrelevant since the components of value are French-derived, non-negotiable "universals." The scientific conceptualization of the project depends on apriori categories; it "out-Murdocks Murdock"; there's an HRAF-type mentality behind it all.

This project raises the same doubts we had last year when we agreed to do a summary of Saramaka life for a multi-volume HRAF encyclopedia. For that, we'd been assigned thirty-six "universal" categories, which we were to address, in order, in a ten page essay. In spite of our intellectual distaste for the whole undertaking, we said yes—largely because saying no would have meant that Saramakas would be documented through a second-hand reading of things that we'd experienced firsthand.

Much the same reasoning lies behind our initial non-negative (but still far from positive) decision about the museum—to participate in a project we don't fully believe in because if we don't someone else will, and the representation of Alukus, Saramakas, and other Maroons (and therefore those peoples themselves) would ultimately be the poorer for it. Who gets enriched (culturally, politically, spiritually, materially) by a project like this, and who impoverished, is very much on our minds. A review in *African Arts* magazine of our 1980 book about Maroon art commented on "[the Prices'] ambivalence in bringing these arts to the attention of a wider and more voracious audience than ever before, as Griaule did with the Dogon" and concluded that "The Maroons' loss is indeed our gain." But this last remark, played in

He replied, "As part of some ceremony, they leave them there to rot."

"What will the farmer think when he returns to his ritual site and the mask isn't there?"

"Oh, he'll probably just think the mask rotted away to earth faster than usual."

"And the ritual objects in the caves?"

"Well, the cave I showed you a picture of . . . I just photographed the masks and other artifacts and left them there."

"Why?"

"Well, it was close to town and well known and people might have gotten upset."

— Betty Faust, "Collectors" (1991), p. 3

A biology teacher in a Parisian lycée gave her students cross-sections of a leek to observe under their microscopes and sketch in their lab books; the result, she explained, would resemble the diagram that she had drawn in red, white, and blue chalk on the black-board. When, however, the one foreigner in the class peered into her microscope, she saw shapes rather different from those on the board; she consulted her lab partner, who confirmed that she was right, but advised her to copy the drawing on the board if she wanted a decent grade. Having recently arrived from a progressive American school that preached methods over results, she rashly bucked the system by depicting what she (and her partner) saw. The teacher, without so much as a glance down the microscope in question, reprimanded her for having "failed to see correctly."

— After S. Price, *Primitive Art in Civilized Places* (1989), pp. 15–16

MISSION. — This is the third *mana* word [after "honor" and "destiny"]. You can deposit anything you like in it: schools, electricity, *Coca-Cola,* maintenance of law and order, police sweeps, death sentences, concentration camps, freedom, civilization, and the French "presence."

Example: "You must know, though, that France has a mission in Africa that she alone can carry out." (M. Pinay at the United Nations)

— Roland Barthes, "Grammaire africaine," *Mythologies* (1957), p. 157

reverse, reminds us that often in the museum business, " 'Our' gain is 'their' loss."

It seems likely to us that the museum will ultimately serve as a significant player on the local political scene and that the representation of the Aluku and other Maroons will have an effect on their collective well-being; if there is going to be a collection and a museum, one might reason, we should help make it as useful to the Maroons as possible. Whether or not this is particularly courageous logic in itself, it might—along with the idea of using the enterprise as a goad to thinking and writing about the issues involved—lend sufficient value to tip the scales in favor of saying a tentative yes.

Among the several aspects of the situation that feel uncomfortably constraining to us is our position as outsiders—doubly removed from the people who are running this show, since we're not Guyanais, nor even French. Being foreigners in a French-defined context is more of a marked category than being foreigners in, say, New York; it constitutes a significant ingredient in who we *are*. Our task, in part, would be to see how well we could act like French or French-educated participants in the project, contributing our insights in terms of ground rules established and sanctioned in the Hexagon. (While at the conference in Cayenne, Sally once strayed from the fold to argue that using the term l'*homme* to refer to human beings around the world is problematical, but she was quickly muzzled by a terse remark that, though she didn't seem to understand it, this usage represents only a convention, and carries no sexist connotations.) Without even raising any subversive thoughts about how we might best contribute to our pre-assigned space in this *mission scientifique*, we have been made to feel as though an obedient effort to conform to a strongly-Gallic definition of how to act, talk, present ourselves is inscribed in the implicit job description. We're frankly unsure of whether we're capable of being

Although he [the man of white race and Western culture] readily recognizes that a number of inventions come from the Chinese (in whom he does not deny a certain wisdom) and that jazz, for example, has been given to him by Blacks (whom he nevertheless insists on regarding as grown-up children), he imagines that in his own being he is self-made and he boasts of having been granted—through his birth, as it were, and by virtue of his very nature—a civilizing mission to fulfill.

— Michel Leiris, "Race et civilisation" (1969 [1951]), p. 11

A Monkey-College to Make Chimpanzees Human. Very Interesting Plan of French Government Scientists to Educate Generations of Primates in the Expectation That Some Day They May Talk and Act Like Human Beings.

FRENCH TO ESTABLISH MODEL VILLAGE, AND TRAINING GROUNDS FOR APES, IN WHICH CIVILISING EXPERIMENTS WILL BE TRIED OUT. Native Women as Nurses and Guides.

— Newspaper headlines from 1924, cited in Donna Haraway,
Primate Visions (1989), pp. 20–21

The artfulness of the ethnographic object is an art of excision, of detachment, an art of the excerpt. Where does the object begin and where does it end? This I see as an essentially surgical issue. Shall we exhibit the cup with the saucer, the tea, the cream and sugar, the spoon, the napkin and placemat, the table and chair, the rug? Where do we stop? Where do we make the cut?

Perhaps we should speak not of the ethnographic object but of the ethnographic fragment. Like the ruin, the ethnographic fragment is informed by a poetics of detachment.

— Barbara Kirshenblatt-Gimblett, "Objects of Ethnography"
(1991), p. 388

Museums betray, in the tiniest details of their morphology and organization, their true function, which is to reinforce for some the feeling of belonging and for others the feeling of being excluded.

— Pierre Bourdieu and Alain Darbel, *L'Amour de l'art* (1969),
p. 165

both culturally obedient and insightful at the same time; all we can imagine doing would be playing out our assigned role as best we could, observing as we went, and trying to pull together the implications of it all once we got back home to our own intellectual space.

And then there's our ever-increasing ambivalence about the mission of anthropological museums more generally. The questioning we, like many other anthropologists, have been engaged in during the past decade about the possibilities of writing/doing ethnography (mainly, Rich) and the implications of art collecting (mainly, Sally) problematize for us the very idea of displaying cultures/artifacts/art in a museological context. Our 1980 exhibit (Afro-American Arts from the Suriname Rain Forest) now seems very much a product of its historical moment. It was able, legitimately we think, to depict Saramakas (and other Maroons) through their art because at that time art was a central concern to those peoples, an integral part of their daily lives. But today, especially when we think of what we'd be likely to find in Aluku territory, such art — woodcarvings, embroidered textiles, carved calabashes — is apparently becoming a dead letter, an activity and a concern to a large extent left by the wayside in a stampede toward Western consumer culture. If in fact we're being asked to engage in the depiction of a culture-that-once-was, in a museum-as-pickle-bottle enterprise, we're less than enthusiastic. And in that case, mightn't the exhibits better be placed in Aluku territory, so that younger generations of Alukus could conjure with their own cultural past rather than displaying a salvaged Aluku culture for tourists in Cayenne, while real live Alukus go about the business of modern life? Or might there be enough redeeming value (in terms of the political and other rewards it would bring Maroons) in simply representing Alukus (and other Maroons) as dignified, cultured peoples to a Cayenne audience

Cultural activity . . . thus comes to carry political stakes. . . . The provisions of Plan VIII for the Overseas Departments and Territories (1980) underscore "the importance of cultural politics for social peace [law and order]."
— Edouard Glissant, *Le discours antillais* (1980), p. 169

For nearly three centuries, a broad and generous trend has been in operation which tends increasingly to bring together the inhabitants of equatorial France and those of the metropole.

. . . And, in the present circumstances, the spontaneously expressed wish of the Guyanais populations and their representatives takes on a special significance when we consider that it has been formulated at once as an homage paid to the genius of France and its civilizing enterprise, and as an act of faith in the permanence of France and of her prestigious destiny. . . .

Gentlemen, in a few minutes Guyane will no longer be an old colony. This former French province, a beacon beamed at this Latin American continent so close to us, will be a young *département*, honored to carry, through its vitality and dynamism, ever higher and ever farther the sublime radiance of the French genius.
— Robert Vignon, first Prefect of Guyane (and later mayor of the new *commune* of Maripasoula), in a speech pronounced upon the occasion of Guyane's becoming a French *département* in 1947; cited in Marie-José Jolivet, *La question créole* (1982), pp. 495–96

Guyane is the oldest daughter of Overseas France. Bound to France, she has received from it her sense of humanity, her culture, her tradition of liberalism, and her conception of values — in a word, her soul.
— Extract from the official presentation of Guyane in 1967; cited in Jolivet, *La question créole*, p. 496

American and European museums teach us that what is most important and intriguing about native cultures here and in distant lands is their outlandish and primitive qualities. The subject people are usually depicted as radically different from the majority of museum visitors, as exotic beings rather than people who might affect or be affected by the larger economic environments that we have shared.
— Edward Chappell, "Museums" (1989) p. 656

that sometimes sees them as only one step up from animals?

As we now understand it, the political project of the museum itself fits firmly within the French design for this former colony and the reaction of its now "decentralized" ruling groups. The museum permits the Conseil Régional to create a lavish, highly visible representation of Guyane both for its own local uses and as "a French show-window in America" (to borrow General de Gaulle's characterization) to be peered into by visiting *métropolitains* (politicians, tourists, missile experts from Europe) as well as by various stripes of "Americans," including Guyanais. Like the Conseil, the museum project is run by the Guyanais (Creole) bourgeoisie—"socialist" in the Mitterand style, fiercely non-independentist, heavily bureaucratized. It seems significant that the Amerindian sections are to be planned by the Grenands (the world's authorities on Guyanais Indians) and the Maroon sections by us—in both cases white outsiders to the local scene—while the decision-making power rests with the Creole (read: "real Guyanais") center. We (anthropologists and outsiders) are appropriate to deal with people defined by the Creole mainstream as exotic Others. The Creoles themselves will—in ways not yet clear to us and probably not to them either—eventually confront the problem of how to represent *themselves* (their problematic past, their much-sought-after "identity") in a museum context, how to deal, in public halls and glassed-in cases and printed labels, with what Bernard Chérubini has glossed as "the bulimic craving of the bourgeois Cayennais for a recognized identity."

A final question of interest to us: how will the contrast between the heroic, historical, mythologized Maroon (Boni, the freedom-fighter) and the modern Alukus (who, under tremendous assimilationist pressure, are moving onto the bottom rungs of the Guyanais social ladder) play itself out? Until the present, the local French-language press (e.g., the Antillian newspapers

The cultural identity of the proletariat of Cayenne could never be the same as that of the ruling class.

— Auxence Contout, *Langues et cultures guyanaises* (1987), p. 3

Permit me to insist on this point: the Creole population of Guyane has nothing but disdain for the tribal populations, about which it nevertheless knows almost nothing, and all of whom it lumps together under the name "Bosch" (that is, forest-dwellers). The Creoles are divided about how to handle them: whether to destroy them by assimilation or to exploit them economically, especially through tourism.

— Jean Hurault, *Français et Indiens en Guyane* (1972), p. 300

As of 1985 (that is, just before the arrival of 10,000 Maroon refugees from Suriname), the breakdown of Guyane's population of 100,000 — which had been but 55,000 a decade before — was roughly as follows: Guyanais Creoles 43%, Haitians 22%, Europeans 8%, Maroons 6%, Brazilians 6%, Antillian Creoles 5%, Amerindians 4%, Anglophone Caribbeans 3%, Chinese 1%, Hmong 1%, Suriname Creoles 1%.

— After Bernard Chérubini, *Cayenne* (1988), p. 13

France-Antilles and France-Guyane) use the English term "Bush-Negro" or Bosch to refer to present-day Maroons, while the word marron is reserved for heroic historical (and especially for mythological/literary) allusions. (And this is equally true of Parisian newspapers, even Libération.)

That evening, no closer to a firm decision, we attend a poetry reading by Derek Walcott, devoted to his recently published Arkansas Testament. Far from the two southern sites where so many of our thoughts and dreams dwell—the Saramaka villages strung out along the Suriname River, and our home in rural Martinique looking out on the Caribbean Sea—Rich jots down some Walcott-inspired poetic contrasts. (We spare the reader.)

In the bland suburban space of our rented Stanford faculty apartment, the idea of embarking on an Ethnographic Mission to the interior of the Guianas exerts that old romantic pull. It's partly the annual attack of pure Kerouacian go-fever ("Whenever spring comes to New York I can't stand the suggestions of the land that come blowing over the river from New Jersey and I've got to go"). And it's partly that Lévi-Stauss and Métraux may have been on to something when they spoke of American anthropology as "a social disease that attacks people unable to tolerate their own culture" (Métraux's diary entry for 13 March 1947). We decide to sleep on it and come to a decision in the morning.

Privileged convicts were permitted enough light to see the vampire bats.
— Hassoldt Davis, *The Jungle and the Damned* (1952): caption to
a photo

The author is to be congratulated for deliberately avoiding references to
Barthes, Bahktin, Derrida, Foucault, et al.
— Eric Hobsbawm, reviewing RP's *Alabi's World* in *The New York
Review of Books*, 6 December 1990, p. 47

"It's rare to find a co-authored art book where *both* the authors are blind!"
— An unidentified art historian, commenting on an earlier Price
and Price book (cited in *African Arts*, November 1981, p. 81)

St. Laurent du Maroni, the decaying heart of the French penal colony, facing the Suriname shore across the broad Maroni River. Rusting iron roofs. Heat rising in waves off the sandy streets. Due to last-minute screw-ups in our pre-arranged lodgings, we've been parked in a room at the Star Hotel (owned by Chinese refugees from Suriname). The rattling air conditioner, stuck in the "on" position, refrigerates the tropical air and competes with our attempts at conversation. Before today we knew the Star only as a hangout of Ronnie Brunswijk and his Jungle Commandos in the early days of the Suriname rebellion, when there were pictures of them in the papers, hanging over the balconies, draped with automatic weapons and a girl on each arm. Drawing the grimy curtains back from our floor-to-ceiling window, we can see past the old prison hospital to the high walls of the *Camp de la Transportation*. Now overgrown with forest vines, the old brick cells have been colonized by recent Haitian and Brazilian squatters whose colorful laundry flutters in the wind from the second story. We recall the persistent rumor, during our last trip to Guyane, that this ruin is to be refurbished some day as an exotic Club Med. We think of Foucault.

Held prisoner here by a promised call from Cayenne with new directives on our lodgings, we've been discussing our personal goals and have decided we'll write an account of our experiences. We'll call it "Collecting Guyane." After considering whether we should keep separate diaries, possibly secret from each other (an erotic game?), or a collective one, we've opted for the latter, on the grounds that our distinctive voices don't provide sufficient counterpoint on the subjects at hand to justify separation. We'll try to write as we go along, every day or two at least. But first, over the next twenty-four hours we're going to force ourselves to write a catch-up diary of the past few days on our trusty Toshiba based on handwritten notes. Divertimento for lap-top, four hands.

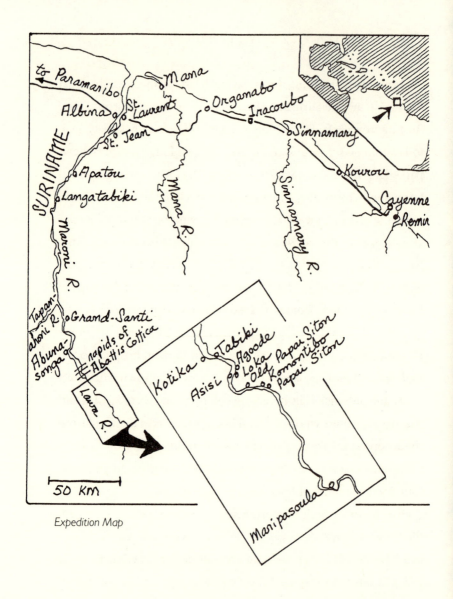

Expedition Map

It is the morning of the third day since we left Barbadoes, and for the first time since entering tropic waters all things seem changed. The atmosphere is heavy with strange mists; and the light of an orange-colored sun, immensely magnified by vapors, illuminates a greenish-yellow sea, — foul and opaque, as if stagnant. . . .

A fellow-traveler tells me, as we lean over the rail, that this same viscous, glaucous sea washes the great penal colony of Cayenne — which he visited.

Ken arrived in Martinique from the U.S. the night of the 18th (a week ago). We spent the next day at our house, making final preparations for the trip—deciding at the last minute to bring a computer and rushing around to find a portable surge suppressor somewhere on the island, trying to close up the house properly in spite of strikes that cut off water and made electricity an intermittent luxury. A good moment to be emptying the refrigerator.

We went over the general itinerary: a few days in Cayenne, a week or two just across the river from Suriname in St. Laurent (where many Maroons live, including nearly 10,000 Ndjuka refugees from the civil war in Suriname), on up the Maroni River to Maripasoula and the heartland of the Aluku Maroons for a few weeks of collecting, then back downriver to St. Laurent, ending with a brief stay in Cayenne. We discussed various moral and epistemological aspects of The Mission, and this continued over the next days. Ken argued that if an Aluku collection were to be made, the three of us were equipped to do a better job than anyone else, so we should probably just get on with the job. Our own participation, he said, was an important consideration in his deciding to join the project.

We talked both *à trois* and (mostly) *à deux* several times a day about the more general questions. Are we wasting weeks or months of our lives in the interests of another trivial show-and-tell of cultural differences? Ultimately reinforcing stereotypes for local political ends? Surrendering our scholarly authority? Replaying the most acquisitive, hegemonic aspects of the Dakar-Djibouti mission? Lots of questions: no reassuring answers.

On the morning of the 20th, after a smooth flight high above the turquoise of the Caribbean, we glide down over the soiled, mud-brown sea that fringes the South American mainland, and into Rochambeau, the international airport of Guyane. No hassles at immigration or customs. As the airport emptied, we stood idly on the curb, surrounded by our bags, for a full hour before Madame

When a convict dies there, the corpse, sewn up in a sack, is borne to the water, and a great bell tolled. Then the still surface is suddenly broken by fins innumerable, — black fins of sharks rushing to the hideous funeral: they know the Bell!

> — Lafcadio Hearn, *Two Years in the French West Indies* (1923 [orig. 1890]), pp. 64–65

We knew that this darkness was Cayenne, because the car had stopped. . . . The room, the swaying, punctured ghost of mosquito-netting, the moon through a latticed window, the chamber-pot, the mildew, the frowsty candle, the twitter of bats echoing beneath the roof of corrugated iron, the sweat in the eyes smarting, and the taste of it, were curiously good again. The colonies I had lived in were blended of these. I was home again, in the dank discomfort which I loved.

> — Davis, *The Jungle and the Damned*, p. 11

The passengers in the van confirm everything I've heard about the destitution and decadence of Cayenne. The descriptions of the city that have been told to me were so unfavorable that I expected the worst, but in fact, Cayenne is even more down-and-out than it was possible for me to foresee. The Place des Palmistes is a wasteland. . . . The houses, mostly of a yellowish or brown tone, are terribly dilapidated. Vultures roam the streets. . . . Talked with a blind convict. A beggar with twisted limbs cries out "God is crazy!"

> — Alfred Métraux, *Itinéraires* (1978), pp. 191–92. (diary entries for 28–30 May 1947)

Even if Cayenne is not yet synonymous with "Parisian perfume" for all Brazilians, it is still true that foreigners expect to find in Cayenne the face of the metropole. Between Rio de Janeiro and New York, the traveler should not consider Cayenne simply as a stopover, but rather as a brief encounter with France, especially if he has never had a chance to cross the ocean. And couldn't whatever holds true for perfume and rum also apply to other products made or assembled in Guyane? And shouldn't it also be French culture that radiates from this *département*? . . . This is where Guyane's future is to be found — in the achievement of this French promotional effort in America, in the rediscovery of Guyanais dignity.

> — extract from the official presentation of Guyane in 1967, cited in Jolivet, *La question créole*, p. 497

La Directrice drove up. No inconvenience, she hoped; she had been in an important meeting and couldn't get away any earlier. She drove us directly to a Creole restaurant near the marketplace that served tapir, anteater, and other exotic Guyanais specialties. There, we were joined by GC, an experienced museum ethnologist from France who had been appointed "Conseiller" for the whole museum undertaking, lending it both expertise and a European-based legitimacy; although we'd never met GC before, we'd read a thoughtful essay of his, outlining the challenges and goals of the proposed museum in the context of recent theoretical writing on the semiotics and politics of museum representation. After lunch, La Directrice put an almost-new Renault at our disposal and we set ourselves up in the rather airless studio, jerry-built as an after-thought in the courtyard of an apartment house, that she'd assigned to the three of us for our stay in Cayenne.

Five o'clock meeting at the office of the Bureau du Patrimoine Ethnologique on the Avenue du Général de Gaulle. There, we quickly saw that the tentative schedule we'd submitted a couple of months before, as a complement to the budget, had since been set in stone. La Directrice had already hired a car and driver to transport us and the expedition supplies to St. Laurent, arranged housing in both St. Laurent and Maripasoula, sent the requisite number of barrels of gasoline and oil upriver for our collecting sorties, and contracted for two Aluku boatmen who would be, as she said, "ours" through-out the weeks on the river. We felt *pris en charge* in every sense; both the schedule and the budget categories were rigidly fixed and firmly controlled by La Directrice. (Moneys for hotels, boatmen, and so on—which we thought we were to manage according to the devel-oping needs of the project—were clearly not to be passed through our hands.) This was to be a true *mission scientifique* in which the hierarchy of command was absolute and unambiguous.

La Directrice invited us downstairs for the "viewing of the expedi-tion trunks," a half-dozen metal containers filled with an odd assort-

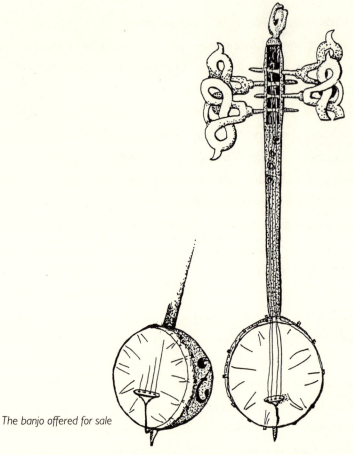

The banjo offered for sale

It cannot be emphasized too strongly that had it not been for the interest and persistence of the private collector in Europe and America, thousands of such objects would simply no longer exist as tangible manifestations of the African creative tradition.

> — Warren M. Robbins and Nancy Ingram Nooter, *African Art in American Collections* (1989), p. 32

15. The *Creole-Bania,* this is like a Mandoline or Guitar, being made of a Gourd Covered With a Sheep-Skin, to Which is Fixed a Verry Long Neck or Handle — This instrument has but 4 Strings, 3 Long, and one Short, Which is thick and Serves for a Bace, it is play'd by the Fingers, and has a Verry Agreeable Sound more so when Accompanied With a Song—

16. Is the *Trumpet* of War to Command Advancing, Retreating &ᶜ—and is cald *too too.*

> — John Gabriel Stedman, *Narrative* (1790/1988), p. 540

ment of supplies left over from the Grenands' last trip: pots and pans, cartridges and fishhooks, toilet paper and scouring pads, butane lamps and stoves, ropes and garbage bags, batteries and candles. The French still know how to mount an expedition.

Another viewing—this time of the museum's collection to date—at the BPE annex, just a few minutes away by car. Lots of Amerindian materials, tagged with the expedition code of the Grenands. A few rather sad looking Maroon objects, acquired here and there. Empty shelves waiting to be filled.

Then the final and most highly-charged viewing of the day, back in the office of La Directrice: the eight antique musical instruments from Suriname that she hopes will become her prize acquisitions. Our task: to authenticate them and thus justify the 250,000F price tag (roughly $50,000) that she has asked the Conseil Régional to cough up. The usual aura of mystery, risk, and intrigue that envelops high priced items on the art market. She explains that the seller, a local collector, has divulged certain tantalizing clues about the original owner—a Surinamer from an old planter family that celebrated the birth of each of its children by commissioning a musical instrument from its African laborers, and had the resulting "Creole orchestra" entertain them on holidays. But because this same gentleman has other instruments and precious objects for sale, his identity is being carefully shielded by the Cayenne collector/dealer, who wants to retain his lucrative position as middleman. Le Conseiller remarks that the instruments are "almost too good to be real," and we agree.

Four of them are available for us to see: A banjo that looks eighteenth-century, very close in form to the slave-made banjo described and drawn by John Gabriel Stedman in 1770s Suriname, but with the sounding-box made of wood in the form of a calabash (unlike Stedman's, which used a real calabash), and embellished with four oversized tuning pegs elaborately carved in an early twentieth-century Saramaka style. Another stringed instrument with a separate wooden bow: wood and turtle-shell sounding-box, decoratively

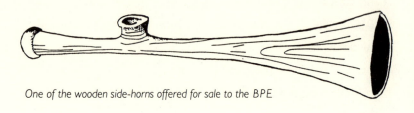

One of the wooden side-horns offered for sale to the BPE

"I once met a man," I said, "who was a dealer in dwarfs."

"Oh?" he blinked. "Dwarfs, you say?"

"Dwarfs."

"Where did you meet this man?"

"On a plane to Baghdad. He was going to view a dwarf for a client."

"A client! This is wonderful!"

"He had two clients," I said. "One was an Arab oil sheikh. The other owned hotels in Pakistan."

"And what did they do with those dwarfs?" Utz tapped me on the knee. He had paled with excitement and was mopping the sweat from his brow.

"Kept them," I said. "The sheikh, if I remember right, liked to sit his favourite dwarf on his forearm and his favourite falcon on the dwarf's forearm."

"Nothing else?"

"How can one know?"

"You are right," said Utz. "These are things one cannot know."

"Or would want to."

"And what would cost a dwarf? These days?"

"Who can say? Collecting dwarfs has always been expensive."

— Bruce Chatwin, *Utz* (1988), pp. 39–40

carved with four tuning pegs in "monkey-tail" style, enhanced with finely whittled sting-ray spines. Both of these instruments have (tuning pegs excepted) a late eighteenth- or early nineteenth-century feel to them. Then, two wooden side-horns. The first a dead ringer for Stedman's *too too*; indeed the shape so exactly matches his drawing that it makes us wonder. . . . We've never seen an example (in museums, in the field) with a similarly raised-up lip—except for the one in Stedman's engraving of musical instruments. In any case, if it's for real, it's certainly a Maroon horn and would seem to be eighteenth-century. The other side-horn is yet more curious, similar in overall form but with three bone keys (as on a trumpet) added. We've never seen anything like it in Suriname, though it's a logical variation on a Maroon *tutu*.

We offer to call Suriname to check out with colleagues the possibility that these pieces have been stolen from the collections of the Surinaams Museum. The call is made on the spot; they haven't been. And we offer to write plantation experts in the Netherlands to elicit feedback both on slave instruments and on the possible identity of the seller in Suriname. We make note of the eagerness with which La Directrice will spend 250,000 francs for these eight "Creole" instruments—five times the amount budgeted for the two-hundred-some-odd objects we are charged with collecting this summer.

In the evening, we drive to the outskirts of Cayenne to visit Kalusé, a Saramaka from Dángogó (the Suriname village where we did fieldwork in the 1960s and 70s), and a twenty-five-year-long resident of French Guiana. The son of Tandó, an important Komantí medium and assistant village headman, and the grandson of Kandámma, who sang for our tape recorder and contributed to our understanding of folktales, Kalusé has become a close friend over the past four years, following our expulsion from Suriname in the initial weeks of the current civil war and our subsequent shift toward French Guiana. His wife is jovial, occasionally hot-tempered and histrionic in domestic conflict, a lively manager of the household scene; by

The turning point . . . came in November and December 1986, when a military campaign in eastern Suriname resulted in more than 150 civilian deaths; in a number of Cottica River Ndjuka villages, unarmed Maroons — including pregnant women and children — were rounded up and massacred. . . . Within a few weeks, more than 10,000 of these Maroon refugees had arrived in French Guiana. Witnesses narrated horrific accounts of defenseless villagers being lined up and mowed down with automatic weapons while they pleaded for their lives. I was there when the refugees began to pour into Saint-Laurent, and I spoke to several of these eyewitnesses, only days after the massacres took place. Of the many atrocities related, one in particular seemed to stand out for its brutality. In the settlement of Moi Wana, not far from Albina, a soldier had torn an infant from its mother's arms, placed the barrel of his gun in its mouth, and pulled the trigger.

    — Bilby, *The Remaking of the Aluku*, pp. 505–506

Saramaka standards of female beauty, which call for ample amounts of flesh on the bones, she's a real prize. When we show up, she welcomes us warmly and shifts her speech hospitably from Guyanais Creole to the language of her Saramaka father, who'd come as a laborer to French Guiana in the 1920s.

The cement house, shielded from the dirt road by a makeshift barrier of rusting corrugated metal, is painted bright pink. A large cage on the front porch is home to a spider monkey who'd been caught in the rainforest, and out back there's a mud yard that comes alive with music, tale-telling, divination sessions, or political debate whenever Kalusé, in his unofficial capacity as "Captain" of the Saramakas in Cayenne, hosts a communal event. Inside the house, various children come and go, amused to hear whitefolks talking Saramaccan, which they understand a little but have never mastered. The living room houses knick-knacks, doilies, pin-ups, boxed bottles of liquor (the local equivalent of coffee-table books), an ornate cupboard with arrays of glasses and goblets of every sort, and a massive color TV, equipped with VCR. Several of the fancy bottles of rum we've brought as presents over the years are still displayed atop the television console. After we've caught up on friends from Saramaka, recent deaths, and skirmishes in Suriname's civil war, talk turns to the funeral celebrations for Saramaka Paramount Chief Agbagó.

Kalusé offers to show us the event "on TV." Technology has made up, in a small way, for the hardships of war, which prevented many Saramakas (as well as us) from being present at the funeral itself. The coffin reflects, by its astonishing dimensions, the stature of the centenarian head of the Saramaka people; its gabled form towers two or three meters above the heads of the twenty men chosen to be its bearers. In addition to the riches packed into it with the body, there are cloths of every description tacked and tied in layers to its exterior, and even the photo-portrait of Queen Juliana and Prince Bernhard that had hung in the Chief's Council Room during his long reign. Before the coffin is lifted for its final journey on the river,

We use media to destroy cultures, but we first use media to create a false record of what we are about to destroy.

— Edmund Carpenter *Oh, What a Blow* (1972), p. 99

Cayenne: the town where the buzzards, those predators with metallic, funereal feathers, half-crow, half-vulture, have appointed themselves as reprocessing agents for the garbage system. . . .

Cayenne: it's an incoherence of races, a confusion of colors, a Tower of Babel of languages, a Babylon of imported vices, a Capernaitical shambles of family, an imbroglio of kinship, as well as a den of gold miners and convicts, a place of force and degradation, dazzle and gloom, gold and garbage!

— J. Tripot, *La Guyane* (1910), pp. 277–78

we see the "dance of death," a slow *adunké* procession, exactly like that described by Moravian Brother Riemer at the funeral of Chief Abíni's widow in 1780 (in *Alabi's World*). The professional video-cam has caught images of friends we haven't been able to see in over a decade—now older, many heavier and greyer, and all preoccupied with the management of this most magnificent of Saramaka spectacles. Dense crowds, piercing mourning shrieks, colorful capes and breechcloths, and intermittent shotgun salutes—it was a burial befitting our wise old friend.

What a contrast with the second of Kalusé's video selections, an RFO-journal segment about the recent funeral of the Aluku Paramount Chief, who had died in the hospital in Martinique (which has facilities its smaller Département d'Outre-Mer sister lacks) whence his remains had been transported back to Guyane. We watched the commercial, mirror-gloss French coffin being lowered into a modern, cement-lined grave, with camera-bearing whitefolks in attendance, and with ready-made *pompes funèbres* wreaths from Cayenne laid on top. (The following week, during the ride from Cayenne to St. Laurent, our Aluku driver assured Ken that "all kinds of other things" had been done during the funeral rites that weren't shown to the cameras. Nevertheless, through our Saramaka-trained eyes, we felt we were witnessing the overwhelmingly long arm of the French state in Aluku, combined with a move toward the "folklorization" of Aluku culture for outside—and even inside—consumption.)

Driving back from Kalusé's in the dark, we pass a twenty-four-hour construction site (apparently destined to be a Chinese restaurant), eerily illuminated by spotlights, where sweating, nearly naked Brazilian laborers are pouring concrete. Then along the sprawling slum in which recent Haitian immigrants have put together shacks from corrugated iron and cardboard, in an area that turns into an inland lake of mud and muck during the rains. By highrise public housing projects, already in decay. Through a mean-looking area of mixed Chinese, Creoles, Maroons, and some longer-established

In the streets of Cayenne as well as in those of the small townships, a diversity of people rubs shoulders. . . . Indeed, the whole world seems to have arranged to meet here. Amerindians, Chinese, Lebanese, Hindus, Laotians, Europeans, Brazilians, Creoles mingle in total harmony.

— Air France in-flight magazine (1990)

One hundred and two years ago, when Saramakas deep in the interior of Suriname named a successor to their recently-deceased tribal chief, a delegation of elders had to set out by canoe down the Suriname River, to continue their journey in a small sailing ship by sea, until they reached Mana, French Guiana, where future tribal chief Akoósu had been working with some 100 other Saramaka men for nearly a decade. In 1936, more than 60% of all Saramaka men, some 2000 individuals, were off in French Guiana working. And in 1968, when we lived in the Saramaka village of Dángogó (the southernmost village on the Pikílío and the most distant from Paramaribo), approximately half of the men from that village were away in Kourou, helping to construct the Centre Spatial Guyanais.

— R. and S. Price, "Working for the Man" (1989), p. 199

As recently as the early 1970's, Kourou slumbered in oblivion as a quiet fishing village whose main distinction was a feature that many of its several hundred residents would have just as soon forgotten.

For decades, the small port here served as the final point of embarkation for hardened French criminals and those convicted of political crimes being shipped off to Devil's Island, the infamous penal colony that lies off in the sunny distance.

— Howard W. French, "Space Center or Not, Some Say It's Still a Jungle" (1991), p. A4

Haitians, as well as some dread-locked immigrants from Guyana, where recorded reggae, kadans, zouk, merengue, soka, salsa, and kaseko pour from various doorways. Across the foul canal that separates Cayenne's poorer areas from "downtown." Under the towering palm trees of the great central square, the Place des Palmistes, we buy salt-cod sandwiches and soft drinks from an open-sided van; like the dozen or so other vans vending pizzas, Indonesian noodles, french fries, and the like, it pulls its light and refrigeration from a noisy gasoline generator set up on the sidewalk.

Saturday, our second day in Cayenne. The three of us spend the morning in our hot little studio, refining preliminary lists of objects we hope to collect: three new stools @ 500F, three old ones @ 1,000F, etc. Then, off for a visit to Saramaka friends who work at the Kourou launch-pad, a hard hour's drive from the capital. On the way, just outside Cayenne, we stop to see Mandó and his brother, Saramaka professional carvers who've been living in Guyane for the past dozen years. Their open Saramaka-style shed, just off the road, is advertised by a rough, hand-painted sign: "SCULPTURE SARAMAKA EN BOIS." Tourist carvings are set out on display — busily carved armadillos, tables, folding chairs, model canoes, two-foot-high Ariane rockets posed on wooden maps of Guyane. After opening pleasantries, we describe the collecting project; they catch on quickly when we explain that we'll want the kinds of objects they make for their wives, not the sorts of things they carve for tourists. (Later on in the project, we'll collect examples of their tourist art; but we want to start with some good examples of contemporary carving made for use in Saramaka.) We promise to come back in a few days to commission some specific things from them, once they've had a chance to think about what they'd like to take on.

Arriving in Kourou, we pass a sign touting "Lingerie Féminine Fantaisie," and drive by the highrise apartment blocks for lower-level employees of the space center, the large French Foreign Legion

Guided by the twofold legacy of its glorious past and the immense prestige of its flag, the 3rd Foreign Regiment of Infantry [the French Foreign Legion] is now well integrated in [French] Guiana, performing varied and valuable missions, training rigorously, and ceaselessly improving its operational capacity. It remains faithful to the words of its regimental march: "Forward the Third Regiment, forward and still forward!"

— Anon., *Kourou: Ville en Devenir* (1987), p. 93 (their translation)

Let's look at how the world of Kourou was organized in 1971 [after its transformation in the mid-1960s from a sleepy Creole village of 650 farmers and shopkeepers into the bedroom suburb of the Centre Spatiale Guyanais]:

— The *quartier* de Roches, separated neatly from the rest of the town, this is the finest residential area. It includes a [seaside] *grand luxe* hotel with a hundred rooms, a restaurant, a bar, and a swimming pool [as well as tennis courts]. Right next door is a private club. . . .

— The white-collar quarter. To the west, but still along the seashore, are 100 identical villas, set in rows, which house the engineers and administrative personnel.

— The "downtown" area. Italianate in style, . . . this includes an interior shopping plaza off limits to cars, decorated with flower beds and ornamental pools and surrounded by arcades giving access to the shops [and] the Prisunic-chain supermarket. . . . The residential buildings, two- to three-stories high, include more than 200 apartments, used by technicians, staff, and storekeepers.

— The "Calypso" quarter. This consists of 300 prefabricated chalets (imported from France), on the eastern side of the shopping plaza. These were the first lodgings built, originally to house the people who set up the Space Center and later for people involved in construction. . . . this quarter, like those mentioned above, is inhabited almost exclusively by *métropolitains*.

— The low-income housing area. These are low-rise multiple-family dwellings that stretch west and south of the center. In these 250 or so apartments, there is a mixture of *métropolitains* and Creoles, mainly semi-skilled workers, but also some schoolteachers. . . .

— The quarter of very low-income housing. High-rise blocks built last, at the entrance to town. Some two hundred apartments for the Creole work force. . . .

— Housing for the relocated. At the edge of town, these absolutely

encampment, and the manicured lawns of whitefolks' villas, before turning into the dirt road that leads to the "Village Saramaka." Visit Amómbebúka (a man from Dángogó we've known for more than twenty years), who receives us in his tiny front room—a 4×7-foot space filled with three folding chairs, a small table, and a gigantic TV-VCR on a shelf just under the low ceiling. We view the same video of the Chief's funeral again, with frequent remote-controlled rewinds and replays to focus on details of particular people and actions. Suriname government soldiers, Amómbe tells us, are moving inexorably up the Suriname River; several Upper River villages are now divided in allegiance, with a strong pro-government contingent—a kind of fifth column—beginning to take hold. Amómbe himself, like many others at Kourou, tells us he's grown tired of the war and now wishes the Jungle Commandos would simply leave the river. He says he argued for four straight days and nights recently, on a visit to Dángogó, with old Captain Kála, who's still holding out for a Maroon victory over the cityfolks. (We feel moved that our old friend Kála is still expressing First-Time values.) We reminisce nostalgically about various people who've died recently, including Bané, a Dángogó boy we've known since birth who died at the age of twenty-five in Kourou after a several-day illness; doctors had intervened only at the very end. All around Amómbe's neighborhood there are flies, filth, green puddles, and kids crawling in the dirt.

After visiting Sinêli, Samsón, and the other Saramakas who had helped refine the folktale transcriptions for our book-in-press, *Two Evenings in Saramaka*, we accompany Ken on two visits in Kourou's small Aluku quarter. We're struck by a different level of material comfort—upholstered armchairs, stereos and records, knick-knacks and china dishes. By chance we meet up with Anton, a Paramaka who'd been Ken's field assistant in St. Laurent four years earlier. Now he's looking for work and discouraged about the prospects, especially since he, like so many other Maroon immigrants from Suriname, has no French papers. He strikes us as a pleasant and seri-

minimal, low-rise concrete structures house the sixty or so families of cultivators whose land was expropriated for the base — the people who lived in Kourou before it was taken over for the Space Center. By 1971, the area already had a decidedly dilapidated look to it.

— The Maroon village. Well-hidden behind the stadium and the empty lots that separate the housing for the relocated from the old town center, this village was built around a water standpipe by Saramakas and Bonis, with the help of recycled materials (old planks, beams) that were "generously" provided for them. In fact, there are two distinct sections; the Saramakas and Bonis do not mix. It is rows of rudimentary shacks which, far from resembling the charming villages along the Maroni, form nothing but a sad shantytown, despite the clear efforts of the inhabitants to make the place nice.

— The Indian village . . . is at the entrance to town, next to the sea, and far back from the road. . . .

— The old town . . . is on the old highway, which is now a dead end street. With its old wooden houses, its quaint town hall, and its little church, the old town retains its flavor as a rural Guyanais Creole settlement.

. . . This, then, is the conception of the new town of Kourou! Could one have dreamed up a more striking demonstration of the expertise of Whites to orchestrate the countless hierarchical encounters that allow them to maintain the ideological bases of their domination?

— Jolivet, *La question créole*, pp. 446–47

The only remaining piece of colonial territory on the South American continent not to have achieved political independence. . . . Geographically, and to some extent culturally, French Guiana can be considered Amazonian; culturally and historically, one might argue, it is essentially Caribbean; politically, like it or not, it is French; economically, it is in some strange sense European. . . . It has often been portrayed in the literature as an oddity, a sort of colonial experiment gone awry. . . . More than 300 years after its initial colonization, French Guiana remains an economic curiosity, simultaneously displaying one of the highest standards of living and one of the lowest levels of productivity in all of South America.

— Bilby, *The Remaking of the Aluku*, pp. 44–47, 68

ous person. We huddle briefly with Ken, who tells us that Anton was always a conscientious helper, and we decide to offer him a few days' work on our collecting project. He's excited at the idea, and promises to call us in Cayenne in a couple of days for details.

At 6:30 the next morning we coax Ken (something of a night-owl) out of bed and set off for the home of our friend AO – Creole politician, sometime *ethnologue*, head of the scientific research bureaucracy for Guyane, and a *grand amateur* of Guyanais flora. On the way, we pass the impressive complex owned by ORSTOM (the French Office of Overseas Scientific and Technical Research), with its various laboratories and library, where AO spends a good deal of his time. AO is an important man. We've occasionally had phone calls from his secretary: "Monsieur Price? Hold the line please; I'm about to connect you with Monsieur O." Pause, then AO's voice, a bit harried [translation]: "Richard! How y'doing? Listen, I'm very busy at the moment, can't really talk. Do you mind if I call you back some other time?" These calls are never returned.

We had been invited by AO, via a message left with La Directrice, to spend Sunday in his garden. Driving up, we hear Mozart on the stereo and see a bare-chested AO sipping tea and reading a spy thriller on his porch, shaded by a grove of dwarf calabash trees. Mozart is silenced, the tea is retired to the kitchen, and we are quickly recruited as labor to load our car and his with brushwackers, jerrycans of gas, machetes, hoes, rakes, and other essentials. Forty kilometers later we arrive in his garden site and are assigned our tasks – Ken, who's the tallest, cutting tree branches with a 1990 model long-reach pruning device, Sally clearing and raking underbrush, Rich using the gas-powered brushwacker, and AO directing, burning piles of brush, and discussing his plans to turn the spot into a botanical laboratory. At breaks, we drink bottled water, eat sandwiches bought at a Chinese grocery on the way, and listen to his dreams about Guyane becoming a country of independent peasant-

The "progress" accomplished since the end of the colonial era cannot be denied. Nevertheless, if the "Land of the Penal Colony" is now hidden behind the "Land of Space Exploration," and if the State has been able (through concerted efforts in matters of infrastructure, the massive growth of a salaried public sector, and social legislation of all sorts) to raise substantially the standard of living of the inhabitants, it is only in order to transform Guyane into a "French show-window" and the Guyanais people into consumers of imported products. In light of this, one might well ask what kind of "progress" is being achieved, and what is the price paid for it by the Guyanais. To be sure, insofar as it is now a consumer society, it is completely French, and from this point of view, the process of *départementalisation* is complete. But this special kind of integration has as an inevitable cost: the complete dependence of the overseas *département* on its metropole.

— Jolivet, *La question créole*, p. 229

NBC-TV broadcast a picture of Lyndon B. Johnson sitting transfixed in front of three television sets, each with a different image of LBJ.

— Carpenter, *Oh, What a Blow*, p. 9

A burst of yells, a whirl of black limbs, a mass of hands clapping, of feet stamping, of bodies swaying, of eyes rolling. . . . They howled and leaped, and spun, and made horrid faces; but what thrilled you was just the thought of their humanity—like yours—the thought of your remote kinship with this wild and passionate uproar.

— Joseph Conrad, "Heart of Darkness" (1902), pp. 539–40

producers, each armed with the latest horticultural mini-kit, which he'll design in cooperation with Japanese and Brazilian engineers; the centerpiece of the plan is a lightweight brushwacker that will supplant the machete. AO, at once thoroughly bureaucratized and an iconoclastic lover of his country, tilts at the windmill of dependence—at least on Sundays. By noon, feeling we've done our part, and marked by the wrath of a disturbed wasps' nest, the three of us take off for Cayenne and turns in the shower.

In the late afternoon we drive through streets of suburban villas on our way to visit DM, the promising young Aluku representative in Guyane's Conseil Régional who we'd met at the conference in Cayenne the year before. He had since spent a day at our home in Martinique; Ken has known him for several years. After a brief conversation in his library/office, he takes us upstairs to a comfortably furnished modern living room, decorated with Maroon carvings and dominated by two identical, framed, floridly-autographed photo-portraits of DM himself. In conversation, DM and Ken speak in Aluku, the two of us in Saramaccan (roughly as close to Aluku as Portuguese is to Spanish); everyone makes token adjustments, and communication is fluid; two Creole women sitting at a table off to the side sip vin mousseux and chat in French. DM tells us about his recent visit to Europe (the Netherlands, Germany, Switzerland, and France) with sixteen Aluku performers; souvenir chunks of the Berlin Wall are now displayed in Aluku villages. We view the video of one of their performances: images of coffee-table savages that could as well have been from highland New Guinea, black faces painted white with kaolin, drums pounding, gaping German onlookers who are invited to come up on the stage to join in the rhythmic dancing for an extended "Children of Many Lands" finale. DM's wife, speaking French, serves sparkling grape juice and hors-d'oeuvres; queried by her discriminating husband on the topping to the canapés, which we would have called caviar, she's uncertain, but does know that "it's not [authentic] caviar." This is clearly a household

The internalization of the Metropolitan Ideal is the final product of this long relationship of domination, at the same time as the privileged means of its continuance.

— Jolivet, *La question créole*, p. 441

I am arguing that at the level of economic relations, aesthetic exchange (the collecting and marketing of artifacts, etc.), and the sociology of interaction, there is no real difference between moderns and those who act the part of primitives in the universal drama of modernity. Modern people have more money usually, but the ex-primitive is quick to accept the terms of modern economics. This may be a practical response to a system imposed from without, against which it would do no good to resist. But it could also be an adaptation based on rational self-interest. The word has already gone around that not everyone in the modernized areas of the world lives a life as seen on television, that many ex-primitives and most peasants are materially better off, and have more control over their own lives, than the poorest of the poor in the modern world. Perhaps a case for difference could be made in the area of interactional competence. Ex-primitives are often more rhetorically and dramaturgically adept than moderns, excepting communications and media professionals. Still, up to this point, it would be tenuous and mainly incorrect to frame the interaction as "tourist/other" because what we really have is a collaborative construction of postmodernity by tourists and ex-primitives who represent not absolute difference but mere differentiations of an evolving new cultural subject.

— Dean MacCannell, "Cannibal Tours" (1990), p. 18

Saturday, January 11 [1992]. We will fly to Timbuctou. . . . In the evening, we will travel by camel to a Tuareg camp to see traditional dances and to eat the traditional roast lamb. **Sunday, January 12.** Morning departure by the same plane to Mopti, which will be our center for the discovery of northern Mali. Our land rovers will meet us at the airport and take us to the comfortable Relais Kanaga on the banks of the Niger River. . . . **Tuesday, January 14.** We will travel to the inaccessible country of the Dogon. . . . **Wednesday, January 15.** We will get up early to hike down the cliff to visit the extraordinary villages on the rocky slopes. After a picnic lunch, we will see traditional Dogon dances performed in the isolated cliff village of Tireli. . . . **Saturday, January 18.** . . . We will spend the night at the Auberge, an unexpectedly comfortable hotel with good French cooking. . . . **Saturday, January 25.** Air Ivoire will take us to Bouake which will be our center for discovery of the Baule people. We will spend the next three nights at

where one does not refer to "champagne" if it's not made from grapes grown in Champagne.

Dinner in a Chinese restaurant with AM, an American Reuters correspondent, who is getting ready to cover an upcoming Ariane launch—his main responsibility in this otherwise marginal outpost of world news. For Sally, who spent much of her year at Stanford reading insider accounts of journalism (*Coups and Earthquakes*, "Has anybody here been raped and speak English?," and the like), the image, even if writ small, of the chain-smoking, expense-accounting foreign correspondent springs to life.

Later in the evening, we read a new proposal for the museum that had been passed on to us by Le Conseiller, announcing that the building will be on six hectares in Remire, a suburb of Cayenne, and will open in 1992. The architectural competition is drawing to a close, and ground-breaking is set for next year. We're startled to see that the size of the exhibition space will be only 500 m^2 (compared, for example, to 830 m^2 for reception, museum shop, and cloakroom). And half of that space has been earmarked for exhibits on the ecosystem and history of Guyane, with the other half divided among Creoles, Amerindians, Maroons, and "Others" (Hmong, Haitians, Brazilians, etc.). At the standard rate of one object per square meter (which we've been told to use as a rule of thumb), very little of what we're about to collect would be on exhibit, making it difficult to present any but the simplest message about art and culture. Late-night three-person huddle, to prepare for the next morning's budget meeting with La Directrice.

Monday morning. We've been told to be present at 8 AM so La Directrice can lay out our final instructions.

At the BPE, we first go over the budget, which we had submitted last year, and which was formally approved in June; modeled slavishly on a proposal that the Grenands had kindly shared with us, the full document was organized in terms of the approved cate-

the comfortable, modern Ran Hotel with its garden swimming pool. In the afternoon we will visit the Baule village of Kondeinu for an introduction to what village life is really like. . . . A chat with the 80 year old chief will give us a chance to talk about the old times with somebody who is a living library of history and tradition. . . . **Wednesday, January 29.** . . . We will continue on to Boundiali, stopping at a village to visit the sacred grove where Poro society rites are held. A high point of the entire trip will be the dance of the marriageable young women and of the men who hurl themselves into a blazing fire.

> — From the Center for African Art's description of its 3-week Mali/Cote d'Ivoire tour package, $6900 per person double occupancy, payable partly to the Center and partly to Magical Holidays Inc.

gories: *Cadre général du projet; Déroulement, itinéraire, lieux de collecte; Appuis techniques;* and *Produit escompté.* As we went through the many lines of budget categories together, La Directrice systematically crossed out all but a few, explaining that she had taken care of those expenses herself. No surprise: the $45 per person per day that had been allocated for hotels in Cayenne had already been transformed into our collective little studio, with the BPE absorbing the difference into its general reserves of available cash. And for those few budget lines that we would control, a series of economies were to be made: the wage for field assistants would be cut from the 190F in the budget to 150F, and the 40F per day *vivres de brousse* ("jungle supplies") supplement that had been approved for them was now to be deleted, although our own identical allowance would be retained. We protest that the Aluku field assistants will be getting less than the minimum wage (which has just risen to 208F), but are told that the 150F figure was arrived at as a compromise between the wage for assistants paid by ORSTOM (which, unlike the Bureau du Patrimoine Ethnologique or museum, is classified as an *organisme de recherche* and is therefore somehow more official) and social security welfare payments. End of discussion. Rich jokes about himself and Ken being Griaule and Leiris; Sally attempts with some ambivalence to see herself as Denise Paulme, one of the female participants in that 1930s expedition, now in her eighties, who we'd gotten to know in Paris.

La Directrice then instructs us on collecting. "Of course," she begins, "you must not dispossess an old woman of a beautiful tray she's using to winnow rice — *unless* the object is functionally replaceable for her." And then, passing quickly from ethics to aesthetics: "But you must nevertheless make every effort to acquire objects that have a *patine d'usage*" — that show evidence of having been used. (Her concern was that, otherwise, people — including members of the Conseil Régional — would find it hard to take the museum seriously.) There's some discussion of the special importance of ac-

This desire for old artifacts was widely shared among Northwest Coast collectors of the time [the 1890s]. The logic was that the old customs were vanishing before the onslaught of Euro-American civilization and thus had to be recorded and collected as soon as possible. . . . Boas and Hunt made a decision to "abstract" past all the change that had occurred since contact so that they would be left with what they hoped would be a description of traditional Kwakiutl material culture. . . . The result was a "memory culture," similar to the verbal pictures of old times painted by tribal elders. This method had its direct visual parallel in the archaic recreation of Edward Curtis's photography. . . . Boas seems to have conflated age with aesthetic value, the old with the well-carved and painted.

— Jacknis, "George Hunt, Collector of Indian Specimens," p. 192

The most common objects are the ones that tell us the most about a culture. A can of food, for example, characterizes our society better than the most sumptuous jewel or the rarest stamp.

One must therefore not shy away from collecting even the humblest and most scorned things. An object might not be worth anything in our eyes or in those of the native and yet be an inexhaustible source of information. . . .

The ethnographic collector [*collecteur*] must rid himself of his European perspective and develop an interest in objects quite different from that of a collector [*collectionneur*] who is only looking for "curiosities." By rummaging through a garbage heap, it is possible to reconstruct the entire life of a society — usually much better than by dealing with rare or valuable objects.

— *Instructions Sommaires*, pp. 8–9

"You don't need the masterpiece to get the idea."

— Picasso, quoted in William Rubin, *"Primitivism"* (1984), p. 14

quiring older Maroon objects in order to underscore the distinction between the future museum and the many souvenir shops of Cayenne. It seems that Amerindian objects, however ethnographically interesting, have the unfortunate quality of being aesthetically uniform, so that essentially identical objects appear in both settings. She therefore warns us that we must not simply commission new objects, which in her hierarchy graze the realm of souvenirs. We do not complicate the discussion by pointing out that although Maroon men carve in a special style they have successfully developed for the tourist trade, they simultaneously carve all kinds of objects for Maroon consumption in a very different style, and that these latter objects will be crucial in representing the contemporary moment in the history of Maroon art and material culture. Nor do we propose a discussion of the venerable tradition in anthropology of collecting beyond the selective realm of the aesthetically attractive, in the conviction that even the humblest and most hybrid of objects reflect on the life of the people who choose to craft and use them.

Le Conseiller has consciously chosen a back-seat role, and generally defers to La Directrice whenever possible. But he also communicates, partly during her absences to answer phone calls or supervise secretaries, a distinctive view. He says he sees the whole museum undertaking as a kind of pari (bet, wager, gamble). His own research interests are in the political processes behind developing a regional museum in multi-ethnic Guyane. At one point, he goes so far as to say that even if our summer's collecting produces few objects (because of the ethical concerns that we've briefly outlined to him), our insights about the process may ultimately be of greater interest and importance to his own intellectual project.

We'd been thinking a good deal about designing a Maroon exhibit that would combine commissioned contemporary objects with older objects borrowed from existing museum and personal collections elsewhere in the world. A few key objects from the storerooms of the world's great museums, plus modest contributions from the

As ethnologists did not generally distinguish between art and artifact—indeed, some still reject aesthetic considerations as unscientific and thus alien to their discipline—the majority of objects they brought back have little or no artistic interest.

— Rubin, *"Primitivism"*, p. 21

living room walls of anthropologists and other old Suriname hands, would permit the presentation of a rather full history of Maroon art. And we could thus circumvent the dubious enterprise of trying to acquire objects that have value for their Maroon owners. We try this out on Le Conseiller and La Directrice, but both make clear that such is not to be. Certainly, no French *musée national*, they say, would lend a single object to a fledgling *musée régional*. Perhaps after the museum has established itself and gained a reputation, limited negotiations could be initiated, but they express little hope. Meanwhile, in the storerooms of the Musée de l'Homme, all the magnificent carvings collected in Aluku over the past century lie gathering dust. . . .

Late morning: La Directrice remembers that there were still several things we'd wanted to add to the expedition trunks, and requests the complete list. A second machete, a rice cooking pot, hammock cords, and made-in-China enamel cups. Sally and Ken accompany La Directrice to stores likely to have the needed goods. In a common Cayenne arrangement for such establishments, the owner, in each case, is Chinese; the employees who watch over merchandise set out on sidewalk tables are Maroons. La Directrice is clearly in a shopping mood, and enjoying the outing; shoulder pads swinging, heels clicking, and key ring jangling, she sweeps into each establishment, confident that she will be recognized and treated according to her station. She is. Our list is handled efficiently, and La Directrice's directives to "put it on my account" are registered with a deferential nod. But no one has the *gobelets* (enamel cups), so the three shoppers make the rounds of every relevant store in the city. Sally resists a strong urge to ask the assistance of the Saramaka clerks, whose language she's more at home with when discussing enamel cups, hammock cords, and the like; it might be seen, she thinks, as an unwelcome intrusion into La Directrice's definition of the situation.

In the afternoon, Rich picks up three Saramaka men, including one elder, and brings them to La Directrice's office to view the

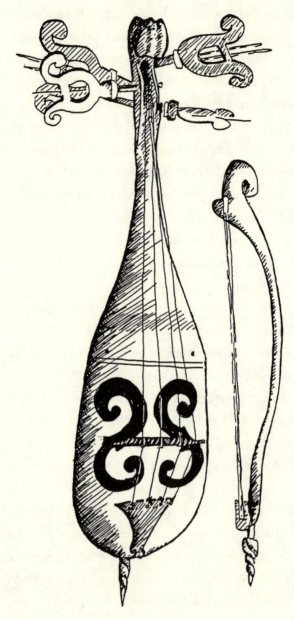

Stringed instrument with whittled sting-ray tails

prized musical instruments. Though we end up learning something about the materials they are made from (the pieces they identify as whittled sting-ray tails, for example, had been a puzzle to us), the men are unfamiliar with the instruments themselves and disinclined to speculate about their origins or age. La Directrice thanks them profusely for their efforts and presents each one with illustrated pamphlets about the Bureau du Patrimoine, as a gesture of appreciation. Many smiles, handshakes, and cordial goodbyes.

Walking along the street in the oppressive heat, the three of us bump into Anton, dressed (as he had been in Kourou) in long-sleeved shirt buttoned to the adam's apple, trousers, leather shoes, and dark socks. This is one Maroon style of wearing Western dress, though we've seen it more often on men born in the 1930s than in the 1950s; maybe it reflects Anton's Paramaribo-Moravian training as a youth. We invite him for a drink and set out to find a sidewalk café. While we're sipping beers and cokes, a raggedy fellow approaches and demands a hand-out. He's belligerent and loud; Anton looks uncomfortable. Rich makes the mistake of answering in English, hoping he'll move on, but of course that's the one foreign language that he's learned the relevant phrases in. He finally leaves. We lay out the project for Anton, and briefly go over his proposed role as a "scout" among the Paramaka, placing special emphasis on our wish to offer prices that "reflect respect" and not to cajole objects out of people who'd rather not sell—an elementary lesson in basic collecting ethics. He listens earnestly; he's a very earnest person.

As darkness falls, sirens fill the air and gendarmes whiz by. A police raid on the drug-ridden section of Cayenne known as "Chicago." Ken goes off with Anton, and we seek out a Chinese meal before turning in.

Tuesday the 24th, our final day in Cayenne. We stroll down a street lined with tourist shops crammed with giant tarantulas in frames, tourist tee-shirts, Saramaka woodcarvings, shell knick-

"There's lots of whites," began Atipa, "who don't know anything about us or Cayenne. But they think they can talk about us, and they think they know more about our lives than us folks whose navel-strings are buried here. . . . There was one white man who came here; he stayed two weeks. If you heard what he said in France, about how snakes here swallow little kids alive, if you had someone read you what he wrote, Compère, you'd even be afraid to go out in the streets of Cayenne!"

> — Alfred Parépou, *Atipa (roman guyanais)* (1885), pp. 175, 179

The only way to acquire these objects [Maroon woodcarvings] is to bargain for them in Dutch money or tobacco, or cheap knick-knacks. Among the more distant villages money is useless. Blue beads are very effective in bargaining, for blue is the Djuka's favourite colour. Ear-rings are also good, but not perfume; they prefer the acrid odour of insecticides.

> — Morton C. Kahn, *Djuka* (1931), pp. 48–49

"Mirrors, beads — that's what they want," he told me. "And the beads must be the right size, and of the preferred color. The more useless something is, the more it pleases them. They're just like children."

> — A gendarme stationed on the Maroni River, giving a French visitor advice about Wayana Indians; quoted in Alix Resse, *Guyane française*, (1964), p. 81

knacks, mounted butterflies, and Amerindian baskets. Then, coffee and croissants in one of Cayenne's several unmistakably tropical but still vaguely Parisian-style cafés, run by métropolitains or possibly pieds noirs from Algeria. There's a threadbare tackiness about these establishments, frequented by a mixture of red-eyed colonial officers (Foreign Legion?), French tourists eagerly seeking the exotic, and down-and-out vieux blancs. We strike up a conversation with PL, an urban Creole we'd met the year before, and tell him a bit about our current doings. He fills our ears with stories of how the Conseil Régional, and its offshoots like the BPE, "really" work: tale upon tale of petty corruption and cronyism. If economies are being made in our budget, he asserts, it's because La Directrice and her associates plan to divide up the excess at the end of the fiscal year. How else did we think she always wore such expensive dresses? From our experience in the "sister" département of Martinique, we're all too familiar with this line, which is leveled at every public figure, from Aimé Césaire to the mayor of the smallest commune, no matter how honest.

The three of us set out to buy field gifts. First, we try the area around the large, bustling market, where we see Hmong women selling Southeast Asian greens, Creoles hawking medicinal plants, and Alukus weighing out grilled cassava meal. We find a Chinese grocery store where they're willing to give us a discount on rum—the most appropriate gift for men—by the case. A few blocks away, at a sidewalk booth on the Place des Palmistes, a Brazilian is selling colorful earrings at 30F; we choose ten pairs, which he gives us for 250F; Sally hopes these will be an appropriate gift for Aluku women, as she knows they would be for Saramakas. Back in the storeroom downstairs from La Directrice's office, we begin unloading and repacking the expedition trunks, choosing from their previous contents and adding supplies we've brought from the U.S. (film, tapes, notebooks, string-tags to identify objects, masking tape for the cala-

Cayenne, le 24 juillet 1990

ORDRE DE MISSION

I, the undersigned, President of the *Conseil Régional* of Guyane, hereby certify that the persons here designated:

- — Richard PRICE
- — Sally PRICE
- — Kenneth BILBY

are engaged, on behalf of the *Conseil Régional* of Guyane, in an ethnographic mission intended to contribute to the establishment of a museum.

I have the honor of requesting that anyone they may encounter in the course of this mission facilitate in every way the successful progress of this project, and thank them for their cooperation.

[signed, Georges Othily, Président, etc.]

bashes, etc.) as well as the results of yesterday's shopping expedition with La Directrice. When we're halfway through the job, Mlle Z (the BPE's well-intentioned technical assistant) shows up, cradles a pad of paper on her forearm, and announces that she has responsibility for making an inventory of everything that we're taking so it can be accounted for, item by item, upon our return. She makes an attempt to peek under the top layer of the half-packed trunks to note their contents, writes down four or five items that her eye chances upon, calling each one out loud as she goes, and adds to her list a few of the things that we're loading in on top. She cannot write as fast as we're packing and Sally, who's been wedging things together like a wooden puzzle to assure their safe passage during the long trip ahead, does not volunteer to empty out the trunks and start again. Mlle Z's assignment is self-terminated within two or three minutes and she trips upstairs to the air-conditioned comfort of the secretarial office.

Our next duty is to receive the expedition cash from La Directrice — a partial advance, equivalent to a few thousand dollars, so that we will not be carrying too much when we travel upriver through the war zone. An official letter/*laissez-passer* has been signed and stamped by the President of Guyane's Conseil Régional, in case we meet up with Jungle Commandos during our river travel. Back in our studio, we divide the daily subsistence cash among the three of us and assign the collecting fund to a special manila envelope; the bills are small and the bulk is great. Spend the afternoon assembling last minute expedition supplies. Then off to see Mandó, who turns out to be in the forest, getting wood for future carvings; we speak with his two co-workers and commission a trial piece from each one, to be purchased in September. They're pleased about the project.

In the evening, Sally takes pen in hand and, after some thinking, enters in a notebook that there's nothing to write, that there have

been no surprises, no real insights about the project since we got here. After reading her open page, Rich counters sardonically that we'd found out how small the museum will be. Sally: That's information, not insight. We both wonder what the point is, and whether all this really matters to anyone other than La Directrice.

The curse of the penal colony. . . . What right has France to corrupt a colony in this manner, reducing it to the level of a "cesspool" for the protection of the mother country?

> — Léon-Gontran Damas, *Retour de Guyane* (1938), as
> paraphrased by Lilyan Kesteloot, *Black Writers in French*
> (1974), p. 232

To be remembered as a penal colony is to be remembered not only as a prison and exotic place of horror, but also as a colony, the object and product of another.

> — Peter Redfield, "The Natural Prison" (1989), p. 28

Guyane's sinister trademark is still alive today despite all efforts to erase it. Just recently, a major airline promoting South American travel decided to symbolize Guyane by a silhouette of a convict in tattered clothing. A vigorous protest by local officials and even a courtroom trial were necessary before another image of the country was proposed.

> — Jean-Claude Michelot, *La guillotine sèche* (1981), p. 25

2

In our room in the Star Hotel, we've just finished wordprocess-
ing our recap of the past week, drawing on notebooks, scribbles in
Sally's appointment book, and mutual recollections. From here on
out, we'll write up each day as it happens.

This morning we made the three-hour drive from Cayenne to St.
Laurent—245 kilometers, built (it is said) at a cost of 17,000 prisoners' lives. La Directrice had hired a large *taxi collectif* with a roof
rack for the trunks carrying the expedition gear. Anton showed up
at our studio early, hoping there would be room for him too, and
there was. The driver was an Aluku named Bwino who had been in
some way "adopted" by La Directrice's family when still a child.

As we left the city, we negotiated a vast traffic circle, built by the
local socialist party in the late 1980s, with a central statue of three
larger-than-life bronze figures: a Creole man (wearing tee-shirt and
shorts), an Amerindian man (wearing a breechcloth), and a Maroon
man (likewise, wearing a breechcloth). In his dissertation, Ken had
discussed the controversies this iconography caused locally, in part
because of its omission of other "ethnic groups"—including *métropolitains*.

Crossed the long bridge over the Cayenne River and leaving the
city behind, we watched the scenery and thought, yet again, about

What a magnificent road! It's supposed to cross all three Guianas. Nobody's been counting the corpses. They've been working on it for more than fifty years. And it's twenty-four kilometers long!

On all sides, the marshes; everywhere, the wavy-grass savannahs. We arrive at kilometer 24. It's the end of the world.

And for the first time, I see the *bagne*! There are a hundred men there, all with sickness in their gut. Some are standing, some lying down, some moaning like dogs.

The bush is in front of them like a wall. But it's not they who will break down that wall; it's the wall that will be getting them. . . .

The real question is whether the intent is to build a road or to kill convicts. If it's to kill convicts, don't change a thing! It's all going smoothly! But if it's to build a road. . . .

> — Albert Londres, *Au bagne* (1923), pp. 89–90, 95–96

The investigator can see emaciated men breaking rocks and digging ditches, naked in stagnant mud contagious with death, naked in the glaring sun. It's a maintenance detail. Once in a while a pickaxe uncovers a tibia or a humerus. The edges of the colonial road are a cemetery.

> — Marius Larique, a journalist, cited in Michel Pierre, *La terre de grande punition* (1982), p. 110

The Madame-de-Maintenon Bridge was inaugurated in 1958. . . . Local tradition has it that Françoise, the future Mme de Maintenon, daughter of Constant d'Aubigné . . . was born there in 1625, during the first colonization efforts of the French Normans under the direction of Richelieu. . . . The first steps of such an illustrious figure would have been sufficient to bring fame to this little town.

> — Resse, *Guyane française*, pp. 161–62

this haunting colonial landscape, so shaped in our minds by the travel-and-adventure books we've read about it and by all the lurid myths that continue to cling to the place. Between Cayenne and Kourou, Route Nationale No. 1, passing through quiet savannahs and grazing country, masks a sinister history, repeated in all the books. The old one-lane road it replaced—Route Coloniale No. 1, which can still be seen in places, winding its way along and across the new one—is supposed to have been paved with the skulls of the prisoners who built it. As we cruise by the innocuous-looking stone marking Kilometer 24, we think, as we do whenever we pass here, of its infamous past.

After crossing the Kourou River, we drive through the Centre Spatial Guyanais, pass the two visible launchpads, and hold our breaths against an iridescent blue and pink cloud of smoke with a fierce chemical smell. The Center, several Guyanais have told us proudly, is as large as Martinique. Heading west from this supreme proof of France's technological glory, the road quickly deteriorates: important people travel only between Cayenne and Kourou. More savannahs and then the steel bridge over the Sinnamary River, where a century ago, Saramaka canoe men fought the rapids to supply the Creole golddiggers from St. Lucia and Dominica who had staked out claims several days upstream. We pass the town of Iracoubo, then Organabo and other Amerindian settlements, until finally the road curves southwest and heads up into the forest. Hills, raw red earth exposed by the force of bulldozers, giant trees and creeping vines, an astonishing variety of palm species, cleared areas where swiddens have been cut. We feel, as we have before on this stretch, a kind of homecoming—if not to Suriname itself, then at least to a close approximation of its environment.

About fifty kilometers outside St. Laurent, near the crossing of the rapids-filled Mana River, where hundreds of Saramaka men monopolized river traffic during the gold rush, we pass the first Saramaka migrant villages. As we approach the town, we see more

Arriving during the early days of the gold rush, Saramakas quickly monopolized major supply routes to the interior and became French Guiana's rivermen par excellence, taking their pay from Antillian prospectors in bags of gold dust and living high off the hog with what their descendants still remember as gorgeous Creole women who were always available, they say, for men with gold in their pockets. When river transport slowed with the waning of the gold rush, Saramakas switched to other forest endeavors — logging, rosewood extraction, and so forth . . . Saramaka men of the generation now past sixty like to say that while Suriname is their "*máma kôndè*" (their matrilineal [home] village), French Guiana is their "*táta kôndè*" (their "father's village," their sentimentally favored place to be).

> — R. and S. Price, "Working for The Man," p. 200

Saint-Laurent is a veritable Sodom.

> — Damas, *Retour de Guyane*, p. 45

St. Laurent is not much of a place. It never was to begin with. Four or five rat-infested streets of decaying wooden houses in the old colonial style — some occupied, some deserted. You can see it all in ten minutes. The whole place reeks of decay. Old Creole women peer out through the windows of their crumbling structures at any stranger who walks the streets. The open sewers are clogged with filth and drowned rats. Stray dogs paw hungrily at the rodent carcasses. The stench is sickening.

> — Alexander Miles, *Devil's Island* (1988), p. 2

Saint-Laurent [was] . . . a town that struck some of the few outsiders to visit it during the first decades of this century as the prettiest in the entire colony. Its wide, shaded avenues, kept immaculate by prisoners, its colonial architecture in brick and mortar, and its carefully tended flower gardens contrasted strikingly with the general dilapidation encountered in Cayenne and elsewhere. For this reason, Saint-Laurent at its apogee, characterized by one author as "one of the most bizarre small towns in South America," came to be known, not necessarily facetiously, by the nickname "Petit Paris."

But this was not to last long. In 1938 . . . an official degree was issued abolishing "le bagne." . . . With this legal act, Saint-Laurent lost its raison-d'être . . . [and its] economy . . . ground to a virtual halt. . . . Saint-Laurent was never to regain the "prosperity" it had enjoyed in earlier times, as

and more small settlements — mainly Saramakas, but also Parama-kas, Creoles, and Amerindians. Then by the police checkpoint at Crique Margot, set up to assure that Suriname Maroons without papers will not travel beyond St. Laurent. Because the border river between Suriname and Guyane provides an easily penetrable bar-rier, the gendarmes have chosen to control the frontier at this spot, several kilometers east, along the only road leading toward Cayenne. We are waved through with hardly a glance. It's only during the past couple of decades that communication by land has supplanted the much traveled twenty-hour-long sea route between Cayenne and St. Laurent; this final portion of the road wasn't asphalted until the mid-1970s.

Hot and dusty at the end of the tedious ride, we enter St. Laurent by the now-idle open-air market, turning onto the wide empty street that leads to the mairie, where we've been told to report for instruc-tions about our housing. A man in uniform signals to Bwino, giving him some kind of instruction about staying to his right at the inter-section, but there are no other cars in sight and Bwino just drives through. As he parks the car in front of the mairie, the man runs up angrily, shouting and gesticulating. Loud words are exchanged and blows threatened, as Bwino defends his right to the public arteries and challenges his attacker's authority to direct traffic, alluding dis-paragingly to his status as a customs official. Once the threatening postures have been played out, the two back off from each other and peace is reestablished; it becomes clear from the comments Bwino mutters over the next few minutes that this encounter was a long-standing personal score being settled, or rather kept alive; its real subject was never mentioned.

To us, St. Laurent seems like "Ken's place"; when we visited him here during his dissertation research three years ago, he had shown us the town and filled us in on its history, ethnography, and local gossip. In our own fieldwork in Suriname, the place had always been the nearly mythical "Soolá" — a faraway site more imagined than

the seat of one of the world's most notorious penal colonies. . . . What kept this former penitentiary community from wasting away and vanishing into the surrounding forest was the economic intervention of the French state. . . . The population of the *commune* . . . grew from an all-time low of 3,020 in 1961 to just under 7,000 in 1982 . . . [when] the town of Saint-Laurent proper [had] an official population of 5,042 — the third largest town in French Guiana (after Kourou and Cayenne).

. . . In 1967, a ferry service was opened between Saint-Laurent and the Surinamese town of Albina on the opposite side of the Maroni River. . . . Vans loaded with rice, fruits, and vegetables regularly traversed the Maroni and passed through Saint-Laurent (now only three to four hours from Paramaribo) on the way to Cayenne. . . . There was increasing traffic in the other direction as well, from Cayenne to Saint-Laurent; imported goods, most of them originating in France, flowed from the capital toward the Maroni. . . . Although Saint-Laurent lacked any productive base to speak of, its shops were nonetheless well stocked with imported food, clothing, and the latest gadgets from metropolitan France.

Along with the imported goods came a stream of people. . . . Joining the earlier Creole majority (consisting largely of descendants of Antillian immigrants) — not to mention the small minorities of Amerindians, metropolitan French, Vietnamese, Chinese, Arabs, and other small populations already there — were unknown numbers of more recent immigrants from the French Antilles, Haiti, Brazil, Guyana, Suriname, Colombia, and the Dominican Republic.

. . . Beginning in the 1960s, hundreds of Maroons — Alukus, Paramakas, and especially, Ndjukas — left their villages in the interior and migrated downriver to Saint-Laurent. . . . In 1987, when community leaders published a glossy coffee table book promoting their town, they decided to title it not "Petit Paris," but rather, *Saint-Laurent-du-Maroni, carrefour des races . . . la ville aux 40 dialectes.*

    — Bilby, *The Remaking of the Aluku*, pp. 281–87

For personal reasons, I felt a need to go off to the end of the world. When I arrived in Cayenne, I realized it didn't do the trick, but as soon as I laid eyes on St. Laurent, I knew this was it.

    — The reply of a Corsican nurse, when we asked what had led her to accept a job in the refugee camps of St. Laurent

imaginable, where Saramaka men were working to earn enough money so that they could load their canoes in Paramaribo with cloth and soap and salt and kerosene, perhaps a new hunting gun, and some Western luxuries like tape recorders and outboard motors, and return triumphant to their home villages. In Dángogó in the 1960s, Soolá's fame was assured by the lyrics of popular songs, by the scandal-mongering names given to cloth patterns, and by an occasional tape-recorded message from someone's husband about his intended schedule for returning home to Saramaka.

Arrangements for our housing were made several months ago; the head doctor of the hospital had offered his guest room for Ken, and we were to be given lodging in a building run by the local mayor's office. Reporting in (according to our instructions) at the mairie, we are told that the man responsible for such visits has just left to catch a plane to Canada, without alerting anyone about our expected arrival. We cajole an office worker into letting us use her phone to call Cayenne; we're on official business, we assure her, guests of the Conseil Régional. La Directrice is clearly annoyed that her carefully laid plans are not going smoothly, but, seeing no alternatives, she authorizes us to take a hotel room until she has time to work out a more suitable (i.e. economical) arrangement. We drive to the doctor's spacious colonial house within the walls of the old prison hospital complex, where we are offered a spontaneous meal in a rustic kitchen opening onto a decaying central courtyard, and chat with French-born Dr. J and his perky Chinese/Creole wife, old Guyane hands. Discussion of where negotiations are on a set of Saramaka paddles from the 1920s or 30s that they know about in St. Georges de l'Oyapock (on Guyane's eastern border with Brazil), where they'd been stationed before arriving in St. Laurent; for some time now, they've envisioned the possibility of acquiring them for the future museum and have mentioned this several times to La Directrice. They had let the matter drop, they tell us, but will ask again on their

An object in a museum case must suffer the de-natured existence of an animal in the zoo. In any museum the object dies — of suffocation and the public gaze — whereas private ownership confers on the owner the right and the need to touch. As a young child will reach out to handle the thing it names, so the passionate collector, his eye in harmony with his hand, restores to the object the life-giving touch of its maker. The collector's enemy is the museum curator. Ideally, museums should be looted every fifty years, and their collections returned to circulation.

> — Kaspar Joachim Utz, "The Private Collector," cited in Chatwin, *Utz*, p. 20

The experience of Louis Shotridge (1886–1937), a Tlingit Indian who was persuaded by the director of the American Museum of Natural History to "infiltrate his own culture to obtain its treasures" illustrates the tensions inherent in the phenomenon of ethnographic collecting (Carpenter 1976: 64; see also Cole 1985: 254–66). Equipped by the museum with a still camera, a movie camera, a typewriter adapted for Tlingit texts, a live-in powerboat, and sizeable amounts of money for his purchases, Shotridge set out to collect for Science.

> When I carried the [Kaguanton Shark Helmet] out of its place no one interfered, but if only one of the true warriors of that clan had been alive the removal of it would never have been possible. I took it in the presence of aged women, the only survivors in the house where the old object was kept, and they could do nothing more than weep when the once highly esteemed object was being taken away. . . . It is not going to be an easy thing to take away the Bear Emblem. . . . My plan is to take the old pieces one at a time. [Shotridge, quoted in Carpenter 1976: 65–66]

Shotridge eventually turned in frustration from offers of money to clan-

next trip to St. Georges. They're sympathetic to the whole enterprise and eager to help out if they can.

As we scan the beautiful paddles, stools, trays, baskets, and other items of Indian and Maroon manufacture scattered casually about their house, we construct a rudimentary *musée imaginaire* based in part on their own collection; Sally thinks back to a New Yorker cartoon in which a monumental museum banner proclaims "Masterpieces from the Golden Age of Tax Deductible Contributions," and fantasizes about a Cayenne equivalent boasting "Masterpieces from the Collections of Guyanais Physicians."

Having unloaded Ken's things, and hauled the expedition trunks into an empty storage room at the doctor's house, we drive to the Star Hotel and check in. We are to call La Directrice tomorrow morning at nine to receive further instructions about housing. With nothing else to do, we set up the lap-top on a little dresser, track down a second chair for our room, and begin to write.

At 5 PM, Anton reports in at the hotel, as we had requested; Ken had come by a few minutes earlier. We go over our collecting experiment: Anton will act as a salaried "scout" for Paramaka objects, using his knowledge of the greater St. Laurent area to visit people, explain the museum and collecting project, view any objects offered for sale, and take notes so that, three days from now, we can revisit those people with him and discuss purchasing anything of interest. We encourage him to look for objects in all media—wood, cloth, and calabash—and to try to find particularly "good" examples of artistry (according to his own best judgment). The real question is whether Paramakas living around St. Laurent have brought much art or material culture with them from their home villages, especially since many are refugees from the civil war. Anton seems pleased with the definition of his job and says he'll start early in the morning. We agree to meet with him after his second day of scouting, to see how he's coming along.

destine theft to acquire the Rain Screen and house posts from the Whale House of his own village. Carpenter describes how

First he offered $3,500. There probably wasn't $100 cash in all Klukwan at that time. He spoke eloquently, at great length, in the Whale House. He said that the museum would protect these treasures, that they belonged to the world and would forever reflect the glory of the Whale House. The answer was an unequivocal no.

Finally, with the museum's knowledge, he laid plans to steal the Rain Screen and houseposts while the men were away fishing. "We plan to take this collection," he wrote, "regardless of all the objections of the community." The reply: "I am glad you have found a way to overcome the serious difficulties in obtaining full possession." But a "gun went off," narrowly missing him. This traditional Tlingit custom, midway between execution and assassination, was no mere warning. Shotridge sponsored a feast to reestablish peace. [1976: 66]

— S. Price, *Primitive Art*, pp. 69–70

THURSDAY 26/VII/90

At 8 AM we called La Directrice, but she hadn't yet arrived at work. After breakfast and some diary catching up, we called again, having pre-thought our position, tone, etc. with care. We very much wanted this to be a conversation where we, not she, would be calling the shots. . . . But that illusion vanished with her first sentence, in which anything we (in this case Sally) were about to propose was rendered irrelevant, and La Directrice proved once again that she was well suited to her title. She had talked to the man at the *mairie* in St. Laurent, she announced, making no mention of his departure for Canada. She now understood that we were balking at the pre-arranged housing site in a place several kilometers outside of town because we felt we would need a car there. We were to stay put for the moment and she would have the whole matter arranged within a half-hour, at which point she would call to give us further instructions. End of conversation. Ken soon joined us; there was nothing to do but sit in our room and wait for orders. They came around noon. A rental car had been reserved for us at Avis; we were to pick it up and drive five kilometers south of St. Laurent to Saint-Louis, where she had arranged for us to have a "studio" in a building used by the *commune* of St. Laurent as a children's summer camp. (Apparently, the outlying summer camp had been part of her original plan; the car was a last-minute concession to our need for mobility.) At Avis, there was some confusion about the car reservation, which had been incorrectly transmitted by the secretary in Cayenne, but a series of phone calls over the course of an hour straightened out the problem, and we drove off to our new home, the *colonie de vacances* of Saint-Louis.

The "studio": three bare rooms in a brand-new and otherwise empty cavernous concrete building. A double bed in a tiny, windowless cubicle, a single cot in an equally windowless alcove, and then a larger space with windows giving on a marshy area next to the

"There are near to two hundred lepers on that island. There's no guard out there and no one in his right mind goes there, not even the doctor. Every morning at eight a boat takes the day's rations, raw. . . . Every one of them's a dangerous murderer."

> — The Masked Breton, a former convict, quoted in Henri
> Charrière, *Papillon* (1969), p. 79

The Flea hands me this tin cup and he says, "Here, don't be afraid to drink the coffee, because this cup is just used by visitors. None of the sick guys drink with it." I take the cup and drink, and then I set it on my knee. That's when I notice that there, stuck to the tin, there's a finger. I'm just seeing this when The Flea says, "Hey! Just lost another finger! Where the hell'd it go?"

> — Charrière, *Papillon*, p. 84

Maroni River. No kitchen, no soap, no towels, no toilet paper or bathroom mirror; an open shower that floods the floor, forming pools at the base of the toilet which then spread out the door and down a step into the "living" space, to collect and remain in place as a large, centrally-located puddle. The bed is made up with a heavy plastic mattress casing partially covered with one (single-size) sheet. The building's watchman, a St. Lucian immigrant from decades back who had come to Guyane in search of gold, kindly offered to loan us an old wooden table and some folding chairs. We designate the alcove with the cot as the "Collection Room," for the storage of our future acquisitions. Not knowing whether to feel nostalgic for "the field" (where roughing it is a personal choice and part of the fun of living out the material culture of the life we're studying) or for research/lecture trips (when we've been put up comfortably by our academic or governmental hosts), we're looking on the bright side and feel grateful to have a car for the dusty five-kilometer trip back into town.

Walking out of the building, past a refectory where several dozen children are engaged in a crafts project, we stroll along a path to the nearby riverbank and look across to a wooded island. Rich remembers why "Saint-Louis" had rung a bell: that island was one of the most infamous sites of the *bagne*—the leper colony.

Lunch with Ken at "le Restaurant du Maroni," across from St. Laurent's tiny but bustling fish market, on the riverfront looking toward Albina on the Suriname side, a town that had been burned to the ground in the recent war. The restaurant is owned by a Dutch pig farmer, now a refugee from Suriname, and frequented mainly by Dutch and French. Like the Hotel Toucan in the center of town, another favorite watering hole of white visitors, it features Stella Artois on tap.

We decide that the two of us should begin Saramaka collecting while Ken renews contacts with Alukus toward the same end. We ask Ken what he expects from Anton's Paramaka collecting efforts, and

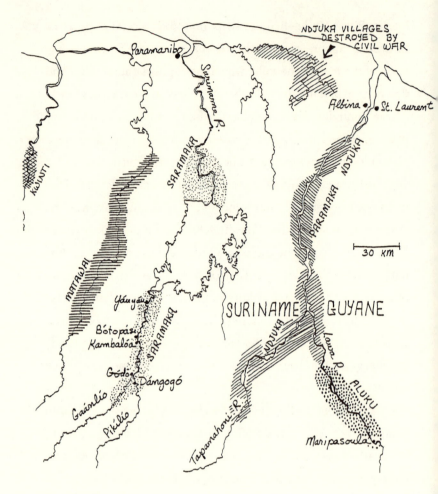

Map of Maroon Territories

he says he's very pessimistic about things being available. He's also not at all confident about finding much that isn't specifically commissioned by us among the Aluku. After lunch, we drive to the older part of Sabonyé (officially, "La Charbonnière"), one of the Maroon ghettos of St. Laurent, where Ken points us toward the Saramaka neighborhood and we split up.

We see two Saramaka women in their twenties and strike up a conversation. They tell us they're from Lángu—the villages along the Gaánlío that are only a day's canoe trip from where we lived during the sixties and seventies. We ask if they know Boiko (Adiante Franszoon), a special friend of ours whose father is from Lángu. Absolutely, they say; in fact, when he passed through St. Laurent a couple of months ago, on his way to his father's "second funeral" in Saramaka, he had left his extra baggage with them before setting off for the trip upriver and the long walk through the forest to reach his father's village.

A bit of personal background for our readers: We first met Boiko, son of one of the captains of Dángogó, in 1967, on our second trip to Saramaka. Then 18, he left for wage labor in Kourou just two months later, so we saw little of him during our stays in Saramaka. But we did receive several brief letters, either dictated to someone or painstakingly inscribed in his own hand. They expressed concern about his future, his job opportunities, and his need for basic schooling, which hadn't been available in Upper River Saramaka when he was growing up. Traveling to Paramaribo to meet with us during one of our visits there, he presented his dream in more detail; in the United States, he would be able to go to school, learn a job skill, widen his horizons. In Kourou, he had hired a personal tutor who was teaching him writing, in Dutch, but he wanted to go further, to learn something useful like welding, to overcome the limitations imposed by his lack of schooling. He had saved almost enough for the air fare; couldn't we help him get set up there? We had heard this plea from others before, but never with such persistence, such

"The soldiers rounded up another group of seven people: six children and one woman. They lined [them] up in the middle of the village. They begged for their lives, but the soldiers shot them all to death. . . . Before the soldiers left, they burned down the whole village."

> — Eyewitness account of a massacre in the Njduka village of Moi
> Wana on November 29, 1986, reported by Adiante
> Franszoon in "Crisis in the Backlands" (1989), p. 36

In June 1986 [Suriname army commander] Bouterse . . . unleashed his military — including field artillery, aerial bombardment, and tanks — on the defenseless [Ndjuka] village of Mongo Tapu. . . . In the following months similar violent actions were taken against other Maroon villages. In December 1986 the *New York Times* reported that 244 Maroons had been killed. . . .

The immediate challenge concerns the fate of the more than 14,000 refugees. At least 10,000 of them . . . have fled across the Maroni River into French Guiana.

> — Franszoon, "Crisis," pp. 37–38

determination. We were about to return to the States, still unencumbered by family obligations; after a cautionary speech about race relations and other realities of life in the U.S. of A., we told him OK.

We flew back first, rented an apartment with an extra room in New Haven, and met him at Kennedy airport one snowy evening in December 1968; a flight attendant had kindly prevented him from disembarking prematurely in Barbados. He lived with us for two years, attending adult education classes and learning English with impressive speed. He sailed through grades one through eight and then, in a single year, passed the high school equivalency exam. After that he lived with roommates, graduate student-style, while attending the local community college. In 1974, we moved to Baltimore, and he came too; after a difficult year as a special student at Johns Hopkins, he eventually finished an undergraduate degree in economics at the University of Baltimore. By 1990, equipped with both a U.S. green card and a Dutch passport (which he had chosen over the Suriname alternative upon Suriname's independence in 1975), Boiko was a sixteen-year veteran of Baltimore, a friend of several generations of Hopkins graduate students in anthropology, an experienced cook who had worked in several gourmet restaurants, an occasional commercial woodcarver, and, since the beginning of the Suriname Civil War, a tireless and outspoken activist for the rights of Suriname's oppressed Maroons.

This past April, he took a month's vacation from his job to attend his father's final funeral rites in Suriname. Knowing he could not pass through the capital because of his public opposition to the regime, he decided to travel clandestinely — flying to Cayenne, getting over to St. Laurent by road, taking a canoe part way up the Maroni River, and making the long trek on foot through the rainforest to the Suriname River and his father's village. His brief stay in St. Laurent had been part of this itinerary. By the time of our arrival in Guyane, Boiko was already two months overdue in Baltimore. His employer was threatening severance, his landlord eviction. His

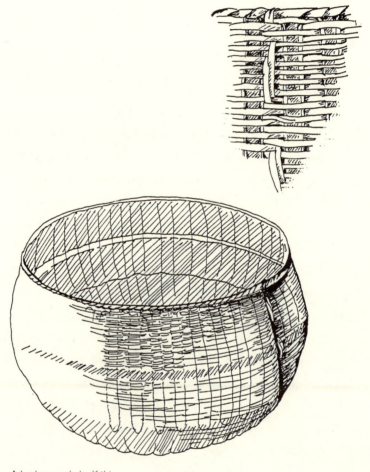

A basket made by Kóbi

friends there had continued to pay rent for him, but Ken – who'd known Boiko for years – reported that they were beginning to lose patience and wondering whether he would, in fact, ever return. He had last been seen crossing the Maroni by canoe, setting out with some other Saramakas for the several-day trek through territory controlled by the Jungle Commandos.

Back in Sabonyé, we ask the two women if there are Saramakas from the Dángogó region around, and they take us to two young men from the village of the Saramaka Chief, who tell us that everyone else from the region is in Kourou. We walk on, through mud and across dried-out planks, semi-rotted during the rains, among the squalid, wooden shacks that people have built on piles in an effort to rise above the filth. Naked kids are running around or pushing coconut sheath "canoes" along the stinking, sandy earth. "Insalubrious" hardly does justice to the living conditions. The poverty is overwhelming; we have difficulty relating any of what we see to the image of a glorious new Regional Museum.

We chat with a group of Ndjuka youths, cutting each others' hair, in the midst of the Saramaka shacks. Walking on toward the riverbank, we greet an old man and he replies in Saramaccan. Although we don't recognize him, he gradually realizes who we are. His name is Kóbi and he's from a village near Dángogó; he remembers seeing us off-and-on in the 1960s. He takes us to his tiny house, set crudely on stilts, nearby. Furnishings include a few rum bottles, three tiny stools, a hammock, some enamel basins filled with leaves for ritual washings, a Primus stove and a bottle of Lesieur cooking oil. Little else. He explains that he's too old to get wage labor, but lives by making medicines for people. Sometimes he weaves baskets to sell. Throughout his life, he's made periodic trips over here to do wage labor. He was in St. Laurent, for example, when the war broke out – the *real* war, he adds, the one with Hitler, not this little squabble that's ruining Suriname now. This time it's been six years; he still has a wife back in Saramaka.

The comb carved by Alimóni's brother, Edy Mayóko

After a while we explain our collecting mission and he says he'll help by "spreading the word." An assistant headman from the Saramaka village of Dáome stops by and old man Kóbi recaps our speech, asking him to help out if he can. We arrange for Kóbi to make us two baskets, a standard-size one and a smaller "sewing basket." When we ask about the price, he says he sells baskets for 50F, which strikes us as very little. Rich says we'll pay 60, and he seems pleased, as much by the gesture as by the money itself. It takes three or four days to make a basket, he says — one to go off in the forest and collect the *báluma* reeds, one to scrape them, and the rest to do the weaving. He offers us rum, first dribbling nearly a whole glassful on the wooden floor in a long prayer to the ancestors, invoking each of the Chiefs since the mid-nineteenth century, his own deceased relatives, and others. He suggests taking us to some good carvers he knows, and we negotiate the wooden planks back out to the car.

First stop: a painted sign signaling professional woodcarvers, on the road to Saint-Louis. An open-sided shed for carving out front, a *têmbe ósu* ("house of art") for storage in back. The middle-aged man who greets us says little and delegates Soomi, in his twenties, to deal with us. He's from the village of Pikí Seéi, where we'd slept over several times during trips on the Suriname River in the sixties and seventies. Soomi can't tell which one of them will have time to carve for us, but together they'll take on responsibility for a curved-seat stool made of South American cedar plus two smaller objects to be carved from *apokéta* wood: a food stirrer and a pestle. They'll go off to the forest Sunday to find wood for their other carving and get some *apokéta* at the same time. No discussion of price, but we said they could set it at whatever they thought fair — it was government money, we explained.

A hundred yards further along the same road, Kóbi leads us down a path meandering through a large cassava field, into a small Saramaka compound where there's a friendly man in his late twenties, Alimóni Mayóko, from the Saramaka village of Gódo. His wife and

Otjútju's daughter's tónton páu

another man are sitting on stools nearby as he carves. The woman recognizes us and introduces herself as the daughter of our old friend Otjútju; she'd known us as a kid. Once Kóbi sketches in our project, Alimóni brings out two round-top stools that he's made, not for sale, but to take back to Saramaka. They're fine examples of current carving styles, but each has chips on the rim; he says he made them a bit too thin. He's started a third, though, with a purple-heart inset on the top. The legs are still unfinished, but it promises to be a beautiful piece. He offers to sell us whichever one of the three we prefer; he'll take the other two back to Saramaka. So we agree to come back after he's made more progress. Again, no discussion of specific price, but a general agreement that we'll pay whatever is appropriate.

Alimóni then brings out a nice varnished comb that was carved by his younger brother, and never used. Although his brother is temporarily away, Alimóni says he could sell it to us, for 50F, if we like it. We consider offering more, but as yet have no idea what the "normal" price of anything might be these days and prefer at this point not to influence the other transactions in the works. Otjútju's daughter whispers to her husband, "Show them the *tónton páu*," and he goes off to get a purple-heart pestle for pounding bananas that he'd once made for her. The other man teases her, "It's always the women who're eager for money!" — or, as Sally comments later, it seems to be *married* women, who can get their husbands to make them replacements, who like to get money for such things. It's a relatively nice piece, but blemished by white spots; Otjútju's daughter says she'll wash it well and show it to us again when we stop by in a few days.

Kóbi then directs us to our final stop, a mini-settlement that belongs to his brother's wife, Sêneki, behind the small local airport. She's a prototypical Upper River Saramaka woman, completely familiar to us in her clothes, discourse, tone of voice, hand motions, and postures. Talking with her carries us back to Dángogó;

When we were not frequenting the market, the shops, and the deeper dives of St. Laurent, exploring for simple viands to eat, when we were not cozening murderers, lepers, and politicians to beguile an egg from them or a cigarette, our days were active, despite a sub-equatorial climate nearly as bad as that of New York in July.

    — Davis, *The Jungle and the Damned*, p. 68

it's an intense nostalgic pleasure. Another woman, from the village of Bótopási, who speaks some French Creole, announces that she has "thirty-five or thirty-seven" combs and would like to sell us a couple, but we don't follow up on it. Sêneki shows us some of the calabashes she has carved, which are very well done but which she needs for household use. She complains that the trees she's planted on the path to her house are still too immature to provide fruit; she'll try to get calabashes from someone else and then decorate them to sell for the collection.

We drop Kóbi off in Sabonyé with profuse thanks, and head into St. Laurent. Exhausted after a non-stop afternoon, we buy a liter jar of orange juice in a Chinese grocery store, chug it in the car, and go to pick up Ken for a beer at the Toucan café. We agree to continue independently the next day, regrouping at 6 PM to pick up Anton and see how the Paramaka experiment is going.

From one of St. Laurent's two pay phones, we finally succeed in reaching Boiko's sister in Paramaribo; we'd tried unsuccessfully a number of times from Cayenne during the previous several days. Sally shouts into the mouthpiece to get through the bad connection, but circumspectly, assuming the phones are tapped by the Suriname military and that they have Saramaccan-speaking listeners. We are given to understand that, according to the news she's had from recent Saramaka arrivals in the city, Boiko is still in Saramaka but not by choice; the soldiers are advancing upriver and have passed the end of the path leading from the Maroni, which Boiko had taken to get there. So he is cornered in his home territory, unable to connect with the outside world. She urges us to have Boiko's friends hold on to his Baltimore apartment a little longer; we later relay the message to Ken, who phones Baltimore to plead for patience.

But if we were not discovered by the enemy, we were almost devoured alive by such a cloud of gnats or mosquitos in this place as I vow to God I had not even met with on board the fatal barges in upper Cottica, and which arose from a neighbouring marsh, while we could make no smoke to drive them away. In this situation, I saw the poor men dig holes with their bayonets in the earth into which they thrust their heads, stopping the entry, and covering their necks with their hammocks, while they lay with their bellies on the ground. To sleep in any other position was absolutely impossible. However, by the advice of a Negro slave, I enjoyed my rest. "Climb (said he), *Massera*, with your hammock, to the top of the highest tree that is in the camp, and there go sleep; not a single mosquito will disturb you, the swarm being too much engaged by the smell of the sweating multitude that is at the bottom." And this I tried, being near a hundred feet above my companions, whom I could neither see by the mist of mosquitos below me, rolling like the clouds under Blanchard's balloon, nor hear them by the sound of their infernal singing music. . . .

So very thick were the mosquitoes now that by clapping my two hands against each other I killed in one stroke to the number of thirty-eight, upon my honour.

— Stedman, *Narrative* (1790/1992), pp. 201–203, 62

FRIDAY 27/VII/90

Last night was nightmarish. Sally slept almost not at all, in our small and airless cubicle. Seemingly hundreds of mosquitos zzz-ing. Heat and sweat on the plastic mattress cover, topped off by a group of Brazilians(?), living next door to our building, who blasted a high-power stereo till 4 AM, picking up again at 7 — heavy metal at many decibels, sending unwelcome vibrations through our room. After this replay of the treatment recently accorded General Noriega in his Panamanian papal refuge, Sally is tired, angry, and mumbling about a premature return to Martinique.

Reactions to our first afternoon of "collecting" yesterday: All the ethical dilemmas that have worried us heretofore take on a different tint when set in the lived context here. Whether or not we buy a comb or basket is no big thing for anybody (except perhaps the museum). Old man Kóbi sells baskets (to other Maroons, to us) when he feels like it, and the same goes for the man who carved the comb. Our participation, our being here, changes nothing. What does matter is that Kóbi lives in a world where 50F seems like a lot of cash, as he has few ways of getting any at all. These people are abjectly poor in a money economy. Sure, some have small gardens, which allows them to survive. But they remain desperately poor. So the obscenity isn't that we participate in "ripping off artists" on behalf of museums, but rather that the system has people selling combs (or a basket that takes three days' work) for the price of two bottles of rum, while the daily minimum wage is five times that. And that most of the people we're dealing with don't have French papers and can't get regular wage work at all. We've also come to realize that the ethical dilemma we anticipated — having to deprive people of objects that have value for them if we're to fulfill our mandate from the Conseil Régional — is in fact overshadowed by its opposite, that of having to say no to people who offer us things we don't want, and who very much need the money it would bring them.

Aluku calabash carved by Ma Betsi [See page 159]

In mid-morning, the two of us drive out the road toward Cayenne, to visit various Saramaka settlements. On our way to St. Laurent two days ago, as we got within 30 or 40 kilometers of the town, we'd begun noticing signs:

```
BONJOUR  LES  ANIS
SOUVIRS   SARAMA
KA TABLES CHAISES
DIVERSESBELLES
CUOSES ————————→
```

```
SOUVENIR·A·VOIR
E·DISPOSITION
ARTISANA·SUR
BOIS·SCULPTER
SUR  COMMANDE
←DIRECTION·MERCI
```

```
I  CI   VOLA
AVENDRE SOUVENIRS
TOBJETS SARAMACAS
CHAISES  PILONS
→IO-KM A ROUTE MANA
```

```
U  R  T  I  S  ∩  N  ∩  T
S  C  U  L  P  T  U  R  E
S  A  R  M  A  .  C  A
E  N  B  O  I  S  D  E
G  U  Y  A  N  E  →
```

Saramakas are, to our knowledge, the only professional carvers established in Guyane, as they used to be the only ones in Suriname.

The Heineken-bottle carafe carved by Simeon Paulus

Just past the French police checkpoint at Crique Margot, we stop at one of the signs:

SOUVENIR EN BOI

A   VENDRE

ARTISAN SARAMACA

BIÈNVENU AGUYAN

Approaching from the road where we'd left our car, we greeted two carvers, sitting in an open shed, in Saramaccan. Stupefied silence. Repeated greetings. Replies from them. What's this? The usual conversation about how could it be that we speak Saramaccan, etc. One of them remarked, "When I saw a white woman walking toward us, I was getting myself all psyched up to see whether I'd be able to get out my few words of Creole so I could sell her something. What a shock!" We were in the new Saramaka settlement of Tjodj ("Georges") and Simeon, two brothers from the village of Bótopási who were there with their wives and some children, renting the land from a Creole farmer. The two men and their teenage sons work in an open shed near the road, with a storeroom/display room in a house further back. We sat and chatted. They'd just heard that the Suriname army was closing in on Bótopási, which had been serving as the base for the Jungle Commandos on the Suriname River, and they were deeply apprehensive. They showed us their carvings, including an item they say they invented—a carved wooden carafe with a removable top, modeled on the crystal kind, in which was embedded (their technique for getting it there a closely-guarded secret) a Heineken beer bottle. They had several of these displayed on a plank shelf. After we talked a while, they asked if we weren't the people who'd written the book about Maroon art, and whether there was any way of getting a copy. We promised we'd bring them one tomorrow.

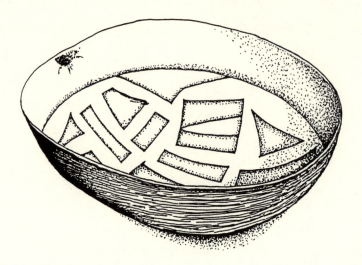

The first of our Paramaka acquisitions scouted out by Anton: a calabash bowl carved by Carmelita Mode Forster [See page 105]

We discussed our museum work and asked if they would each make us a Saramaka object of their choice—not tourist style but as if they were making it for a wife. One proposed a woman's paddle, the other a round tray. One of the teenagers volunteered to make a couple of combs. All these, we said, would be picked up at the end of August, on our return from upriver. Sally went in back to visit with the women and came upon a patchwork cloth in progress—reminiscent of either Saramaka patchwork from the early twentieth century or (perhaps more to the point) the revival of that style as seen in Matawai in the 1970s—strips constructed out of triangles of contrasting solid-color cloth, which were then sewn together to make the whole. It was predominantly blue and yellow but otherwise looked almost exactly like the Matawai examples we'd illustrated in a color plate of our 1980 book. The woman sewing it, Malvina, gave the name of this kind of sewing as *abéna kamísa* and the men added that it had been in style in Bótopási for the past few years. We expressed interest in buying it, but the woman pleaded a lack of cloth to finish it and changed the subject, so we dropped our request.

Drove farther east and eventually came to Gotáli Kôndè, a large Saramaka settlement that has been there for over a decade. It looked much like a small Saramaka village in Suriname. We were taken to a large open-sided shed where a bunch of women were working and relaxing. Some of them recognized us from twenty-odd years ago, since most of them were from the village of Gódo, not far from Dángogó. Saasíni, a brash young adolescent who'd sung for our tape recorder in the sixties, was now in her thirties and considerably more mellow. She tried to persuade us to stay overnight, since they were having a big snake-god ceremony that evening, but we said we had to get back. (Are we losing our ethnographic curiosity? Getting old and lazy? Or is it, rather, a kind of information overload— we can't deal with so much at once?) The men were off in the forest working or hunting; we left without broaching our collecting project.

. . . in the world anthropologists have lost, in the dreamtime when it was still acceptable to believe that there was "no more thrilling prospect for the anthropologist than that of being the first white man to visit a particular native community" (Lévi-Strauss 1955:325–26). Such romantic Western self-inflations, and their racist and sexist conventions, were dying—if slowly—by the 1930s, as Claude Lévi-Strauss' 1955 comment

Several other stops at Saramaka woodcarving signs, but none of what we saw inspired us to commission other objects.

Back in St. Laurent, Rich picks up Ken and they go off to meet Anton, to see how his two days of Paramaka scouting have been going, and to make plans for the next day. Meanwhile, having heard that Diane Vernon is in town working on a government-sponsored AIDS project and housesitting for a doctor in the hospital complex, Sally goes off to visit with her. Next door to Dr. J's, it's the spacious upstairs of a house in the same classic colonial architecture. Rich and Ken arrive before too long, and we all have drinks on the verandah, served up with special enthusiasm by Diane's high-energy eleven-year-old, Benji. Exotic tropical birds in a giant cage, screeching for attention. Fifteen-foot-high ceilings, tremendous slabbed wooden jalousies, peeling paint, hanging hammocks, painted Maroon paddles and other *objets d'art* on the walls. The rear faces the eery, forbidding surgical ward—a tall, long, two-story wooden structure; this is the heart of the penal colony and, by moonlight, it's an unforgettable sight. From Diane's verandah, we look down, across a tall cast-iron fence, on the Boulevard De Gaulle, where a few local *clochards* spend evenings with a bottle sitting on the curb and listening to a transistor. In all, an overpowering ambiance of bygone colonial decadence. After a while, Ken and Rich bring some take-out Chinese food and beer back to the verandah. Hearing about the serenade we endured last night at the summer camp, Diane offers us a bed on her back porch, which we accept most gratefully.

During her visit with Sally, Diane, who's slated to join us for the second stage of the museum's collecting program next summer, raised a problem that's been very much on her mind. Ndjukas are happy to sell objects of art or material culture to her, since she's been going there for extended stays over such a long period and has become close to so many of them. But if she were to broach the idea of a museum, she thinks their attitude would be completely different.

indicates. So does Rabinow's account (1977:68–69) of his 1968–69 sexual conquest—symbolic domination—of a "Berber girl" in the field. . . . Today the promise and premise of a world anthropology in its liberal or more radical universality is visible reality. Other-fucking in its more vulgar forms is drawing to a close.

— Roger Sanjek, *Fieldnotes* (1990), pp. 39–41

The relations between tourists and recent ex-primitives are framed in a somewhat forced, stereotypical commercial exploitation model charac- terized by bad faith and petty suspicion on both sides. . . . The dominant view of white Europeans and North Americans expressed by recent ex- primitives is that they exhibit an unimaginable combination of qualities: specifically, they are rich tightwads, boorish, obsessed by consumerism, suffering from collectomania. . . .

As degenerate as these exchanges [between tourists and ex-primitives] might at first appear, there is no problem here, really. . . . All these behav- iors are recognizably boorish, so the "problem" as represented is entirely correctible by available means: counseling ("don't use ethnic slurs"); edu- cation . . . ; etiquette. . . . With a bit of decency and sound advice these "problems" . . . would go away.

Or would they? I think not. Because I detect in all these reports on exchanges between tourists and others a certain mutual complicity, a co- production of a pseudo-conflict to obscure something deeper and more serious: namely, that *the encounter between tourist and "other" is the scene of a shared utopian vision of profit without exploitation, logically the final goal of a kind of cannibal economics shared by ex-primitives and postmoderns alike.* The desire for profit without exploitation runs so strong, like that for "true love," even intellectuals can trick themselves into finding it where it does not exist, where, in my view, it can never exist.

— MacCannell, "Cannibal Tours," p. 15 (our italics)

I thought it was important that my business concern itself not just with skin and hair preparations, but also with the community, the environment and the big wide world beyond cosmetics. . . .

Simplicity has a lot of appeal in an increasingly complex world. So does honesty. . . . The Body Shop has many stories to tell, because the ideas and the ingredients for our formulations come from such a rich variety of sources—everything from folkloric recipes that have been tried and tested by human beings for thousands of years to tips harvested by our visits to

First, she says, they would raise their asking prices significantly. And besides that, once they hear that the object will go into a museum, many will say they don't want to sell at all. She's concerned and unsure whether the whole enterprise can work. Sally, who has been engaging over the past couple of days in a kind of internal sales pitch for optimism (at least as a working hypothesis) in order to be able to follow through on the summer's project, gives a short-form reply: Well, if people want higher prices than what they would charge a friend, the museum budget can be written accordingly. And if they don't want particular things in a museum, it's surely their privilege to keep them. Diane seems taken aback when the debate ends so abruptly and Sally experiences the uncomfortable feeling of having swept a large ball of dust under the rug.

One thing that's bothering all of us—surfacing at different moments, in slightly different modes—has to do with the changes that "collecting" threatens to introduce into relationships that we care very much about. The two of us are not in precisely the same position on this as Ken and Diane, since, for the moment, we're not talking about fulfilling the museum's charge with "our" people, the Saramaka; for us to adopt a particular role (as agents of a museum in Cayenne) among the Eastern Maroons is one degree less disturbing to our field rapport than were we to carry it out in the Saramaka villages of Central Suriname. Among Ndjukas, Paramakas, and Alukus, we're not, for the most part, known. No one particularly expects Sally to observe menstrual taboos or to skin monkeys; no one assumes that Rich will hunt and fish for our suppers or know how to discuss the particulars of eighteenth-century battles. We're new kids on the block; there's not all that much—in the way of reputations to uphold, friendships to treat with special affect, etc.—that will be placed in jeopardy if we walk into villages simply as polite, articulate visitors and turn out to be engaged in a project of government-sponsored acquisition. Both Ken and Diane, on the other hand, are concerned about turning one kind of relationship, which they've

tribal cultures around the globe. I don't think The Body Shop will ever lose the sense of adventure that is attached to the pursuit of knowledge.

— Anita Roddick, founder of a chain of 600 stores in 40 countries and major sponsor of the television series "Millennium: Tribal Wisdom and the Modern World," in "What is The Body Shop?" (1991).

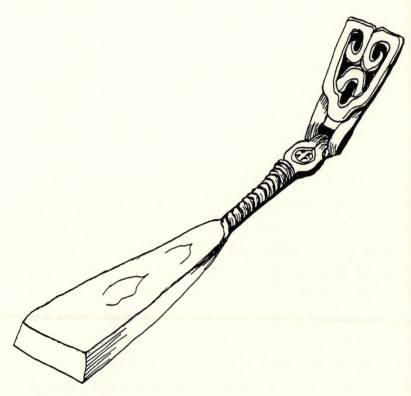

Captain Tafanye's folding laundry-beater [See page 169]

each worked hard to shape over the years, into another, much more problematical one. That's why Ken has proposed introducing us as his "bosses" on this venture. That way, he's reasoned, if there's any awkwardness about buying and selling, about conducting visits in a "business-like" manner, and so forth, Alukus will still be able to see him as a special friend who's simply accepted a temporary job that was offered. It's also why Diane continues to waver about joining the project at all.

Their feelings resonate strongly. When we were living in Dángogó in the 1960s, we were contacted informally about making a collection for the Smithsonian, and because one of our interests was material culture and aesthetics, we considered it seriously. In fact, we put together, not one, but two complete Saramaka collections— some two-hundred objects for the Smithsonian and about half as many for the Surinaams Museum in Paramaribo. These were backed up with careful ethnographic documentation on several hundred types of objects (not all of them "collectible"). The enterprise of putting these collections together was enormously useful to us in arriving at an understanding of Saramaka life. But in the end we froze it at the stage of field notes, documentary photos, and technical sketches; the objects were never actually acquired, the collections never collected. Concerns over upsetting the delicate balance of our presence in Dángogó—a village where non-Maroons had never been allowed to spend the night before we came—made us opt for a musée imaginaire only; there simply seemed to be too much at stake to play with turning the stuff of everyday life into commodities, and us into customers.

Now we're in a different time and place—a different world both for us and for the people whose life we say we're going to document for Science . . . or for their grandchildren . . . or for tourists flying in on Air France. . . . The balance is tipped ever-so-slightly from when we were in Dángogó; enough to have made us say yes to the enterprise, not enough to erase a lot of doubts. And personal

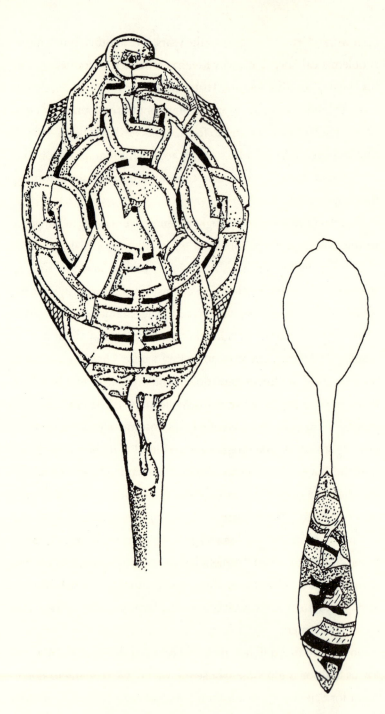

Anton's nephew's paddle, carved for his grandmother by Thomas Muli [See page 107]

field relations aside, there remains the broader issue of whether complicity between respectful collector and willing native may not mask underlying violence of a deeper kind.

The three of us meet Anton at nine to hear what he's been able to track down, and then set out to make the rounds for potential purchases, following the notes (person's name, place, kind of object) that he has penned with great effort and care in his notebook during the preceding two days.

Our first Paramaka stop is a house on the sandy slope of Sineisi Pasi, a twenty-meter-wide band of shacks on stilts squeezed between the high brick wall of the old penal colony enclosure and the polluted riverbank. The four of us stand as a group for five or ten minutes while neighbors try to find the woman who, according to Anton's notebook, has an embroidered textile to sell. We feel terribly self-conscious, socially out of place. All of us (including Anton, an experienced field assistant) are used to personal, individualized encounters as the stuff of fieldwork; this relatively anonymous "team" approach feels awkward and intrusive, more what we imagine being part of a team of medical researchers or census takers would be like. When the woman can't be found, we leave word that we'll return later, and dutifully file off to the second address on Anton's list.

At the other end of Sineisi Pasi, we stand on old planks serving as walkways above the mud and slime and talk to a woman who has two calabashes, made by other women, to sell. She asks "five thousand" (50F); they're handsomely carved and she's living in utter squalor; we give her 60F, and interview her for the documentation requested by the fiches. What an incongruous enterprise.

On to the older part of Sabonyé, where we visit at length with a fifty-four-year-old Aluku named Dooi. Appointed local "Captain"

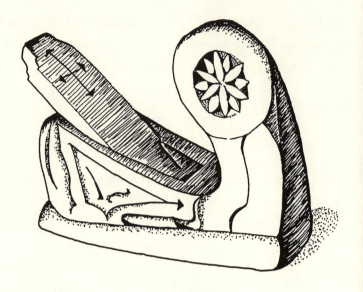

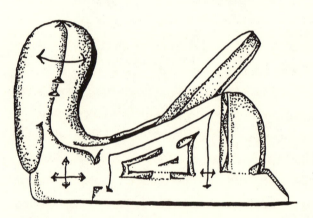

Captain Dooi's plane

by the French in 1989, he receives 30 percent of the minimum wage as his government salary. His mother is Aluku, his father Saramaka. Expansive, he switches easily between his parents' languages, and is equally comfortable in French. He proudly shows us official French papers attesting to his status as a "licensed woodcarver." "*Dati da mi fak*" ("That's my profession"), he insists repeatedly in Sranan, the lingua-franca of coastal Suriname. He talks about making something new for us, but Rich is much taken with the carved carpenter's plane he sees in a corner, which Dooi uses to smooth planks; when asked, he says he could sell it to us since he's got another one almost finished. The handle of the one we buy is rounded on one side, flat on the other, and each has distinctive decoration. We interview him for the *fiche* and get further technical information about manufacture. One of his four wives has some calabashes, he volunteers, and we arrange to return in the late afternoon to talk with her when she comes back from working in her garden.

Still in Sabonyé, Anton takes us to see a "very, very old" paddle that a nephew of his has inherited from his grandmother. Going over its ownership history more precisely with the nephew, we determine that it was carved in 1970. Not a bad piece, though it's chipped at the tip. We buy it.

Back to the woman with the embroidered cloth, who's now at home and receives us in the little room on stilts over the muck. Her white-cloth wrap-skirt is embroidered with flowers, her name (Helena Jotje), and various phrases in Sranan: "Don't worry your head," "I don't know what I'm doing," and "Sugar." She smiles coyly and tells us that "they really showered me with compliments when I danced [in a stage performance] in Paramaribo wearing this skirt!" We agree to buy it, but pass on the second more ordinary one she also wants to sell. Then suggest taking her picture wearing the skirt, which we say we'll send her. Some confusion. Take my picture, but not wearing this skirt, she says. The whole thing's more than a little awkward. We think back to picture-taking in *Cannibal Tours*, a film the

What we saw as we cleared the overhanging foliage literally mesmerized us. Standing several yards ahead of us was a young [Saramaka] girl who looked so thoroughly African that she might have been standing on the banks of the Niger or the Congo or some other African river. Her color was deep black . . . and she was naked to her waist. . . . We could not contain our delight at this evidence that we had found the culture we sought. We expressed our excitement so loudly that the child immediately spotted us and ran into the bush, but not before we could snap a photograph of her.

> — S. Allen Counter and David L. Evans, *I Sought My Brother* (1981), p. 32

Helena Jotje's embroidered skirt

two of us saw while at Stanford. We don't really have to take a picture, we suggest. The subject is dropped and the textile paid for and documented.

Anton directs us out the road toward St. Maurice ("Sémóisi" to Saramakas working in Guyane a century ago, who took the name for one of their largest Suriname River villages). There we're shown a collection of Paramaka calabashes that are more gouged and scratched than carved. Saramakas we know would dismiss them as the work of a child, or of a woman just beginning to learn to carve. (And we know it's not just a question of Paramaka-Saramaka stylistic difference. The two calabashes we'd just collected, like those John Lenoir brought back from Paramaka fieldwork in the 1970s, were different from all those we'd seen in Saramaka but still thoughtfully conceived and executed — completely free of the jerky contours and stray gouges that Sally, a novice calabash carver, recognizes all too well.) We explain that the proposed bowls are not exactly what we had in mind, and feel badly about the reaction of clear disappointment. Similar discomfort when we say no to two people who want to sell us painted Ndjuka paddles — nice enough, but not "museum quality" according to our discussions in Cayenne.

We drop Anton at his house and conclude the shopping tour with three visits in Sabonyé. The first to Sama Mma, Captain Dooi's fifty-six-year-old Paramaka wife, now back from her garden, who brought out a sack of well-carved calabash bowls and spoons. A nice antidote to the gouged Paramaka bowls we'd just refused. Friendly conversation and problem-free negotiation: she named prices for each of ten items and we agreed. Then to the house of a young cornrow-coiffed Aluku man in a neighborhood called Sabana-ini who had two stools and a tray to sell. The carvings were borderline in terms of quality, so we said we'd get back to him after our trip to Maripasoula. While we were talking, his wife arrived pushing a child in a French stroller.

The door we commissioned from Dakan for the museum

We walk by Bakaloto, a large corrogated iron shed that comes alive as a Maroon nightclub and dance place on weekend nights. Nearby, we make our final visit of the day: an old friend of Ken's, Papa Dakan, an Aluku carver who has lived for some years in St. Laurent. Buy a stool from one of his wives, but because it needs a minor repair that he won't be able to make until he gets the proper glue, we arrange to pick it up when we come back downriver. And we commission two wooden doors, one for the museum, one for Ken (actually, a door Dakan promised to make for Ken several years ago), to be picked up after our upriver stay.

The three of us go off to find Peter Redfield, a graduate student from Berkeley who'd taken a class with Rich and was arriving that afternoon to get a preliminary look at St. Laurent, before deciding on a dissertation research topic. We found him sitting at the sidewalk café of the Hotel Toucan. After a beer, we all head off to Diane's verandah in the hospital complex. Friendly shop-talk among five anthropologists. A couple of Ndjuka men drop by to chat and we listen in on their conversation with Diane, understanding perhaps 80 percent of what they're saying. Later, the government psychiatrist invites us all to dinner at a local Creole restaurant, along with the head of the hospital — half a dozen whitefolks out on the town, fulfilling all the local stereotypes.

SUNDAY 29/VII/90

Like every Sunday morning of this expedition, we diligently swallow down our mefloquine pills, designed to spare us from the falciparum variety of malaria that almost killed Ken during his fieldwork with the Aluku. Then the tedious process of logging in the objects we've acquired (attaching tags or masking-tape labels with the catalogue number, filling out the *fiches* from our on-the-spot interview

In May 1990 some young Saramakas formed a new armed group called "Angula," which quickly built close ties with the National Army. The army then undertook a campaign for the first time south of the lake, and on 23 July 1990 captured the medical post of Debiké, which had served as a base for the Jungle Commandos. On 24 September 1990 the army, as a punitive measure, burned down some twenty houses in [the neighboring village of] Bótopási.

> — Ben Scholtens, Gloria Wekker, et al., *Gaama Duumi, Buta Gaama* (1992)

notes). Renewed annoyance at having to squeeze the Maroon world into standardized French categories.

We visit Sêneki in her Saramaka garden behind the airport. A pleasant moment just chatting in the cool of her open-sided shed. We ask after the Bótopási woman who'd said she had thirty-odd combs to sell, and are directed down a path where we find her at home. Linoleum floor, refrigerator, coffee table covered with lace doily and knick-knacks; her husband has been working at a steady job. She serves soft drinks and little crackers. Her husband has left her combs to sell, she says, and she brings out a sack filled with brand-new, identical, tourist combs crudely-carved on one side only. Once again, we feel badly that we have to say no.

We head out the road, wondering whether collecting upriver in Aluku villages is going to be more interesting than the experience so far in St. Laurent. Visit Tjodj and Simeon's atelier, where we discuss the latest war news from Suriname. They report, with emotion, that the Suriname army has arrived in Debiké, just below their home village of Bótopási, and they fear the worst. After engaging for a half hour or so in animated discussion of the war, and picking up the carved wooden carafe for the collection, we double back through St. Laurent to visit Alimóni, who shows us his progress on the pretty round stool we hope to buy. A ten-year-old boy, sent out by the men at Soomi's atelier a hundred yards down the road, runs up and delivers his message: we mustn't forget to come by for the several objects we'd commissioned on Thursday. We buy a nice winnowing tray he's carved for us, with his name incised in large capital letters as part of the design, but refuse a stool whose carving seems both unexceptionable and repetitive with the tray. He's carved both of these in only three days — by sitting up nights, he says. Yet another awkward moment of refusal and disappointment; but we feel sure that he'll find someone else to sell it to. We pay his asking price for the tray.

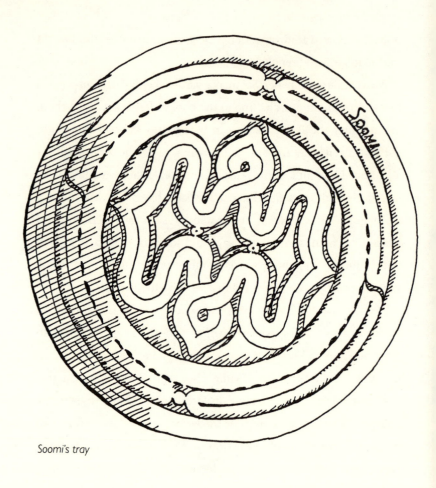

Soomi's tray

This was a real Chinese restaurant, and as friends of the house we were given places of honour between the pig-run and the duckpond, where two Chinese laid on a doubtful-looking cloth about ten dishes which looked more doubtful still. From somewhere hidden a Chinese singer burst into nasal song, and in the kitchen an ex-convict hurried through the last round of a slipper fight with the cook.

      — Henry Larsen and May Pellaton, *Behind the Lianas* (1958), p. 9

Meanwhile, Ken has been spending the day at Diane's, talking anthropology with her and Peter Redfield. Working in Aluku and Ndjuka gives Ken and Diane much more common ground with each other, in terms of people, places, even language and ethnography, than with us, and they haven't had a chance to catch up on things for a couple of years. Peter, newly arrived in his first "ethnographic setting," plays the part of the fascinated observer, using the opportunity as a kind of symbolic bridge from library-based graduate studies to anthropology as lived experience. We meet them on Diane's verandah for early evening drinks and all go out for some Chinese food (dished up, like much of St. Laurent's restaurant food, including Italian pizzas and French crepes, by Saramaka cooks).

MONDAY 30/VII/90

Six straight hours of diary writing on the computer. At 3 PM, we leave to get sandwiches at the Suriname-run snack bar on the main drag, then to pick up Peter (who's been continuing his apprenticeship by watching Ken's interactions with various Alukus) and drive off together to visit Saramaka carvers to commission more objects. At each stop, animated discussion of the contradictory information arriving about the war in Saramaka. Back in St. Laurent, we continue to nurture Peter's introduction to being in the field by eating tjoptjoi in one of the town's hole-in-the-wall Chinese eateries. Ken and Diane, who've spent a lot of time over the years in St. Laurent and know the local dignitaries, are the guests of the Sub-Prefect for a formal dinner in a fashionable restaurant.

Three of Sama Mma's calabash bowls [See page 109]

Woke up after a hard night, not blameable on ghetto-blasters or an airless room, but only on our continuing doubts about what we're engaged in, and our feelings of frustration at not having sufficient time, in the midst of running around after objects here and there, and keeping a detailed record of it, to think the whole enterprise through to our satisfaction. Rich has dreamed that he's driving a car backwards and out of control, the steering wheel only loosely connected. Sally has woken at intervals, dreamed petty arguments over dirty laundry, and engaged involuntarily in repeated calculations of how much of the fifty-day commitment is still left to be discharged. We decide to divide efforts in order to get things done faster, perhaps to ease the unpleasantness of it all, and to arrive at a more contemplative stage a little sooner. Rich will join Ken in making the rounds with Anton to potential artifact-providers, and Sally will word-process our handwritten notes into the computer. Our little studio is looking increasingly shoddy, with sand and mud tracked in, and water from the shower standing in large pools on the floor. The bug life is gradually returning after the watchman's initial fumigation with Baygon, and there's no equipment available to us to effect a tidying up.

In the late morning, Ken, Rich, and Anton return to the studio with a new idea. The Paramaka Chief's son has offered to accompany us on a one-day upriver trip to Paramaka where there are, he says, a number of really fine old carvings that no one's interested in anymore. We agree on logistics and attempt to call La Directrice for authorization of this serendipitous mini-expedition and its purchases. She's not reachable at any point today, her secretary says. While Rich, Ken, and Anton set off to see and perhaps buy several textiles that Anton has located in the wider St. Laurent area, Sally stays behind in case La Directrice's secretary calls back about our proposal. Not five minutes elapse before the phone rings in the

One of the two Paramaka skirts bought outside St. Laurent, embroidered by Lusia Beebe Masana. At some time in the past the cloth had been cut, through part of the embroidered design, to shorten the skirt.

watchman's quarters; it's La Directrice herself and Sally wonders (now that we are beginning to understand the system) whether she hasn't been there all along. She is fully supportive of the Paramaka idea. "I grant you carte blanche," she announces with the expansive generosity that we are coming to expect whenever museum acquisitions, rather than researcher's lodgings, are concerned. Sally gets an absorbent rag from the watchman's wife, mops up the puddles on the floor, and returns to her word-processing.

Meanwhile, Rich, Ken, and Anton have gone off to collect. A couple of kilometers outside St. Laurent on the road toward Cayenne, they track down a Paramaka woman, about sixty, with whom Anton had talked previously. She sells two embroidered skirts, volunteering that she'll use the 200F to buy rice to cook for her son, who's about to visit. Polite inquiry about her son's whereabouts. He's getting out of jail (or hospital?), she explains, because he'd taken up the practice, while working at the space station in Kourou, of "shooting a needle of white powder into his arm." Then a fruitless search down a long dusty red-earth road, looking for one of Anton's sisters who might have something to sell. Finally, a quarter-hour walk off the main Cayenne road, through the forest, into Anton's father's garden-camp. Eight or ten children and grandchildren. People lying around in hammocks. A pleasant, familiar sight, more reminiscent of Saramaka than what we've been seeing around St. Laurent. A half-hour of relaxed conversation before returning to Ken's lodgings at the doctor's house for several back and forth trips in the car to transfer the expedition trunks to our summer-camp housing. We've decided to repack them there for the trip upriver.

The American threesome then makes an attempt to secure a French flag to fly from the stern of the canoe on the day-trip to Paramaka; we've been told that neither Suriname soldiers nor Jungle Commandos mess with canoes on official French business. In Sabonyé, we find an appropriate flag, but the Aluku owner is unwilling

The French flag is the only one to have a staff a thousand feet tall.

> — Gustave Eiffel, cited in Joseph Harriss, *The Eiffel Tower* (1976), p. 140

Wasn't it common until recently, among the Creoles of St. Laurent, to use the term "Boni Indians" to designate Maroons? "Indians," in the Creole sense, referred to a status, that of an excluded group, considered to be on the lowest rung of the social ladder. The semantic amalgam "Boni Indians" set in stone for Creole society the equivalence of the two minorities.

> — A. Hublin, "La proletarisation de l'habitat" (1987), p. 22

Montaigne's classic essay "Of the Cannibals" plays off his favorable impressions of *Africans* against French ethnocentrism, using cannibalism as a test case.

> — Marianna Torgovnick, *Gone Primitive* (1990), chapter 1, sentence 1, footnote 1 (our italics)

to loan it out, even for a day; the same story with our second possibility. French flags are a precious and not easily relinquished means of protection for travel on the river. Ken says he knows another Aluku with a flag who might lend it to us, and volunteers to go see him the next day.

We're invited for drinks *chez* the psychiatrist, at the hospital. Ken, who's been based in the hospital complex since our arrival, tells us he's had his fill of doctors and begs out. The scene: a decaying, high-ceilinged gem of French colonial architecture, ca. 1906, strewn and bedecked with painted paddles, carved stools, dusty basketry; table laden with gin, rum, Johnny Walker, wine, peanuts, and an impressive assortment of fancy patés and terrines (of goose liver, smoked salmon, etc.) flown in from Paris. A few Paramakas (including the pregnant fiancée of the psychiatrist's young son) are lounging on the rattan sofas; metropolitan French guests are sitting around the drinks and paté. Would it have looked any different fifty years ago in this colonial prison hospital? Perhaps the dress would have been more formal. . . .

Among the guests are Dr. J and his wife, who is a nurse. In a general discussion of what St. Laurent was like when they arrived at their posts a decade and a half ago, she describes the hospital's long-established custom of taking outpatients who came for consultation, regardless of time of arrival, in "racial" order: whites first, then Creoles, then Amerindians, and finally Maroons. She tells us proudly how her first act, upon taking up her duties, was to install a stack of numbers and institute a strictly-observed first come, first served policy. It caused considerable scandal.

Condemned, Without Rights

For more than two years, in a French *département*, Guyane, many thousands of Surinamers have been "parked" in camps under the control of the French army, without rights of residence, the right to work, the right to attend school, any guarantees that they won't be sent back to the land they fled because of persecution, the right of free speech, and so forth. . . . These Maroons have been placed outside the law . . . without the official status of refugees to which both normal French law and international law entitle them.

— *Libération* (9 May 1989), p. 25

We make two early-morning collecting forays, while Ken continues the search for a flag. The first, in Sabonyé, results in the acquisition of an embroidered cloth used to cover a meal during the interval between a woman's setting it out and her husband's eating it; the Paramaka man who sold it to us declined to pronounce the name of the woman who made it for him, since she had been his lover, and one of his wives was sitting next to him, giggling in embarrassment at the whole situation. We acquire a second textile on the outskirts of town, from an older Paramaka woman who explains that she bought the materials and then asked a Saramaka friend to design and execute the decoration.

Then off to a meeting with the psychiatrist, who has asked our assistance in communicating with a fourteen-year-old Saramaka patient currently incarcerated in a Ndjuka refugee camp. The background, according to the psychiatrist: Young "Baala" was brought to the hospital by an older brother a few months ago, after having suffered a nervous crisis one night. The doctor tranquilized him and, after several days, interviewed him, eliciting a story about a broken calabash that had been made by his mother. The doctor told us that the boy's condition was due to his relationship with his mother, symbolized by the broken calabash, and he spun out for us various Freudian implications. ("What's it like to conduct a psychiatric interview when you don't speak the patient's language?" we queried. "Thank goodness for the universal language of symbols," the good doctor replied.) After several days of chemical treatment, Baala was placed in Camp A (no literary abbreviation; the official name is "Camp A")—the refugee camp next to the St. Laurent airstrip. The psychiatrist ended his summary of Baala's pathology by recounting how the boy stopped speaking as soon as he arrived in the camp. RP remarks to SP, under his breath, that this case makes him think of the incident described by Stedman in which a fourteen-

The above Mr. Ebbers [an overseer] was indeed peculiarly tyrannical, tormenting a boy of about fourteen, called Cadety, for the space of a whole year, by alternately flogging him for one month, then keeping him laid flat on his back with his feet in the stocks for another, then making him wear an iron triangle called a pot-hook around his neck, to prevent him from escaping or sleeping for a third month, and chaining him to the landing place in a dog's collar night and day without shelter, with orders to *bark* at every boat or canoe that passed, for a fourth, &c., &c., till the youth had almost become insensible to his sufferings, walked crooked and, in a manner, degenerated into a brute.

 — Stedman, *Narrative* (1790/1992), p. 147

year-old Suriname slave had been deliberately deprived of speech and driven mad by a sadistic overseer. SP: "*Ou malin!* [Martiniquan creole, roughly: Don't be such a smartass!] The psychiatrist is just trying to pull Baala out of what he sees as a psychotic episode. How can you compare torturing a slave with the practice of modern psychiatry?"

Since Baala had been abandoned by his relatives, who never came to see him, the psychiatrist hoped that we would be able to give an opinion and help him figure out what to do with the boy. (The immediate concern was that the psychiatrist was about to leave St. Laurent for several weeks and he needed to be able to give some kind of instructions to the people who would be holding the fort during his absence.) With the psychiatrist at the wheel, the car was waved through the military checkpoint at the entrance to Camp A which, like the other Ndjuka refugee camps, is run by the French army. At our approach, Baala's behavior confirmed the doctor's summary; he was silent, and he seemed disturbed. We asked the doctor, in French, to leave us alone with him, and greeted him in Saramaccan. Suddenly, a broad grin, a normal fourteen-year-old. We introduced ourselves and said we were interested in what had happened to him.

He'd been held there against his will, he said, for many weeks, surrounded by Ndjukas who spoke a language he could barely understand. The words came tumbling out. The white doctor scared him; the white nurses scared him; the soldiers scared him. His brother, he said, had been visiting him every three or four days, sneaking in across the back fence because he was scared of the soldiers and the nurses and the doctors; he had no French papers and, like many Saramakas in French Guiana, lived in constant fear of discovery and deportation back to Suriname. And the broken calabash? Baala explained that he'd had an argument with his brother, who then went off to wash the dinner dishes at a creek and, on purpose, broke Baala's drinking calabash. He was furious. That night some sort of "god" had come into his head and made him cry out violently. His

The only heroes of the book are Richard and Sally Price.
> — IK, *Museum News* (July–August 1990), p. 66 — referring to one of our earlier books

brother delivered him to the hospital the next morning. Since then, he'd been fine and simply wanted to get out of this awful place. Did his brother and the rest of the family want him back? we asked. Of course! he said. We told Baala we'd see what we could do and went off with the psychiatrist, who agreed that we should visit the family to confirm that they were prepared to receive him back.

Off we drove to a Saramaka settlement ten kilometers out on the road to Mana, just past the largest of the Ndjuka refugee camps. Baala's friends and relatives were delighted that he could be released, and confirmed the story he'd told us. Nothing would please them more, they said, than to be able to have him back, but they'd been too frightened of the soldiers and the doctor to try to arrange his release themselves. We took one of Baala's brothers with us and drove down the road to the giant refugee camp where the psychiatrist was consulting. A menacing aspect to this place, where white crew-cut soldiers live on a central hill surrounded by a heavy barbed wire barrier hung with a large skull-and-crossbones warning sign. We persuaded the psychiatrist to release Baala into his brother's custody that very day, and he wrote a note for us to take, along with Baala's brother, back to Camp A.

Before leaving, we couldn't resist a comment or two on why Baala had been silent—no one spoke his language, he was terribly frightened of the soldiers and the doctor, he was incarcerated in a squalid camp—and we tried to explain what French colonialism, backed by automatic weapons, looked like from the perspective of a fourteen-year-old boy who'd grown up in a Saramaka village in the interior. The psychiatrist protested that he'd never been anything but kind toward the boy (which was certainly true). We drove back to Camp A, and Baala was soon on his way home.

In the afternoon, meet up with Ken, who still hasn't found a flag. Together, we try a couple of possibilities without success, but Ken has yet another idea, and later that night he finally succeeds in getting the precious piece of cloth.

Large calabash bowl carved by the late Ma Titia and sold to us by her sister's daughter, Chief Difou's widow [See p. 221]

Up in the dark at 5:30 to pack, pick up Anton and then Ken, and be at the river by 7:00 for the day-trip to Paramaka. When we arrive at Anton's, his wife says he didn't sleep in their house that night, so we head into town to buy bread in the only store that's open, wake up Ken, and install ourselves by the river to wait for Anton, the canoe, and the Paramaka boatmen we've hired for the day to materialize. Anton shows up at 7:30; he'd been stranded without a ride somewhere along the Cayenne road. We wait several hours, skipping stones in the river, listening to a weird buzzing monotone which we eventually trace to a French woman in a nearby row of flats reciting her morning mantras, and finally decide the trip is ruined. So we adopt Plan B—to leave the next day in the expedition boat (which is due to arrive in St. Laurent today), taking Anton with us as a guide to the Paramaka garden camps and having him hitch back to St. Laurent with some downstream-bound canoe while we proceed upriver for our stay in Aluku territory.

The rest of the morning is spent tracking down the two expedition boatmen, who've been spotted in St. Laurent, and running a series of errands for Anton—picking up fish and bread for his family, etc. Catch up with "our" Aluku boatmen-to-be, Ba Manku and Ba Nyolu, who agree to leave the next morning at seven. A flurry of last-minute food- and supply-buying for the expedition, with Ken and Sally suffering intermittent attacks of diarrhea. We speak to the Avis man and arrange to leave the car and the keys by the river at seven the next morning.

Evening: the trunks are finally packed, but there are two more hitches. Manku and Nyolu report that the eight barrels of gasoline to be used for the duration of the mission are nowhere to be found. They were neither upriver in Maripasoula nor are they here in St. Laurent—nor is there a purchase order to buy them. They also report that they lost the cap (the metal cover) of the outboard motor in

Creole-style broom made by Papa Aputeiki for his daughter, bought for the BPE August 12 in Maripasoula

a difficult descent through a rapids on the way downstream, and the one they had borrowed to replace it earlier in the day has just been repossessed by the owner, who has been having a personal quarrel with Manku. We immediately phone La Directrice in Cayenne, but it's already 6:30 and she's just left the office for the day. Rich decides to use personal funds to buy a barrel of gas that evening and a motor cap the next morning so we can get going on schedule, worrying about the additional gas once we get to Maripasoula. Manku knows a Ndjuka who owns a truck, so we head off to find him in the new part of Sabonyé where the French have constructed rows upon rows of prefabricated houses. They look like a cross between old-time Aluku A-frames and Swiss chalet ski lodge bungalows. We're able to rent the truck for an hour to transport the gas, which we buy at a Texaco station, to the boat, where we say goodnight to Manku and Nyolu. The three of us eat a last Chinese restaurant meal and engage in an intense discussion of linguistic questions having to do with comparative Saramaccan, Sranan, and Aluku. A pleasant change from the rest of the day's program.

FRIDAY 3/VIII/90

It's 5:30 PM; we're writing this at Diane's house, high in the prison hospital complex. It's been another hairy day of *imprévus*. Up at 5:30 AM. This time, Anton's ready and waiting at his house when we come by. Ken nearly ready and waiting at his. Bought bread for the second day in a row to take in the boat; we'd given yesterday's to Anton's children when the trip was aborted. Nyolu and Manku load the canoe. We're struck that they push the motor in a wheelbarrow (rather than hefting it on a shoulder) and take two men to roll the barrel of gas; compared to the men we've known in Saramaka, who take pride in shows of physical prowess, the self-image here shades toward that of a *fonctionnaire*. The landing place is filthy, the sand

Captain Tobu's fishing arrow [See page 207]

strewn with broken bottles, bunches of palmfruit, plastic refuse, feces, and old shoes washed up by the tide; Ndjuka mothers wash their young children in the foul water. Other Ndjuka women use garden rakes to clean debris from under their houses-on-stilts, not far from the water's edge.

The question of the motor cap comes up. Boatmen blasé, more or less ready to leave with or without the cap, and see whether or not it really interferes with the motor's performance. Ken worries about getting stuck out of reach of a village, with the war going on. A little history: Thursday Manku had borrowed a motor cap from the warehouse belonging to the Département ("state government") garage, but a man later came and reclaimed it. There was some kind of personal fight between him and Manku.

We decided to go to the Département garage to persuade him to return it for our use. Unequivocal refusals; hostile remarks. So, at 7:15, off to the store that sells outboard motors, following information from three people that (a) it opened at 7:00, (b) it opened at 7:30, and (c) it opened at 8:00. Arriving and finding it closed, we inquired at the bar next door and were told that (d) it opened whenever the owner felt like opening it. But there was, we were told, a second outboard motor store, so off we went. The clerk sitting at the computer said that her boss hadn't arrived, and she was not able (lacking either the authority or competence—it wasn't clear) to quote us a price for the cap (which we wanted in order to phone La Directrice and ask for authorization to buy the thing). More trips back and forth, too numerous to remember with accuracy. The boss returns to Store #2 and tells us that he has Evinrude, but not Johnson caps; our motor's a Johnson Seahorse 45HP. Return to Store #1 and, with uncharacteristic good luck, we find the owner just pulling up in his car. Discussion. Evinrude now owns Johnson, or vice-versa, he informs us; the cap will fit both brands because they're just one thing with two names. Our spirits rise. He, however, doesn't have either in stock. Would we like to place an order for one from

I am well persuaded that while some of my readers wish me in Greenland for these digressions, others wish me at the Devil for dwelling at all on the expeditions &c., but I have read the fable of the man, the boy, and the ass,* and while I am well convinced that I cannot please all the world, I will at least, by those varieties, have a chance to gratify a few of every denomination without exception. This is my plan and, assuredly, a better one than to be tied down to the whims of one particular set of people. Thus I will ever (gentle critics) proceed in my own way.

*One of Poggio's fables, concerning the difficulties of an old man who, with a boy, took an ass to market and, by trying to please every person he encountered along the way, ended up displeasing them all and losing his ass in the bargain.

— Stedman, *Narrative* (1790/1992), pp. 236, 331

Cayenne, which he could have in a couple of days? Back to Store #2: Could we buy an Evinrude cap? Long wait. Computers consulted. Back room calls to Cayenne. There is one cap in Cayenne, . . . etc.

Returning to the Département garage, we phone La Directrice, who phones a state government official in St. Laurent who's higher up than the men at the Département garage, and he orders them to lend us one of their motor caps. Victory. Rich walks over and picks up the cap but gets barked at by the very angry *mécanicien*, who tells him to get his dirty hands off it, that he (the mechanic) is in charge there. We are finally given one of the two available caps and leave. Back at the boat, the cap is installed but keeps pulling off; the latch doesn't latch. Deciding to press forward on the Département garage front, we return and try to sweet-talk the Amerindian-looking man who uses the office and phone. But the offended mechanic, who had originally taken back the loaned cap, has gotten to him in the meantime and he says the answer is an absolute and unnegotiable no. Arguments. Counterarguments. President Georges Othily's "Ordre de Mission" is flashed, as an ultimate invocation of authority. But it does no good. We call La Directrice and explain the situation. She asks to speak to the Amerindian guy, who tells her that "*C'est le mécanicien qui commande.*" Sally figures that this remark will be enough of a challenge to La Directrice so that she'll move mountains to prove that she, not the mechanic, commands. But in the end it turns out that he does.

Many phone calls via the satellite link to Maripasoula (where the boss of the St. Laurent office now happens to be), from both La Directrice in Cayenne and the Amerindian office worker in St. Laurent. The mechanic is called to the phone and rants about the white man who had the audacity to barge into his space, grab his equipment, etc. Sweating profusely, face twitching, very angry. Tells chief in Maripasoula that there IS no alternative cap. Meanwhile, Rich, Ken, and Nyolu have gone to Store #2 to see if the latch on the borrowed cap could be fixed. Rich asks the manager if we could pay his

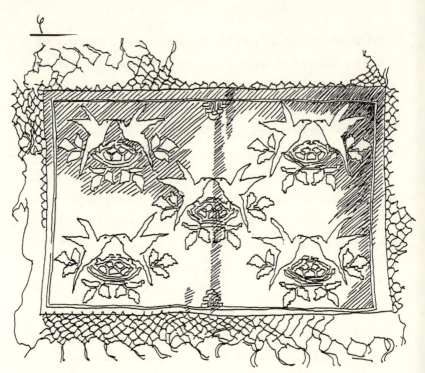

The Paramaka textile embroidered by an unnamed lover of the man who sold it to us
[See page 123]

mechanic (who is standing idly by) to spend ten minutes with us at the river diagnosing the latch problem. "Out of the question! We are not authorized to make service calls." By trying the borrowed cap on a new showroom motor, they realize that it's an older model cap and that's why it won't latch on our relatively new motor. Return to the Département garage, where Sally has been closely following the phone call tug-of-war. La Directrice phones and tells Rich that the Département's second (good) cap, the one Rich had tried to pick up, was apparently (read: allegedly) "reserved . . . though they are unable to give me the name of the person who reserved it" — thus saving face, since she had not been able to force her orders. It's now 10:15, three hours past our planned departure time: she proposes buying a cap in Cayenne and sending it to us by an "express taxi" at 11 AM. We suggest that she have it delivered c/o Dr. J at the hospital. Nyolu volunteers helpfully that perhaps she should send it by airplane. We drop off the useless cap at the Département garage and return to the loaded boat. Decide to regroup, with the new cap, at 2:30 to make the two-hour run up to Apatou, a militarized Aluku commune harboring a large number of Paramaka refugees, and to sleep there.

Anton, who'd been told by Rich that he'd be paid for the day as if he'd been working (because the screw-up wasn't his fault), then requested that we drive him back to his house outside of St. Laurent, since he "had no place to go in town," and would we also come pick him up at 2:30? And on the way, he had just a couple of quick errands if we'd wait in the car for a few minutes.

While we were still at the boat, the Avis clerk, looking disgruntled, appeared on the scene. He'd come to pick up the car as we'd arranged and saw it sitting there locked, but he also saw that the keys had not been left as we'd promised. We explained, apologized, and set up a 2:30 drop-off. After chauffeuring Anton around to his various destinations, the three of us had beers, plus some of the bread we'd bought for the trip, spread with a chocolate bar that had melted

Then professionally envious, Fortune suspected that Bateson was favored there [at Cambridge, where both had worked under Haddon] for hereditary reasons. "Haddon is very kind to me," he had written Margaret, "but he gave Gregory Bateson his mosquito net."

    — David Lipset, *Gregory Bateson* (1980), pp. 135–36; cited in
       James A. Boon, *Affinities and Extremes* (1990), p. 177

It was said of him that in that same bedroom he'd murdered a man he found sleeping with his wife, that he'd buried him secretly in the courtyard. The truth was different: Adalberto Asís had, with a shotgun blast, killed a monkey he'd caught masturbating on the bedroom beam with his eyes fixed on his wife while she was changing her clothes. He'd died forty years later without having been able to rectify the legend.

    — Gabriel García Márquez, *In Evil Hour* (1980), p. 31

That night we drank *yagé* by the sick boy's bed, Santiago and I. . . . It was an uneventful night with soft chanting and talk of hunting in the Putumayo, what it was like in the forests for Santiago when he was a kid by his father's side, how he'd killed an anteater with a lance, but never a tiger, whether or not there was envy in the countries where I had lived, and so forth. He couldn't conceive the notion that envy as a maliciously wounding force capable of even killing people did not exist in the places I came from. Years later I began to see how right he was, especially with regard to academics.

    — Michael Taussig, *Shamanism, Colonialism, and the Wild Man*
      (1987), p. 349

Be wary of the history that claims to be separate from the circumstances of its telling or to have only one meaning.

    — Greg Dening, *History's Anthropology* (1988), p. 15

as it sat in the idle boat. Then, after a short pause, a Vietnamese restaurant meal, on the theory that we wouldn't eat that night in Apatou. Finally, to the hospital for the motor cap.

At 1:30, the motor cap still hasn't arrived and Sally has stomach cramps, so she lies down in Dr. J's guest room while Rich and Ken go off to intercept the motor cap when it arrives at the hospital gate. Sitting on a wooden bench in front of the white-washed colonial admissions office, Rich and Ken talk about publishing and linguistics, but mostly they exchange anthropological gossip. Rich realizes that they must look very much like the cover photo of Larry Fisher's book, *Colonial Madness*, in which a couple of inmates sit, draped on a similar hospital bench, on the porch of the Barbados insane asylum.

Diane bikes up, smiling; Ken goes off with her to her house while Rich remains on the bench, waiting for the motor cap and watching the sky blacken; a tremendous tropical downpour is gathering force. As the deluge begins, he cowers on the porch by the gate. Meanwhile, back at the doctor's, rain blowing through the wooden jalousies wakes Sally, tummy somewhat calmer, and she walks into the living room where the doctor is talking with his daughter. She explains, when he looks startled at seeing her, that she's been napping in the guest room and tells why we hadn't left that morning as planned: "It's a long story involving a motor cap." "Motor cap?!" he says. "That's funny. Because someone delivered a brand new motor cap to my house a little while ago and I have no idea what it's for." Sally explains. The doctor phones the admissions office next to where Rich is waiting. Rich runs back to the doctor's house, arriving soaked to the skin. The cap had been delivered to a back entrance.

It is now 3 PM, and black as night. The rain continues to pour down. No way to leave at this time in this weather. We retrieve Ken and drive off to tell Anton, who asks for a lift into town. Then to Avis for another postponement of the car's return, and off to the boat and boatmen, who are eager to get started since the rain appears finally to be abating. They strongly protest our decision to leave early

Both colonial and ethnographic situations provoke the unnerving feeling of being on stage, observed and out of place. Participants in such milieux are caught in roles they cannot choose. . . . Ethnographic liberals, of which there are many sorts, have tended to be ironic participants. They have sought ways to stand out or apart from the imperial roles reserved for them as whites. . . . Many have in one way or another publicly identified themselves with exotic modes of life and thought or cultivated an image of marginality. . . . Ethnographic liberalism is an array of ironic positions, roles both within and at a certain remove from the colonial situation. Its complete dramaturgy remains to be written.

— Clifford, *The Predicament of Culture*, p. 79

the next morning, arguing that (a) Apatou is only an hour and a half away, (b) the gendarmes there would be willing to watch the boat overnight so they wouldn't have to unload it, and (c) the man who has the storage place where our stuff had spent the previous night has since had a fight with them and wouldn't give them the key, so we have no place to store the baggage here. Clearly, they'd prefer not to have to unload the boat now and reload it tomorrow morning. We hint at more phone calls to La Directrice in Cayenne. But eventually Nyolu comes up with a solution: a friend's storeroom nearby, fairly full already with black-market barrels of gasoline (from Suriname). Despite a lot of grumbling, the canoe is unloaded and everyone is in better spirits. Nyolu suggests that it would be a good moment to buy a liter of beer to share, and Rich does. We agree to meet the next morning at 6:30. The three of us go off to Diane's, in search of some R&R. She generously provides beds for the night.

Now, whoever tried to deny that anthropology is the handmaiden of colonialism? In St. Laurent, even more than Cayenne, we have been living pretty much the way visiting colonial whitefolks would be expected to: and when we're feeling tired or blue, we find ourselves heading for the old prison hospital compound and seeking out the company of other whitefolks (admittedly, themselves anthropologists). There's something about the definition of our role, and the way the town is set up, that leaves little choice, unless we decided to live more like Saramaka or Ndjuka migrants — which is the kind of choice the two of us, as well as Ken, have always made in the past, when we were not on a French mission scientifique.

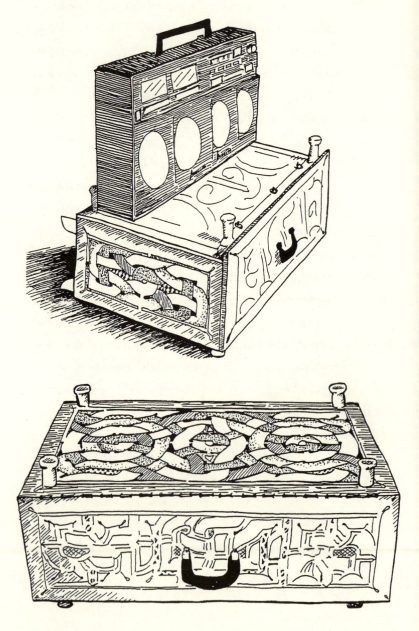

Obentié's wooden chest, from our first day upriver [See page 153]

3

Up at 5:30 for the third straight day. Once again, we go to pick up Anton, but we find him still asleep. Climbing into the car, he mentions in passing that Captain Akilingi of Langatabiki (the Paramaka "capital," on an island several hours upstream from St. Laurent) received a letter the previous night—delivered by an Amerindian runner—from Suriname's military strongman Desi Bouterse. It warned that the Suriname army was encamped only five kilometers away, at the last creek-crossing before the road reached Langatabiki. If he wanted the village to remain standing, said the letter, he must expel the Jungle Commandos who were based there. But, whether he did or not, the soldiers would be moving into Langatabiki.

Anton suggests that we restrict today's Paramaka collecting to settlements on the French side of the river below the island of Langatabiki, since the fighting wouldn't touch those areas. We buy a large supply of bread for the third straight morning. Back to the hospital, where Ken is making tea. We hurry him along and fill him in on the Bouterse letter. He says that, under the circumstances, he doesn't think we should go to Paramaka at all, because of the danger. While Ken finishes his tea we go back to Anton, who's been waiting in the car, and tell him that Ken wants to cancel the Paramaka collecting. Anton protests that even if the expected battle at Langa-

As extremely nervous passengers in dugout canoes, they went skimming through trecherous rapids, watching the thick boulders against which obviously any collision would immerse all hands into waters abounding with man-eating piranha — not to mention their near panic each time the dugouts passed under overhanging jungle vines and foliage from which large snakes could fall into the dugouts.

> — Alex Haley, describing a 1970s upriver expedition to visit the Maroons, in Counter and Evans, *I Sought My Brother*, p. x

Bare-breasted women washing clothes on the muddy banks take passing notice of canoes making their way down stream; further up in Indian country there is no washing since there are no clothes.

> — Miles, *Devil's Island*, p. 1

tabiki takes place, the settlements downstream from there should be safe. Ken arrives and argues with Anton that it's too dangerous. Anton, the faithful field assistant, agrees. Rich tells Ken that the two of us are inclined to go and feel out the situation but that, as *chef de mission*, he's not about to take responsibility for bringing Ken into a war zone against his will. Ken says he's not only concerned for his own safety but also feels strongly that we have an obligation to protect Anton from danger; we would end up leaving him there without an assured ride back downstream. We suggest that Anton is capable of making that decision on his own home ground. Ken protests that if anything were to happen to him, this kind of reasoning would offer little consolation, that the responsibility is ours. Rich reluctantly cancels the Paramaka collecting for now. We talk about the possibility of doing it after we come downriver in a few weeks.

We find Manku and Nyolu by the river and watch the uneventful (re-)loading of the canoe, with its new motor cover installed and the French flag flying near the stern. For the first couple of kilometers, we give a lift to an Aluku man, who tells us that French artillery pieces are poised on the hill across from Langatabiki and that Jungle Commandos are hidden in the bush there, ready for an ambush.

Apatou, two hours upstream from St. Laurent, a *commune* with its own mayor, gendarmes, etc. A mixed group of Ndjukas, Alukus, and Paramakas chat with us in front of a store while Ken takes pictures of the gendarmerie for a future publication.

Second stop, the garden-camp of Paramaka Chief Forster, below Langatabiki, where we decide—despite earlier discussions—to approach Captain Akilingi. He is sitting in an open-sided house above the river, surrounded by children. He speaks to us with emotion about a battle, some three weeks before, with a Suriname helicopter-gunship firing rockets down on Langatabiki. He tells us how much he has on his mind because of the war and shows us a 24 July letter from Commander Bouterse requesting his presence at a meeting in Paramaribo. He speaks of the noise of battle and how scared the

Today fell into a muddy puddle. Beastly. The fault of the man that carried me. . . . Getting jolly well sick of this fun.

— Joseph Conrad, "Congo Diary" (1890); cited as an epigraph in Christopher L. Miller, *Blank Darkness* (1985), p. 169

[We ascended] stretches of the river which were thorny with rapids, walled with immaculate timber, but quasi-civilized. Canoes spurted past us, and the naked Bonis or Boschs [Ndjukas] in them would salute us with tremendous cardboard helmets, which they had painted and silvered in the same deviously phallic designs which made all their wood carving remarkable. . . . As we approached the confluence of our river Maroni with the Tapanahoni on the Dutch shore . . . the rapids charged like white wolves at us from every side.

— Davis, *The Jungle and the Damned*, pp. 106, 127

children had been. We realize how inappropriate it would be, under the circumstances, to bring up our collecting project, and we leave after saying brief goodbyes. Ken later tells us that he heard Captain Akilingi complaining to Manku and Nyolu that it seemed as if the whitefolks didn't understand the seriousness of the war and the extent of his people's suffering, and that Ken felt called upon to reassure him, as the two of us headed toward the canoe, that we all felt deeply for their plight. We reflect on how subtle the cultural cues are for the proper expression of emotions, and how our Saramaka knowledge only half prepares us for our encounters on this river.

Smooth trip upstream. All the excitement of river travel again. High water, wide river, fast canoe, most rapids fairly flat, though we almost went under in the largest one through incompetence. Nyolu is an inexperienced bowsman; we took lots of water but Manku was able to keep the canoe upright. Passed many gold-prospecting barges, Amazon-like, sucking mud from the bottom of the river, and run by an assortment of Brazilians, Indians, and Ndjukas. Motor canoes filled with French soldiers, uniformed and in life jackets, pass us occasionally. With the war going on, and the French intent on establishing their presence, the whole river feels like a semi-militarized zone. We pass what seem like scores of Ndjuka garden-camps (and in one area, Paramaka camps), stretching all the way from St. Laurent past the confluence of the Tapanahoni and the Maroni, where we finally enter the Lawa River.

5:30 PM. Stop at Grand-Santi, an administrative post. French military camp with sandbagged machine-gun emplacements off to one side, main grassy areas of doctors' houses, clinic, school, engineers' camps, a building marked "Maroni Tours," the gendarmerie, etc. Ken says about one-hundred Ndjukas live here, many with French papers. We can't find space to hang our hammocks—the place is chock full of whitefolks—so we continue upstream for an hour or so and find a Ndjuka garden-camp where we are welcome to sling our hammocks in a shed. Nyolu and Manku go off to an all-night *dansi*.

An expedition leaving civilization is a delicate thing, a machine which, to function properly, must be perfectly balanced, in work, relaxation, nourishment, diversion, and in co-operation in all of these. The crochets of one man can throw the whole machine out of alignment, and in the jungle you can find no spare parts.

 — Davis, *The Jungle and the Damned*, p. 113

Thinking back over all that's happened since this morning, when we set out from the summer camp for a collecting trip in Paramaka with Anton, we jot down some reflections on being in the field as a team:

Ethnographic research is an art that involves a strategy, individually molded according to personal temperament, for balancing several potentially conflicting things—intellectual questions, ethnographic goals, conformance to local etiquette/conduct, as well as personal comfort, privacy, and schedules (eating, sleeping, drinking, bathing, relaxing . . .). Even when handled with supreme care, this balancing act is tremendously delicate; it walks thin lines on all dimensions. It shouldn't be surprising that engaging in it with someone else produces tensions, or that marriages often break under the weight. Questions of status, authority, judgment, initiative, and priorities, however subtle, are inevitable; in the present case, there are also moments when differences between Saramaka and Aluku ways risk being drawn incongruously into matters of personal pride, into questions of respective expertises. Among the three of us, the Aluku are "Ken's people"; Ken is "Rich's student"; and Sally's the one who's been writing on the ethics of ethnographic collecting. All three of us know that, in the larger scheme of things, none of this really matters. But all of it is capable of seeping in imperceptibly when we're tired, when defenses are down and unrelated petty annoyances are up, or when (like this morning) there are potentially stressful decisions to be made. Ken is a terrific partner for a project like this one: perceptive, energetic, knowledgeable—a damn good ethnographer, and fun to be with. But it's still a different dynamic when we add a new member to our habitual team.

Just like all primitives in contact with whites, the Boni are especially prone to take on the more harmful and undesirable aspects of civilization. They never borrow our better qualities.

    — Tripot, *La Guyane*, p. 149

The spectacle of *francisation* at its most visible: small groups of [Aluku] villagers, as they take a break from the tedium of peeling or grating cassava tubers, huddled over the soiled pages of the latest offering from [the cata-logue of] *La Redoute*, admiring the digital watches and bikinis, the patent leather belts and frilly party dresses. At night, and sometimes even during the day, they come out to sport their new booty, in a disconcerting pag-eant of alienated Frenchness. . . . An official government boatman, a man of means, shows off his newest acquisition: a bright blue pair of overall shorts, with cuffs at the thighs and a flaring collar, the *fantaisie* of an anonymous metropolitan beachwear designer. A middle-aged mother of seven thinks nothing of parading about the village in a flouncy three-tiered miniskirt of the sort usually associated with clean-cut French teenagers. An elderly vil-lage chief wears a puffy pair of tinselly gold running shorts, three sizes too large, on top of ankle-high sneakers. The occasional passing boatloads of adventure-seeking French tourists from the coast keep an eye out for the few remaining loincloths and wonder about the *bouffonnerie* being passed off as "les populations primitives."

    — Bilby, *The Remaking of the Aluku*, pp. 182–83

My friend, George Hunt, will read this to you. . . . It is good that you should have a box in which your laws and your stories are kept. My friend, George Hunt, will show you a box in which some of your stories will be kept. It is a book that I have written on what I saw and heard when I was with you two years ago. It is a good book, for in it are your laws and stories. Now they will not be forgotten. Friends, it would be good if my friend, George Hunt, would become the storage box of your laws and of your stories.

        — From an 1897 letter that Franz Boas wrote for George Hunt
            to read to the Kwakiutl, cited in Jacknis, "George Hunt,
            Collector of Indian Specimens," p. 224

As we wake up, Manku and Nyolu return from the dance, together with a bevy of teenage girls, dressed to kill in the latest mail-order creations from France. We head upriver, entering Aluku territory. We think back to the early 1960s and our reading of *Les Noirs Réfugiés de la Guyane Française*, a book about the Aluku by the French geographer Jean Hurault, which first sparked our interest in doing fieldwork among Maroons. We were especially taken with his photographs (which we now know were heavily retouched)—Riefenstahlesque, heroic bodies, exotic-looking art. But now, after twenty-five years of Maroon studies, this is the first time we've set foot in Aluku territory.

We stop for an hour at Abunasonga, a garden-camp, where we meet an Aluku in his early fifties named Obentié, who Ken knows to be an accomplished carver. Just before arriving, we've discussed our self-presentation for the Aluku phase of our project. Ken reminds us that, in the interests of preserving his field rapport, he'd feel most comfortable if he could present us as his "bosses," in charge of what to buy or not buy, how much to pay, whether to hurry along rather than lingering for small talk, and so on. We assure him that's OK.

Sitting on little stools in front of Obentié's house, Rich—with support from Ken—explains our mission in a formal speech (in Saramaccan, tinged with an attempt at Aluku inflection):

The French government in Cayenne, the *Conseil Régional*, is putting up a big building near Cayenne in the place known as "Remire." The French call it a *musée*, the Dutch a *museum*. They're going to put objects made by all different kinds of people in it. There'll be one area for the Aluku. There'll be one for Saramaka. There'll be another for Ndjuka, and one for Paramaka. And so for every group, including one for each of the different kinds of Indians— Wayana, Galibi, Palikur . . .—to house their baskets, firefans, cassava presses, bows and arrows. You know how Aluku ways of

"Often," said Torday, "you give away some keepsake to a white man, but what becomes of it? It is lost, or in years to come no one will know what it is or whence it came. Everything that you or your people will sell to me will go to the big house I have mentioned, and there remain for all time as evidence of the skill and greatness of your race."

> — An anthropologist/collector explaining the British Museum to the king of Kuba (Congo Free State, ca. 1908); cited in John Mack, *Emil Torday and the Art of the Congo, 1900–1909* (1990), p. 69

"Take it!" the Granman said. "What else is it you ask?"

There was the apinti drum. In the house where objects of all peoples of the earth were brought for men and women to look at, there were none of the fine carvings the Bush Negroes make. When we returned, we would place beside the African and Indian objects which were there those of the Saramacca people. As yet, we had not been able to buy an apinti drum. This one was more beautiful than any we had seen. Could he not sell it to us, so that everyone might know that the finest of drums had come from the council house of Moana Yankuso, Granman of the Saramacca people?

This time he did not hesitate. He smiled, and shook his head.

"No, no, white man," he said, "this drum is not for me to sell. This one I cannot part with, not for all your goods. . . . This one no gold can buy."

> — M. and F. Herskovits, *Rebel Destiny* (1934), p. 269

Often Westerners have difficulty accepting the idea that Africans traditionally produced art just for its aesthetic value. . . . The corollary, that African art that was made *as* art had to be tourist art, has been damaging and demeaning to African artists, who may have taken pride in making beautiful objects simply for pleasure.

> — Enid Schildkrout and Curtis A. Keim, *African Reflections* (1990), pp. 15–16

To simplify the problem, I can state that a Negro art object cannot be definitively classified as a fake unless it is expressly copied from the original for commercial purposes.

> — Henri Kamer, "The Authenticity of African Sculptures," (1974), p. 32

doing things are fast disappearing? How these little kids here [pointing to a couple of small children outside the door] go to [French] school and aren't learning Aluku ways? Well, many years from now, when these kids have children of their own, and they no longer remember Aluku ways as we know them today, the things in that building will still be there. They'll be able to go there and look at the things, and say, "So that's the way our grandparents used to do things! Look at how well they made things!" There's another point too: For every object that's on display in that building, there will be a card with the name of the person who made it, that person's village, and whether the object was made in Aluku or Saramaka or Ndjuka. It wouldn't be good for Aluku to be upstaged by those others! The name of Aluku should be big. And another thing: We're not taking these things away for nothing! The French government gave us money to buy them, so the person who sells will be paid as is fitting, with proper respect. And it's not that we're buying things like other whitefolks to carry off and sell at a profit. These things will remain forever in that building. Anyone will be able to come look at them, but no one will be able to buy them and take them away.

Invited to bring our stools into Obentié's house, we're immediately struck by a beautiful, ornate, wooden chest, carved on some surfaces, painted on others, with legs on three sides so it can be set down in various positions to display each of its six uniquely decorated surfaces. He shows it off proudly, explaining he'd made it for his portable stereo system. Though he can't sell it, since he uses it to carry his massive stereo when he travels, he promises to make us a similar one for the museum. (In fact, he says, he's already made a second one for his brother; this one will be his third.) We discuss the details and set the price of this major commission at 2,000F. Then we buy (from his Ndjuka wife and two other women) a fine

Eddies swell the river, break it, crisscross it with foamy waves that turn it into an overflowing sea: it's a strange spectacle under the clear blue sky. . . . Sprays of water shower us, toboggan-like bumps jolt us. . . .

With the width of the Lawa more than six kilometers here, I expected, if not the boundless ocean of the mouth of the Amazon, then at least some kind of vast expanse like Stanley Pool.

The sight that greets us is completely different: a throng of islands rob us of any distant view by their impressive succession of shorelines. . . .

For some twenty kilometers, the rapids of Abattis Cottica spread their network of sinuous arms cluttered with islands.

— Resse, *Guyane française*, pp. 117–18

paddle he'd carved, as well as some smaller objects (two decorated pestles, two hammock threaders, and a cassava spatula). The paddle has a purple-heart inset into which Obentié has incorporated a few balls of shot, which shake like a rattle whenever the paddle moves. We leave behind, with the same wife, a second, equally nice paddle, with an ornately pierced handle, thinking we won't want too many pieces made by a single carver and unsure what range of objects and carving skills we'll find upstream in Aluku villages.

Back on the river, up through the fierce rapids known on maps as "Abattis Cottica." In a water-smudged notebook, in shaky hand, we write some thoughts on collecting in Abunasonga, which we feel somehow was our first real, in situ, "field collecting" of the summer: Regarding Rich's initial speech, we're struck that such a discourse, while perhaps an appropriate tool for the task we've agreed to do, is loaded with implicit ironies and contradictions, concepts of anthropology and museology that, in other circumstances, we wouldn't endorse. We were also surprised by people's behavior, as they literally rushed from their houses with things to sell, once Rich had made a little clarificatory speech specifying that it wasn't just new things we wanted. The three of us sat in Obentié's house and looked, decided, bought, and wrote down data, as women gathered wooden objects and calabashes in their houses and brought them to us for sale. We reflect that such collecting is completely "non-violent" on a *personal* level. The objects being offered have already served (1) aesthetic gratification to the artist, (2) as conveyors of social/sentimental value in gift-giving, (3) functional use and display by the owner. A woman who decides to sell (to us, a gendarme, a tourist—it's all the same to her) thinks of it as no big deal. She'd simply rather have the money than the extra paddle. And in contrast to Saramaka, there was no reticence about giving names.

2 PM. After canoeing past all seven "traditional" Aluku villages in the course of a rainy hour and a half, with Nyolu, Ken, and us each huddling under a piece of tarp or plastic, we arrive at the "new

What is Maripasoula?

A charming oasis at the end of a "forest wilderness"? But what else? A challenge? A sort of infinitessimal, microscopic Brasilia, at the mercy of airplanes and linked with the coast by five hundred kilometers of a rapids-strewn river? . . .

I had left the other side of the virgin forest equipped for several weeks, with a hammock and anti-venom serum in case of snake bites. I find a fully equipped dispensary, a modern hospital, and a villa with every convenience where I'm served vegetables parachuted in from France!

— Resse, *Guyane française*, p. 70

There was no permanent [French] administration on the Maroni until 1940 . . . [when] a small administrative post was founded at Maripasoula.

— André Sausse, *Populations primitives du Maroni* (1951), pp. 42–43

From 1949 to 1969 the post was administered by gendarmes. . . . In 1969, Maripasoula was transformed overnight, as was the rest of the interior, by the policy of *francisation*. As the *chef-lieu* of a new commune, it became the site of a town hall, a new school, and an expanded clinic. . . . It was chosen as the main administrative center for the entire region encompassed by the Lawa and its tributaries. . . .

By the mid-1970s, Maripasoula had metamorphosed into the largest settlement in the Lawa River area . . . [and] had the distinction of simultaneously being the largest and one of the least populated communes in the entire republic of France. . . . In 1974 the commune included: 248 Wayana and Emerillon Indians, 387 Maroons, almost all Aluku, and 168 Creoles. . . .

The Aluku were living in a dizzying world that had been abruptly and radically remade by forces beyond their control or comprehension. . . .

Many Aluku remember with great clarity the visit of Jacques Chirac, then Prime Minister of France, to Maripasoula on Christmas Day, 1975 . . . [when he] danced *awasa* arm-in-arm with his Aluku fellow citizens. . . . [He] was accompanied by a detachment of the French Foreign Legion from Kourou. For this special occasion, a "live" Nativity scene was staged, complete with manger, "virgin," and infant, and with a cow, donkey, and goat added for effect. During [his] speech . . . Chirac is reported to have said: "Here in Maripasoula, men of totally different racial, religious, and cultural origins live in the most perfect harmony. They have France in common, and I have seen nothing but peace and gaiety here."

— Bilby, *The Remaking of the Aluku*, pp. 268–69, 139, 623, 195, 615

town" of Maripasoula, our base for the next phase of the mission. Heavy, heavy tropical downpour. Long wait for a truck to transport the expedition supplies to our pre-arranged lodgings, during which we realize that we're missing the two cases of rum, intended as gifts to village headmen and other Aluku dignitaries. For the first time in our experience, we see streets and roads and cars and lawns in the interior; we also see an Amerindian family, dressed traditionally, silently debarking from their canoe, followed by their lean hunting dog. We help Ken get set up at a new, and as-yet unoccupied, municipally-owned hotel, out in a field of mud beyond the soccer goalposts. Then install ourselves in two rooms built under the house of a West Indian store-keeping couple, owned by a friend from Martinique with ties to Maripasoula, and kindly put at our disposal for this visit. The three of us eat a pleasant meal upstairs from our apartment, on the porch of the very West Indian home/shop/sometime-restaurant of Miss Iris, who was born in Georgetown, Guyana. After dinner, we listen to the shortwave radio we've brought along: Iraq, we learn, has invaded Kuwait and there are rumblings of a war in the Middle East.

MONDAY 6/VIII/90

Early morning, over to Ken's to raid the expedition trunks for food and supplies, walking along a street lined with the ramshackle dwellings of West Indians who'd arrived, decades ago, in search of gold. The three of us returned to our place for breakfast, then met with the young Aluku deputy mayor in his modern, air-conditioned office. Called Mme J in St. Laurent, who confirmed that our two cartons of rum had been left behind in her storeroom and promised to have them sent upriver by the next government boat. Outside the mairie, we see a large garbage can overflowing with empty bottles of Moët et Chandon.

Since 1985, Maripasoula has, quite literally, been connected not just to the coast [by daily air service] but to the rest of the world. In that year, an automatic telephone station, linked by satellite relay to the world communications network, was officially inaugurated. . . . The breakthrough was celebrated with a conversation between the *maire* in Maripasoula and two government ministers in Paris.

— Bilby, *The Remaking of the Aluku*, p. 275

When we suggested that we might care to acquire the board, the woman became apprehensive. She took up the board, and excusing herself, disappeared with it inside her hut.

"No, no," she called from the house, when her brother went to tell her of the offer we had made for it. "I don't want money for it. I like it. I will not sell it."

The sum we offered was modest enough, but not inconsiderable for this deep interior. We increased it, then doubled our original offer. There was still no wavering on the woman's part, but the offer began to interest her family. Such wealth should not be refused. Basia Anaisi began to urge her in our behalf.

"With this money you can buy from the white man's city a hammock, and several fine cloths. You should not refuse this."

The old woman took up the discussion, then another sister, and a brother. At last the bassia took us aside, and asked us to leave his sister alone with them.

"We will have a krutu [meeting], and tomorrow you will hear. She is foolish not to sell. But she cares for the board. It is good, too, when a woman loves what her man has carved for her. We will krutu about it, and you shall hear."

Three days passed before the woman's permission was given to dispose of the piece.

"When they see this, your people will know our men can carve!" she exclaimed in a voice which held as much regret as pride.

— M. and F. Herskovits, *Rebel Destiny*, p. 281

Lunch *chez nous:* instant "Oriental" noodle soup. Found out that DM, who was supposed to come on the plane bearing the remainder of our collecting funds, had not taken the flight. We phoned from the deputy mayor's home and DM said he'd arrive in several days, in time for the funeral rites in the village of Loka, since the person who'd died was a relative of his. The three of us visited with several Alukus on "the Mountain" (the Aluku section of Maripasoula which, to look at it only, has little distinctively Aluku about it except an occasional carved door or some drums lying about). Bought eleven calabashes from Ma Betsi, a woman in her fifties who was wearing only a long, bright pink tee-shirt and a head-tie. We stood at the door of her house-on-stilts and conducted our museum speech and calabash buying there. Ken said afterwards that, in the context of Aluku etiquette, she was not being particularly rude keeping us on her doorstep, just casual and not very interested, one way or the other. Ken also mentioned that she was the mother of Bwino, our coastal taxi driver.

Manku came by and said he wanted to take us to see where he was staying and to visit his two aunts. We walked down a long concrete-paved road, lined with streetlights, past the *mairie* and gendarmerie and a number of wooden houses inhabited by Creoles. A couple of streets over, this time unpaved, we found the house of Manku's family, and we all sat on stools in the dirt yard. Considerable amusement at our ability to speak Saramaccan; the double exoticism of Saramaka and whitefolks provides special entertainment. Discussed the museum project but they had nothing to sell. Ken went back to his hotel, nearby, and Manku took us inside his own little house to taste Aluku *konsa* — fermented cane juice used for funerals. Dinner *à trois* at the small restaurant run by Mme Jeanne, a sixtyish-year-old woman born in Guyane of Guadeloupean and St. Lucian immigrants. Then packed our bags for tomorrow's day trip to Komontibo and Papai Siton.

Here, then, is a move toward a methodological treatise. It urges a moral and aesthetic practice: Do radical ethnography, one that gets you closer to those you study at the risk of going native and never returning; it is hoped, at least, that you will not again embrace the received assumptions with which you, inheriting your academic texts, methods, and corporate academic culture, began.

— Dan Rose, *Living the Ethnographic Life* (1990), p. 12

The major division within the discipline for the past decade has been between those who engage in practice and those who do not.

— Joan Vincent, "Engaging Historicism" (1991), p. 49

Further thoughts on the enterprise we're involved in: Even though hand-washing calabashes, rice-rinsing calabashes, etc. aren't used here any more, many middle-aged Alukus have them and all know about them. People seem very matter of fact and apparently unconcerned about this "loss." Ma Betsi was as blasé about selling us a calabash spoon made by her grandmother as she was about the price of the whole transaction. She showed some feeling for a calabash she said her *mati* (formal friend) had once given her, but essentially said, "Take it, it's just lying there in the sack, I never use it." After we bought our several calabashes, she was still left with a sackful in her house. Manku's aunts say they have no calabashes, though he had told us they did.

We've now logged in twenty-one Aluku objects. At each one, Sally curses the *fiches* out loud. Among other things, we feel as if we're closing the barn door in Aluku. These people have already been bought off. None of it really matters anymore. There is neither much social significance attached to such objects nor financial significance in their sale to the BPE (or to anyone else).

Nor, for our part, do we feel that we're in any sense ethnographically *engagé*. What we're doing this time isn't fieldwork, it's a job. We're on the outside, trying to be friendly visitors looking in, but we're in no way putting our own ways of thinking and feeling and believing and acting at risk—which is prerequisite to true ethnography.

TUESDAY 7/VIII/90

A few early-morning thoughts, while waiting at the boat for some minor mechanical problems with the motor to be resolved. One thing people do care about and lavish aesthetic attention on is motor canoes, which are stunningly painted with care and pride by young men. Boat naming is also pervasive, often consisting of aphorisms,

We were astonished at the luxuriance of the forest which cascaded down to the water on both banks in an indescribable tangle of greenery and flowers. Mangrove blossoms as red as rose-hips swung above the creamy cones of moucou-moucous, which rose from a wonderful background of shining leaves. There were tree-ferns and aouara palm trees, and tormented and knotted roots seen through the green, translucent water, like submerged snakes. At one point a flock of turquoise-coloured parakeets flew overhead uttering small cries, and as they disappeared into a thicket flushed out of it a flight of pink and grey tropical kingfishers. This was truly the empire of vegetation and mystery, and it was difficult to imagine that man could ever conquer it.

— Larson and Pellaton, *Behind the Lianas*, pp. 25–26

for example, "Life is good—but love is better." Most are in English and many are from Bob Marley songs. Some are in Sranan and a few in French. We also note another difference in general from Saramaka: people tend to live inside more than outside their houses here. This is clearly related to the relative spaciousness of rooms in these Western-style, plank-constructed homes.

The hour-long canoe ride down to Papai Siton is magical. Mist blankets the river, creating mysterious shapes around the black river rocks. We glide through rapids and shiver in the damp, but soon the sun burns through, revealing spectacular walls of forest. Our passage disturbs flocks of parakeets and wild ducks that scatter as we descend. Pass the strange new settlement of Wacapou, on the site of an abandoned Creole village, apparently inhabited by Alukus and some Ndjukas belonging to an American-based fundamentalist mission that had earlier converted a number of Wayana Indians upstream from Maripasoula; its houses are dominated by a rickety, very tall wooden platform—perhaps a watchtower used to scan the skies for the Second Coming? Pass Benzdorp and Bellevue, recently-abandoned Creole goldminers' villages established a half-century ago; the inhabitants have either grown old and died or moved to Maripasoula. Broad swatches of the fast-moving water are filled with foam, and we see fish jumping.

Spent the day in Komontibo and Papai Siton (officially called Pompidouville), which are contiguous settlements—the first, a "normal" Aluku village, the second (like Maripasoula) the French-mandated center of a commune and, as the wooden sign at the landing says, "Capitale des Boni"—the home of the Paramount Chief, boasting a gendarmerie and a large mairie under construction. We disembarked at contiguous Komontibo, where Ken had lived during his dissertation fieldwork four years ago. Greeted by Captain Tobu and invited into his sitting room. The two of us are struck by the lack of demonstrativeness compared to Saramaka. Ken was welcomed back quite matter-of-factly. No hoots, no hollers—almost closer to

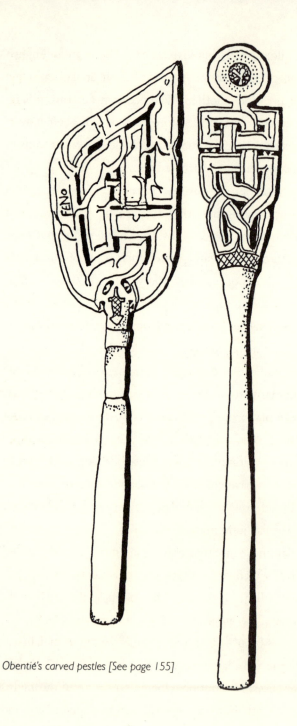

Obentié's carved pestles [See page 155]

Creole (Martinique) style than to Saramaka. On Ken's recommendation we'd brought food for the day, but Tobu invited us to share in a morning meal and we enjoyed fine dishes of boiled plantains and cassava bread dipped in spicy crab and meat sauces. We presented the captain with a bottle of rum we'd bought in Maripasoula, and he poured libations on the floor. We are struck in Komontibo that libations are much more truncated than in Saramaka, and that men frequently knock down jiggers of rum without ceremony. Women also serve and drink rum, in contrast to Saramaka.

At one point early in the visit, Rich was "tested" by the women in the neighboring yard of Ma Atubun, who first poured a libation and invoked a list of her ancestors and then passed the bottle to Rich, saying they wanted to know how Saramakas did it. They seemed surprised and impressed when he followed suit, though in Saramaccan and calling upon a string of Saramaka ancestors. As we walked around the village, we saw no thatched roofs; there was not a single traditional (non-store-bought) skirt, very few bare breasts, and no breechcloths, though children were often naked. Lots of lawn areas where grass is cut by machine that reminded us of the Moravian mission stations on the Suriname River. No "traditional" (1950s-style) Aluku houses like those illustrated in Hurault's books, though we did see a few painted doors and a couple of carved ones. Like Maripasoula but on a smaller scale, Papai Siton has paved and unpaved streets and a number of vehicles. Many people are employed by the commune, doing maintenance work, etc.

The two of us engaged in some five or six collecting encounters, several while Ken was trying to send a telegram to Julia (in Washington), from the gendarmerie, on the occasion of their second wedding anniversary. Ma Legina, from Ken's old neighborhood, pulled two sacks of calabashes from her house and spread them out for our viewing. She'd been selling them off to gendarmes and tourists but still had lots left, including many dozens of calabash spoons. Prices seem well established by all this trade, generally ranging from 10F

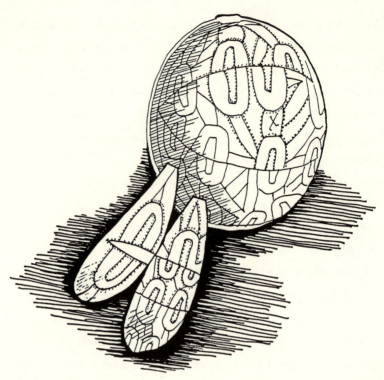

Calabash bowl carved by Ma Betsi and two spoons carved by Ma Legina

to 25F per piece, depending on size. We select a dozen. No tension, no particular joy. No reticence when we ask to write down names, ages, etc. The idea of a museum doesn't seem to matter one way or the other.

Then on to Ma Atubun in her two-story house, where the walls of her front room were covered with a display of enamel plates and bowls, glass mugs, shining kitchen ware, enamel buckets, and so forth. She brought out several cloths and calabashes she wanted to sell. Again, very matter of fact. We bought a calabash bowl, a calabash spoon, a breechcloth she'd made around 1943, and a neckerchief sewn at the same time; she asked 50F for the lot. This seemed awfully low, but we're still not far enough into our Aluku collecting to feel we know what's really appropriate. Sally offered a pair of colorful Brazilian "parrot" earrings as a gift; Ma Atubun looked at them without enthusiasm. It looks like extrapolating from Saramaka to Aluku in matters of taste doesn't always work.

Then back to the house of Captain Tobu, who had offered to give a breechcloth to the museum. The breechcloth never materialized but, together with Ken, we negotiated the purchase of an earthenware pot that he'd bought from an Amerindian woman way upriver a few years ago. He told us he'd paid her 150F, so we offered 200, which he accepted. (Back in Maripasoula in the evening, we found similar vessels for sale in a Creole store for 50F.)

Going on to Papai Siton, the three of us sat with the elderly Captain Tafanye in the upper room of his two-story house, sitting around a Western-height table on which he had placed various bottles of room-temperature beer and sodas. He engaged Sally in a flirtatious way familiar to us from Saramaka, where it's also common for an octogenarian to tease a younger woman. He seemed to think the museum project was a good idea, and we arranged a return visit the next Monday to spend the day together going through his trunks of textiles in Papai Siton and then proceeding to Old Papai Siton, a village abandoned fifteen years ago when the commune was built,

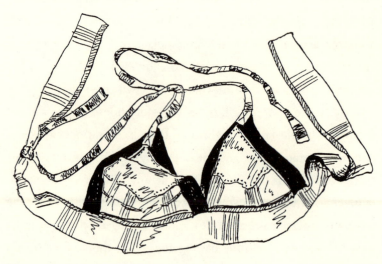

The patchwork bra sewn by Ma Sokodon

where his old wooden objects are stored. The two of us were then called downstairs to a tiny room where Tafanye's twenty-one-year-old grandson, Dinguiou, lives.

Dinguiou is becoming a professional artist. Several of his geometric, vividly colorful paintings (in the style of Aluku doors and boat decoration) were exhibited in Cayenne by the Aluku cultural association "Mi Wani Sabi" ("I Want to Know") and his similar mural-paintings also embellish the new (as yet unused) market building in Maripasoula. He sold us a laundry-beater that Tafanye had made some sixty years ago for his first wife, Dinguiou's grandmother. Before giving the object up, however, he set it on a cluttered shelf and photographed it quickly with an instamatic camera and flash. We proposed that he make us something in wood to be hung in the museum next to his grandfather's piece. He liked the idea and said he'd make us a tray. He also wanted to sell us one of the two paintings on canvas that were lying on his bed, nearly finished. The large one would cost 3,000F, he said, but we thought the smaller one was nicer and arranged to buy that, once he'd finished making the frame.

Back to Komontibo, where several objects had been left for our scrutiny in Captain Tobu's house by a woman who gave her name as Rachel. We had her called and tried to interview her in order to document the pieces. She was either reticent or irritated by our questioning, but straightforward about conducting the sale itself. (On the way back to Maripasoula, Ken told us that "Rachel" is normally called Ma Sokodon, that she's Tobu's wife, and that she's often a bit gruff.) We bought several calabashes and four sewn textiles, including a patchwork bra that Tobu insisted on having fitted on Sally before we bought it. Meanwhile, a nine-year-old showed up with three toys that Ken had commissioned earlier, finished with his work and eager to be paid. His slingshot and noisemaker were acceptable, but when we tried to photograph the artisan illustrating the use of the stilts he'd made, he couldn't stand on them, and when

In 1957, one clever Boni succeeded in building and furnishing a house that approximated European norms, with a floor, double walls, furniture with drawers, a bed, and a mattress. . . . After less than a year, this house was so infested with rats, cockroaches, spiders, and ants that it was uninhabitable.
— Jean Hurault, *La vie matérielle des Noirs Réfugiés Boni et des Indiens Wayana du Haut-Maroni* (1965), p. 70

I soon realized that using Boni laborers [on the river] requires a great deal of patience and flexibility on the part of the gendarmes.
— Resse, *Guyane française*, p. 103

Nyolu helpfully jumped on to demonstrate, the stilts broke. The kid, looking dejected, promised to make another set for next week.

In the middle of the day, while Ken was visiting friends, we asked a child to take us to the house of Ma Anaaweli, an Aluku woman who had been married to Saramaka Captain Kala and had lived, along with her adolescent granddaughter Maame, near our house in Dángogó during the 1960s. We had been told that Anaaweli, now in her eighties, was blind and living in Papai Siton with Maame, who was now a grandmother. Greetings with strong emotion, many hugs and even, eventually, French-style kisses on both cheeks. Maame prepared a rum, lemon, and sugar drink and served us a special confection made from coconut and sweet cassava. They made us promise to return for a real meal later. When we did, after a couple of hours, accompanied by Ken and Manku, they gave all of us stools in Anaaweli's house, served mounded rice and a delicious bird cooked in sauce, and pressed upon us presents of cassava meal and carved calabashes. Anaaweli showed us the pile of lumber she's been buying with her various allowances from the French state (money for being old, money for being handicapped . . .); she plans to replace her "traditional style" house—one of the few remaining in Papai Siton—with a "modern" coastal style dwelling of the type that has become the norm here. Anaaweli was hungry for news of Saramaka and genuinely interested in everything we could catch her up on.

Back upriver as darkness falls. Considerable griping by Nyolu about not having days off. He has a cold and a bad toothache. He's been agitating to sleep over for a few days in his home village of Loka, using it as a base rather than having to travel every morning and evening. As we arrive in Maripasoula, he confronts Rich with a belligerent speech about how, whether we like it or not, he's going to Loka on Friday to sleep over. The funeral rites are for someone in his family; work or no work, he's going to be there. Later, Manku takes us aside to say that he's given Nyolu a dressing-down for his

And I, being firm, would say "No." They were testing us, these first few days, to find out how pliable we were and how much they could get away with for their own fun on the river. And, as with all other primitive servants, the best politics at the beginning of a trip, which would inevitably end by their being your masters, was to get at least the first week's hard work out of them by consistently saying "No." You would, of course, give in at last and be lenient, because you had grown to like them . . . and once you said "Yes" they had you.

— Davis, *The Jungle and the Damned*, pp. 90–91

The village founder's stool from Asisi

outburst, which he takes as a lack of respect and a sign of bad attitude toward work.

WEDNESDAY 8/VIII/90

We delayed the morning departure until around 8:30 so that Ken could get off his anniversary telegram from Maripasoula; he wasn't able to reach the outside world from Papai Siton yesterday. Then downstream to Asisi, a quarter of an hour past Komontibo/Papai Siton on an island in the river. It looks like a good part of the island has been washed away by the river over the years, leaving houses perched right next to the steep yellow-clay bank.

We met old Captain Adiso, who offered us stools at his doorstep. After we made a formal speech about the museum project, he told us he had a relevant stool, made by Gwentimati, the man who'd founded the village (which Ken places at ca. 1860). He brought it out: a worn and once-termite-infested stool with a cocked seat and a solid base, carved from a single piece of wood. Visibly, an historic artifact. As we continued chatting, he called over several other older men as they wandered by, and some women gathered to watch too. A lot of hemming and hawing, insignificant comments, inaction. Then a couple of the men started proclaiming that they didn't want to have anything to do with this museum business. The flavor caught on. Others told the captain that he shouldn't sell the stool. It should stay where it was, they insisted, and not be carried off to some place in Cayenne. The captain proposed that we photograph it for the museum, which we did.

Two women took Sally off to show her their houses. One brought out a few calabashes and a cassava sieve—an object shaped like a round winnowing tray, but with only the rim made of wood. The rest was tin, crudely pierced at regular intervals. The whole was decorated with large copper tacks and painted designs. There was

We say: "*Me wanny buy timbeh*" — "I want to buy wooden pieces."

The [Maroon] Negro's common reply is that he has none to part with: "*Me no habbe, massra.*" The word *massra* is a corruption of "master," a vestige of the slave days.

We point to a pierced and inlaid stool and say "*How many?*" meaning, how much does he want for it.

"*Me no wanny fu selly*" — "I don't want to sell it."

To show him we mean business, a concrete offer is made, "*Me gon gibbe sixa banknoto*" — "I'm going to give six banknoto."

The bargaining is in silver half-guilder pieces, called *banknoto*. The Djukas do not understand large sums of money, except when counted in half-guilder pieces.

If he refuses six coins, we offer seven, eight, nine, and throw in the added temptation of some tobacco leaves. To each of these offers he shakes his head in negation, saying doggedly, "No, no."

Finally, in a tone of voice that indicates we are amazed at our own generosity, we say: "*Me gon gibbe tena banknoto, nanga twee weefee tabak.*" — "I'm going to give ten banknoto, as well as three leaves of tobacco."

The reply is short and spirited.

"*Gimme.*"

Which does not have to be translated.

— Kahn, *Djuka*, pp. 48–50

real ambiguity and uncertainty about whether these were being shown off or offered for sale. Finally, they said the sieve was something we could photograph if we wanted, and the woman asked Sally which of the calabashes she liked best. She chose one which they carried back to the house where the men were. The calabash was still in the hands of its owner, in a strangely ambiguous status. In the meantime, an older man whose hands were damaged by leprosy brought out a stool he'd made and placed it at Rich's feet, apparently for sale, though Rich didn't think it was "museum quality." The sieve was photo'd. Sally finally asked the woman whether she wanted to sell the calabash and she shook her head. OK. But then she pressed it on Sally and said simply, "Take it, I want you to have it." The leprous man, after watching the photographing of the sieve, declared that he'd only brought the stool to show Rich so that it could be photographed. When Rich made no move to photo it, he simply took it away, saying that since he was sick he couldn't replace it anyway.

Some other women then took Sally off to their houses—an expedition that resulted in ten more calabashes bought for the Bureau du Patrimoine. One woman offered a mediocre laundry beater for sale; it turned out to have been made by a Ndjuka, so we didn't buy it, explaining that we were only buying Aluku-made objects. She pouted but said nothing. The men sat around in a semi-hostile silence. Looking back a few hours later, Rich felt as if, had he cared about acquiring objects for the museum the way he had once cared about gaining older Saramaka men's confidence about historical knowledge, this encounter would have been a very mild version of some of the more adversarial group interviews that he described in the Introduction to First-Time. The big difference: we didn't much care and they didn't much care. Little was at stake. But the rhetorical relationship was like a pale imitation of those other, highly charged, encounters.

Meanwhile, a boatload of French soldiers in jungle military garb and life preservers motored up and disembarked—hair close-

The life we're leading here is . . . like that of a circus troupe that's always on the move, but only to present the same show over and over.

— Leiris, *L'Afrique fantôme*, p. 43

By the mid-1980s, roughly one-half of all Alukus from the Lawa River region were living in one of the two new communities built in the interior with [French] government funds (Maripasoula and Pompidouville [Papai Siton]), while nearly a third resided in coastal towns; the rest of the population, less than a fifth, remained thinly scattered in the interior, divided between the old villages and the few horticultural camps still in use. The amenities offered by . . . the coastal way of life — wage-earning opportunities, Western medicine, running water, electricity, and consumer goods, to name a few — had made their way to the [new towns in the] interior and drawn most Aluku away from their ancestral villages.

— Bilby, *The Remaking of the Aluku*, pp. 151–52

cropped, heavy boots. Handshaking and bonjours to the captain and
to us. The leader accepts a large glass of the old captain's rum and
knocks it down in one motion. Sally is struck by the lack of a sense
of Aluku ownership of villages. Anybody can come and go as they
like—from soldiers and gendarmes to tourists and ethnobotanists
and museum collectors; it's France. In Saramaka villages, such visitors are guests; it's Saramaka territory.

The three of us set off for a walk through the village. Chatted with
some women in an open shed; saw nothing to buy. Visited the man
standing in for the absent captain at the other end of the village. Yet
another description of what a museum is; we could as easily just
put it on tape and play it back each time. Several objects are carried
in to the open shed where we're sitting—by Manku, by the wife of
the man we're speaking with, and by some other villagers. We decide it's time to draw the line on calabashes, which now represent
by far the greatest bulk of what we've got, though when one really
nice example shows up, we go ahead and buy it. Then another textile. Bought various wooden objects of marginal aesthetic quality
and physical condition, since Ken insists that there's very little left
in Aluku. The wood we've bought looks like the poorest pieces in
the storerooms of the Surinaams Museum. In contrast to our discussion at the captain's house, the encounters at this end of the village
were without a trace of tension. Just general indifference and lack
of interest one way or the other.

Across the river to Loka, the village that's involved in preparations
for a major funerary celebration and therefore, Ken says, uncharac-
teristically filled with people. To our Saramaka-trained eyes, it still
seems not very bustling. This is Nyolu's matrilineal village. As we
approach the house where one of Ken's older friends, a man named
Ateni, is staying with his wife, Nyolu emerges with two food stirrers and asks if we want them. He has simply grabbed them off the
wall in brash "grandchild" fashion. The three of us are invited in
and given stools, and we chat with Ateni. Nyolu wanders in and asks

"How are we to know what they are worth to you? The price you will pay seems to us to depend, not on the things, but on the persons who buy them. You say this thing is worth two pounds to you. It might be worth two hundred to someone else. How are we to tell what it will fetch except by trying?"

> — Sir Martin Conway, *The Sport of Collecting* (1914), p. 64,
> quoting a veteran antique dealer in Damascus. Cited in
> Christopher B. Steiner, "Transnational Trajectories" (1989),
> p. 5

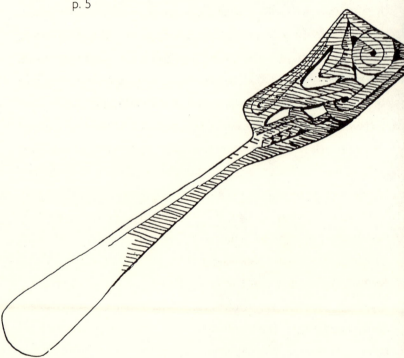

The food stirrer requisitioned by Nyolu, carved by the late Afuudi

Rich privately if we want the two objects he's holding. When Rich says yes, Nyolu calls out abruptly to the woman, holding up the two food stirrers and asking, "Wanna sell these?" She quickly answers; no to one, yes to the other, and Sally elicits data for the fiche.

Manku calls the two of us to the door to go see a cloth he has located. A young woman with a baby, distinctly untalkative, has told Manku she'll sell her cross-stitch skirt for 500F. Since we've already bought other, nicer, examples, for 200–250F, we apologize that it's out of our range. She suggests 450F. We counter that it's better for her to keep it and find another buyer someday. She accepts our decision but is clearly unhappy, and Manku seems disappointed.

Walking on, we catch up with Ken in a large open shed containing eight or so young women all busily embroidering wrap-skirts with cross-stitch patterns, in some cases two women to a skirt, in anticipation of the funeral celebration. An older man lounges in a hammock. We exchange pleasantries and indicate an interest in buying things. Chaotic scene as people start to offer for sale first cloth, then combs, then a tray, then a laundry beater. No place for us to sit, so we stand pressed together amidst the sewing women, the man in the hammock, a retarded ten-year-old drooling on the floor, and babies of various sizes, trying to deal with these offers, pull the cash out of Rich's wads of banknotes, and jot down the museum documentation. End up with various purchases of wood, plus a cross-stitch skirt, nicer than the first one we were offered, which we buy for 200F. We eventually extract ourselves from the village since it is getting late, leaving various offers hanging until our projected return on Friday for the all-night dance. As we disembark at Maripasoula at dusk, Rich tells Nyolu and Manku that they've got tomorrow off, but that we'll go to Loka early Friday and sleep over there that night.

Maripasoula?

Was it not a grand and generous idea, born of the conviction of a few men of courage? . . . A great idea alive with devotion, faith, and love? . . . And is it not the conscious generosity of France, which gave everything without asking or taking anything in return?

— Resse, *Guyane française*, p. 75

Up early. Sally washes some clothes. Rich walks down one of Maripasoula's side roads to the bakery to pick up an Aluku-French ba-
guette. We boil drinking water, then write up fiches from yesterday.
At 10:30, just as the last object is being logged in, Ken shows up
and starts out by taking a shower, since the water has been cut off
in his hotel. Manku stops by to tell us an involved story about how
our boat and motor were stolen last night. Someone saw it happen
and alerted the gendarmes. The culprits, Aluku joyriders, were apprehended and the boat repossessed. Manku leaves and the three
of us plan our general collecting strategy. Ken takes on the long list
of ethnographic material culture items, plus the drums. We concen-
trate on the rest. Cook up some instant soup packages and sardines
for lunch. Ken returns to his room and the two of us go off to commission a painted canoe, one of our projected *pièces de résistance*. At the
landing place, we find Daniel Ateni (the son of old man Ateni, whom
we'd met in Loka), whose new canoe, which we've been admiring
for the last few days, is just now being launched. We watch it motor
back and forth in front of the landing. He agrees to make a nine- or
ten-meter boat, a really nice one, within the next two months. He
asks 6,000F and we agree. The whole thing very friendly. We serve
considerable entertainment value for the men who've been helping young Ateni with the boat-painting, because of our command
of Saramaccan. It's a language that, in itself, sounds exotic to Aluku
ears; hearing whitefolks using it so easily is strange indeed.

The deputy mayor happens along and suggests taking us to be
introduced to the mayor, who has just flown in from the coast, and
is fiddling with the dashboard of his white luxury speedboat. He's
thirtyish, affable, expansive, on his way up. He automatically greets
us in French, but we're soon talking Saramaccan and he Aluku. He
says there'll be plenty of time to talk at our leisure about the museum
project once the festivities at Loka are over. At Iris's place above

The patchwork breechcloth bought from Ma Atubun
[See page 167]

our apartment, which engages in a sometime commerce of drinks, peanuts, a few household items, and local trinkets, we buy beers as well as two Amerindian pots to take home as presents. A little later, we see Ken walking by, on his way to begin commissioning ethnographic objects on "the Mountain." We retire, with three 1F packets of popcorn and a 130F bottle of whisky, bought at a house-front shop run by a former goldminer from St. Lucia, to write up notes.

In terms of our general state of mind, the constant "What are we doing this for?" of St. Laurent has given way to a "Let's get this thing over with as efficiently as possible." We keep holding out the hope that we will come up with some significant insights about the act of collecting, about museums, etc. But in the meantime we continue to be impressed by the project's relative lack of redeeming social or intellectual value. The three of us eating bland, packaged noodle soup under a Creole house in Maripasoula seems a world away from that highly charged, mythical anthropological moment when Bateson, Fortune, and Mead were cooped up in their famous "eight-by-eight-foot mosquito room," in 1930s New Guinea, eagerly discovering each other, as well, they thought, as the exotic peoples around them. We've had no really surprising encounters and local people seem rather blasé about selling off their possessions. We have not yet answered our own Big Question of why we're involved in this undertaking, though it comes up idly several times each day and night. Sally says she's recurrently bothered by a sneaking suspicion that many of her negative feelings may derive more from personal complaints — matters of comfort, where she'd rather be, what she'd rather be doing — than from her nobler ideological concerns about imperialism, oppression, cultural integrity. . . . As we keep writing, there seems to be an absence of issues. Nothing matters much one way or another. To us or to them. Rich feels the same. We're paying the prices people ask. We're not asking for objects they don't want to sell. And we'd rather be in Martinique. Make a bumper sticker? At each stage, we keep going in part because we don't feel like making

Peanut masher carved by the late Papa Adan

Whereas the voyage to the coast once took weeks, or after the introduction of the outboard motor, days, one can now make the journey to Cayenne in a leisurely 50 minutes, at an affordable price. . . . The shrinking distance between coast and interior has made possible certain novel living arrangements. An Aluku individual may, for instance, reside most of the year in a coastal town, but at the same time may maintain a garden in the interior to which he or she returns periodically, for brief stints. A man may have two wives, one upriver and one on the coast, between whom he divides his time. . . . Certain individuals fly between Maripasoula and Cayenne routinely, carrying deliveries and news back and forth.

— Bilby *The Remaking of the Aluku,* pp. 273–75

the decision to stop—which would be disruptive and would mean reneging on agreements. So, we'll try to finish the damn thing well, and maybe shave off a few days of unpaid labor at the end.

Dinner with Ken at Mme Jeanne's. We pack up for tomorrow's overnight trip to Loka. More disconcerting radio news about the Middle East.

SATURDAY 11/VIII/90

Late afternoon. Just back from our overnight stay in Loka for funerary rites. Much to report. We'll start with what happened today and then catch up on yesterday.

We began this morning with an assortment of collecting chores: arranging for drum purchases (we ended up with two—one made nearly seventy years ago, the other from the early 1980s), viewing two combs that were said to be Aluku but which were clearly Saramaka (and turned out to have been made by the Saramaka husband of an Aluku woman), buying a skirt with cross-stitch embroidery and rejecting two others, finding and buying Obentié's second paddle (the one we had rejected on our first collecting stop in Aluku), buying a cylindrical peanut-masher and an old but very worn round tray (that might look all right if the museum lights it so the remaining bas-relief casts sufficient shadow), and getting from a thirteen-year-old a better slingshot than the one we'd bought at Papai Siton.

But at the same time we were thinking ahead to a special opportunity—a man named BM who works for the government sent us word last night (via DM, who had just flown in from Cayenne for the occasion) that he would show us "some really old things." We hung around the area where DM's mother lives, and where BM said he couldn't get at "the things" until the woman who had the house woke up. We couldn't quite figure why an older woman

Do not be afraid to collect doubles, nor even triples, which are always useful in a museum.

— *Instructions sommaires*, p. 9

would sleep so late—even after an all-night "play." The mystery was solved around 11 AM when MF, French graduate student in ethnobotany, emerged from the house—she was the temporary occupant. With considerable grumbling, she untied her hammock as the three of us plus DM and BM moved inside.

BM ferreted among trunks piled high and pulled out four or five moldy pieces of wood from ground level—including a stool with a leg missing carved in "owl's eye" style, a barely decorated pestle, and an undecorated, deteriorating peanut-grinding board, all of which we bought. The other pieces were too far gone, decoration washed nearly off. Then DM's mother came in, indicated the two trunks that contained textiles, and left. In the semi-darkness of the cramped house, DM and BM opened the trunks; Rich quickly unfolded each cloth and did the preliminary triage, handing out to Ken anything that looked interesting and leaving in a separate pile the mediocre and undecorated cloths, as well as those that seemed unnecessarily redundant, which DM and BM refolded and returned to the trunks. Ken passed the cloths Rich gave him on to Sally, sitting near the door; she served as the "textile lady" for this session, examining each one in turn, and making a further separation into more and less desirable purchases for the museum. The trunks were filled with breechcloths, men's caps, patchwork sacks of various sizes, and a few skirts, mostly from the second quarter of the twentieth century, we guessed. But there was one example of openwork embroidery that reminded us immediately of the 1880s cloth from the Tropenmuseum that we'd illustrated in our art book.

The embroidered cloth inspired the most "Leiris-like" moment we've had so far: Rich did not indicate by words or gestures that this one was special. Nor, when the price of the lot was being calculated, did he call attention to it. Caught up in the fever of collecting for the first time (or, if collecting is to be considered violent, "in the heat of battle". . .), he replied to BM's query about how many cloths we'd chosen by counting them in their once-again-folded state, keeping

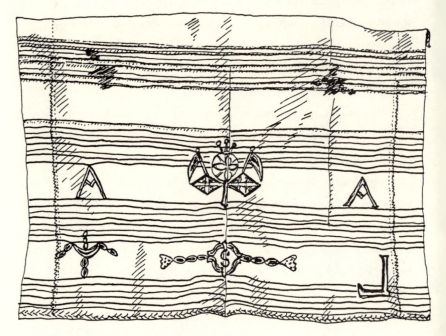

The old embroidered cloth from Loka

the old embroidered textile in its unmarked place in the stack. It, like the much more ordinary garments above and below it, was figured at 100F, and no one was the wiser. Sally watched the exchange and said nothing. Ken was quiet. Who, if anyone, was being ripped off? Hard to say, since BM, who was not in any clear sense the owner of the objects, was the one who pocketed the 3,100F we paid for the whole bunch of cloths plus the wood. Would anything have been different if the cloths had been left unfolded?

We could have bought many more cloths if we'd wanted. Maybe we should have? It was purely our discretion—not BM's or DM's—that limited us to twenty-odd examples. We think that the old embroidered cloth is the nicest "museum quality" piece we have collected thus far in any medium.

We've noticed that when cloths are sold more than a few at a time, the asking price drops considerably. And there's a striking discrepancy between Aluku criteria for pricing and those traditionally used for the appraisal of objects in the art market or a museological context. People ask from 50 to 100F for old cloths, which are rare and especially valuable to a museum but obsolete in terms of Aluku fashion, and 200–500F for newly-sewn ones that, from a "museological" perspective, are of relatively minor interest. This was also true in Saramaka where, once Sally made clear her interest in patchwork and embroidery, men offered gifts of old textiles from their trunks without a second thought but were reluctant to part with a cross-stitch cloth from the 1970s, which could be worn in style to community events.

We later learned that BM is the son of one of the women who was being honored in the funeral rites then underway, and that the house where we bought the cloths had once belonged to her mother. DM and Nyolu are the sons of BM's mother's sister—so, all three men are grandchildren of the original owner of the trunks. Later in the day, when Rich told Nyolu (who'd been absent) about finding some beautiful cloths in his grandmother's house, Nyolu

However, they were entering the country of the river Tietê, where boodle regulates everything and the traditional money is no longer cocoa beans but what is described at various times as cash, coin of the realm, gold, dollars, pelf, lucre, dough, jack, brass, bullion, tin, sterling, boodle, farthings, joeys, tiddlers, tanners, bobs, florins, half-crowns, pence, quids, fivers, ponies, monkeys, dimes, quarters, fins, greenbacks, frogskins, bucks, iron men and zacs. . . . Macunaíma was much dismayed by this discovery.

— Mário de Andrade, *Macunaíma* (1984 [1928]), p. 32

perked up and said, "Terrific! Sometime I'll just ask my mom for the keys and take what I want too!" We suspect that our transaction with BM was initiated by DM, who as a Conseiller Régional is directly interested in the museum project; DM sat there during the selection of cloths, but when Rich began to discuss money he made a point of leaving that to BM—avoidance of the appearance of conflict of interest. Whether any of the money was given to DM's mother or her sisters is unclear. It's as if DM didn't want to know. There's definitely a pattern of younger men simply taking things from their mothers or aunts and selling them off. When Sally later pressed DM about exactly whose cloths we had bought, he told her only that "they belong in general to our family."

The squalor of the Maroon areas of St. Laurent is not entirely absent from Aluku villages today—in marked contrast to the meticulous tidiness of Saramaka villages we knew in the sixties and seventies. Some areas really stink and there's refuse—plastic coke bottles, lots of broken glass, cardboard beer packaging—all around. Personal demeanor, dress, and hygiene is also very loose by Saramaka standards. And the sharing that characterized so much of social life in Saramaka (and, according to all accounts, in pre-commune Aluku) has given way to rampant monetization and commodification: things that used to be divided up among kin—hunting and fishing kills, various imported products—now all have their price; the heart of intrafamilial morality has been pierced.

The quantity of imported goods displayed in front of the funeral hangar, all destined for eventual redistribution, is staggering. Our final count is 160 cases of rum, 180 cases of beer, 70 cases of soda, and 70 of "Sunkist." And there are scores of baskets of Aluku cassava cakes, with bowls of ground peanut sauce, to boot.

On Friday, shortly after we arrived in Loka, Sally separated off from Rich and Ken to wander around and was soon taken in by an Aluku woman, who offered her a warm beer, then fed her a meal, and finally insisted on "delivering" her back to Rich and Ken. All this

Today, thanks to *francisation*, [the Aluku] are a "subsidized" people. . . .
In 1983, 1,800,000 francs (a little less than U.S. $250,000 at the time),
which had originated in metropolitan France, passed through various inter-
mediaries in Cayenne and made its way to the *commune* of Grand-Santi-
Papaïchton. . . . Since that time, yearly budgets have increased. . . . In 1986,
the standard monthly amount paid out for old-age pensions was 1,500
francs [=$300] per person. In contrast, agricultural allowances varied to
some extent. One woman received 7,500 francs in such payments over a
period of three months. . . .

The influx of "free" (or "cheap") money has helped create an enormous
appetite for gain, and has sparked what at times seems like a frenzy of
buying and selling. . . . There remains almost nothing that cannot be sold.
— Bilby, *The Remaking of the Aluku*, pp. 173–74, 178–80

was familiar from Saramaka — a proper playing out of the beginnings of a *máti* (formal friend) relationship, right down to the responsibility toward the husband to show that the woman wasn't off with another man.

Meanwhile, DM, who'd just arrived, presented Rich with two packages for which he'd served as courier — one envelope with the remaining 50,000F from the collection-buying portion of the summer's budget, and another with the Dutch translation of *Primitive Art in Civilized Places*, in manuscript, which Sally's publisher in the Hague had sent via the BPE for her comments and corrections.

One window on Aluku life was provided by the several Saramaka men who are in residence. Sinêli of Dángogó (a sister's son of our late friend Asipéi) didn't have too much to say, having been here for a couple of decades, taken a wife, and generally gotten used to the way things are done. But two younger men we met in Loka, one from Gódo and one from Bundjitapá (in Aluku as carpenters, working on a large project in Maripasoula), were hungry for a chance to vent their reactions to this strange place, where women sat with their knees bared and thighs open, where funeral salutes were fired with loaded cartridges, where women drank beer and rum as if they were men and men drank to excess, where people didn't know how to cook tasty rice (and manifested a peculiar preference for grilled cassava meal), where gossip was frequent and nasty, and so on. (We had heard some of these same comments from our Saramaka friend Sêneki in St. Laurent, when she confided her assessment of the neighbors she had there, who were Ndjuka.) It was all spilled out in whispers, the two of them sticking together for solidarity in an alien environment, and latching onto us as a rare chance for more corroboration of their perceptions, for banter with people who knew and appreciated the "proper" way to live. On Friday night, while Ken ate with the French ethnobotany student, the two of us had a fine dinner of howler monkey and cassava cakes in the house of an Aluku woman who had a Saramaka father. The two young Sara-

This is surely the heart of Boni wisdom. Through an instinctive selectivity that reflects the vitality of their tribe and the awareness they have of its originality, they borrow from civilization only those elements that will improve the smooth workings of their society, without disturbing its foundations: . . . their women have adopted the dishware of European housewives, but not their dress. . . . They have not slavishly imitated the image of modern man that is held out to them by St. Laurent and Maripasoula; rather, they have reacted to it by countering with their own image, born of independence and a sense of their own dignity.

— Resse, *Guyane française*, pp. 110–11

Maroons lose their discrimination and their aesthetic sense as soon as they come into contact with European influences. Then they're seen wearing shirts and shorts in yellow, red, purple, or green that come from the atrocious tawdry commerce that rages on the coast of the Guianas as much as it does in Africa. . . . In recent years, hideous jockey caps were all the rage on the Maroni River, along with jerseys adorned with ads for outboard motors and other designs that are equally ugly, ridiculous, and vulgar. Sadly, Chinese storeowners from Suriname gain renown in this business. It sometimes seems as if there are firms that set up research centers, with experts in the art of uglifying and degrading men.

Between 1958 and 1964, the problem has increased considerably, and it is now clear that the Boni have almost completely lost their picturesque allure.

— Hurault, *La vie matérielle*, p. 85

maka men, who were staying in that house, had arranged for us to be invited. We repaid the hospitality by entertaining them with whitefolks' Saramaccan.

At the Friday evening *dansi*, not a wrap-skirt in sight, and it would clearly have been inappropriate to wear one. Women in glittery sequined dresses, in complex French dressmaking extravaganzas, many in high heels, all in elaborately braided or carefully straightened hairdos. Actually, there were two women's costumes during the day: for the afternoon ceremony in which young women and girls danced and hooted in six or seven long motor canoes that circled around and around in the river before the landing place (as passive spectators on shore used cameras and video cams—a recent token of Aluku conspicuous consumption), the costume was cross-stitch-embroidery skirts, a broad black elastic belt (no more waist kerchiefs) and blouses; the glitter-dresses were for the evening play, where there wasn't an embroidery stitch in sight. For all men: long pants. At the evening dance, we saw several jackets (as in sports jacket), and at least one tie. Everyone wore shoes (not sandals, but shoes). The children (equally be-shoed) were likewise dressed to the hilt in frilly dresses for the girls, pants and shirts for the boys. The evening music began with a couple of hours of *aleke* singing and drums, a recent Aluku style for which we have not yet acquired a taste. Around midnight, fifty or so people (largely young, largely female) crammed into the funeral hangar—an open shed draped with embroidered cloths, with drums at one end—and began to "play *mato*." This distant cousin of the narrative folktales that Saramakas introduce with the words *Mató!/Tongôni!* rang unfamiliar to our ears. Brief shouted vignettes, brief songs, lots of hooting, backed by drums. Many of the stories recounted recent local gossip, scandal stories that Saramakas would have fed into popular songs or cloth names. Much more raucous than Saramaka tale-telling, much less attentive listening.

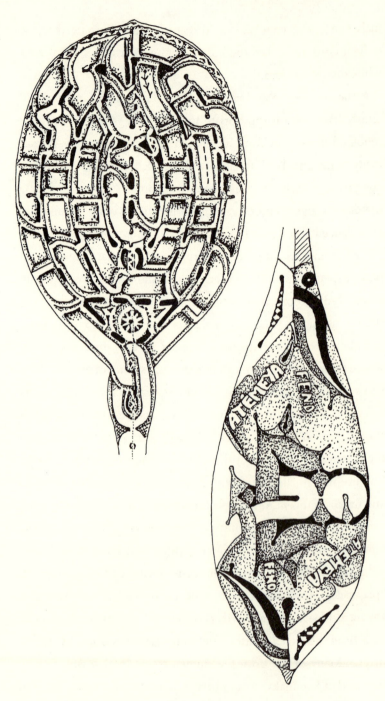

Carved handle and painted blade of Obentié's second paddle [See page 185]

After an hour of *mato*, we retired for some sleep. Because we were carrying so much cash (the 50,000F of collecting money that had been brought by DM), the two of us had been given a room with a lock on the door in the dispensary. A gasoline generator, located on the other side of a flimsy wall from our hammock, was going full blast and our room was brightly lit. The generator wires had been strung directly to our high-ceilinged light bulb, bypassing the light switch. We considered turning off the generator but knew that others, including DM, were using the house. Getting to sleep under the bright light with the generator roaring a few feet away seemed unlikely, but we were exhausted, and managed to drift off, waking early on Saturday to face yet another day of collecting.

Continuing thoughts about (lack of) purpose—almost an aggressive indifference.

There are, nonetheless, occasional observations of mild interest. Sally thinks about the changes (from Saramaka-then to Aluku-now) in art, conjugal relations, and social exchange patterns: "then" the best men's art was intended for women, the best women's art for men; "now" the best men's art (elaborately painted motor-canoes) is for men, and the best women's art (elaborately cross-stitched, and sometimes fringed, wrap-skirts) is for women. Reciprocity has given way to a me-generation pattern in the context of a monetized economy, where cash flows in to both men and women through the French welfare system, and relations based on a two-way exchange are rendered obsolete.

Second ethnographic insight: A woman gave Sally a little speech yesterday, much like the ones we used to hear in Saramaka villages, about the difficult social problem of women who "hide their periods." She made clear that even though Alukus don't observe the kind of rigidly regulated seclusion that's practiced in Upper River Saramaka, they do have milder restrictions based on the same theory of female pollution. Sally, who's just read The Book of Laughter and Forgetting, has been thinking about the feminist (re-)vision of menstrua-

Among the Djuka of Dutch Guiana (Kahn 1931:130) . . . menstrual seclusion has been seen as bringing women sexual autonomy and opportunities for illicit love affairs.
> — Thomas Buckley and Alma Gottlieb (eds.), *Blood Magic* (1988), p. 13

[And the cited passage (Kahn 1931: 130), in its entirety:]
Menstruating women are required to leave their homes and retire to a separate hut situated outside the village on a by-path; they may not return until three days after the period is over. Under no condition are they allowed to go to the provision fields during this time.

If you think you are emancipated, you might consider the idea of tasting your menstrual blood — if it makes you sick, you've a long way to go, baby.
> — Germaine Greer, *The Female Eunuch* (1971), p. 42

One [American] woman said, "There should be celebration around menstruation. If done right it could be wonderful!" . . . Maybe we could restore a feeling of wholeness about the process and reduce in and of itself some of the disgust. . . . Some have urged us to revel in menstrual blood and make it a matter of spiritual delight by developing new rituals, "bleed-ins."
> — Emily Martin, *The Woman in the Body* (1987), p. 111

To see and feel the warm, tender blood that flows naturally from oneself, from the source, once each month is happiness. To be this vagina, open-eyed in the nocturnal fermentations of life, ear alert to the pulsations, to the vibrations of the primal chaos . . . to be this vagina is bliss.
> — Annie Leclerc, *Parole de femme* (1974), p. 48; see also Milan Kundera, *The Book of Laughter and Forgetting* (1981), pp. 56–57

[In Saramaka] reference to the menstrual hut as the "bad house" (*táku ósu*) and the fact that a single expression (*dê a baáka*) means "to be in menstrual seclusion" and "to be in mourning" are true reflections of the tone of a woman's life during those times.
> — S. Price, *Co-wives and Calabashes*, p. 22

tion—especially its lack of fit with her own extended experience in Maroon menstrual huts in the company of Saramaka women. If menstrual seclusion is such a joyous sisterly retreat, why do women cheat? She thinks about writing an article called "The Curse's Blessing: Feminism Redecorates the Menstrual Hut."

More on collecting: we could acquire tremendous numbers of calabashes (which remains a lively and fairly generalized art among women) and cloths (from both old men and old women, for whom they are relics to be used in [and often received in] funeral exchanges but to whom they don't have great social meaning anymore). At $2–6 per calabash, and $10–20 per old cloth, we could fill several canoes . . . but that's hardly what the museum wants or needs, nor are we inclined to do much more of that. So, we'll see what Captain Tafanye has in his trunks in Papai Siton—he said he'd show us Monday—and probably halt on cloth-buying as we pretty much have already for calabashes.

The "problem"—in terms of doing our job for the museum—remains one of getting "museum quality" wood objects. The difficulty so far results from several things: (1) For some time in Aluku, wood has not been part of the expected male-female exchange system, though a few men still carve—so some currently (recently) made objects are available, but they're in relatively short supply and aesthetically they're not anything to write home about; (2) *really* old objects either have sufficient sentimental/social value so that they're not for sale or (and this is frequent) have been scrubbed so often with sand over the years that their bas-relief carvings are barely visible; and (3) as we have been told time and again, the best objects that people had have by now all been sold to the myriad whitefolks who wander through asking to buy woodcarvings. These people (# 3s) seem for the most part to be curiosity/souvenir hunters—tourists (of which there are many), doctors and nurses (ditto), and gendarmes (the most frequently mentioned)—who come through asking for things to bring back home, rather than professional dealers, runners, or

The request for "good, old" pieces is a constant refrain in Boas's instructions. . . . "I wish you could get more of these old carvings. They are much finer than the new ones. . . . What we need most are good old carvings" (Boas to Hunt, 9/13/1899).

— Jacknis, "George Hunt, Collector of Indian Specimens," p. 192

collectors. The result is the same, however: the very great bulk of "museum quality" woodcarving ever made by Alukus that is still extant is either in museums or in people's living rooms, mostly in France. What's still here on the river is truly the leavings.

Gendarmes, by the way, have a reputation in Guyane as particularly avaricious and unscrupulous collectors of Aluku art. La Directrice had told us in Cayenne how gendarmes, at the end of their three-year tours of duty, fly back to France on military planes, with no police or customs checks of any kind. We asked why this would make a difference, in that Guyane is officially part of France and we were unaware of laws that prohibited export from this overseas *département*. She replied with a story, which we don't remember in detail, about a large drum the BPE had bought upriver and left with gendarmes for safekeeping. The drum disappeared, apparently along with some men whose tour of duty had ended.

6:45–7:45 PM. As we're writing up notes, Ba Manku comes by and spends an hour talking, with interest and expertise, about the various rapids in the river. He relives the upriver trip we made from St. Laurent, discussing in animated detail the choice he made of which channel to take through each rapids, how Ba Nyolu's indications of which to follow would have sunk the canoe if they had been listened to, etc. He shows considerable knowledge of many individual details—from particular stones and whirlpools to watch out for to places where the sideways current whiplashes the canoe. We're reminded not only of Saramaka men's love of such talk but of Mark Twain's Mississippi river pilots.

Trouble getting to sleep. Sally is restless and wants to talk about our leaving earlier than planned. If Monday's collecting with Captain Tafanye goes well, mightn't we be able to put together a "rounded collection" by a week from now? We finally drift off but wake up thinking the same thoughts.

The avocado pear grows on a tree above forty feet high, and is not unlike our walnut trees, but the fruit, which is about the size and colour of a large pear, viz., a purple or pale green, is in my opinion, the most exquisite of any in the colony, or in the world. It is yellow inside, with a soft stone like a chestnut, and so good is the flesh or pulp of this fruit — so nutritious and salubrious — that it is often called the vegetable marrow (a name given it, it is said, by Sir Hans Sloane), and is usually eaten with pepper and salt. Nor can I approach it to anything so well as to a peach, it melting in the same manner in ones mouth; but though not so sweet it is incomparably more delicious.

How great thy fame, O vegetable pear.
What fat, what marrow can with thee compare?
Long known to fame, till now unknown to song,
Though Britain sigh, and Britain's monarch long

as this fruit can never be transported.

— Stedman, Narrative (1790/1992), p. 134

Amazing — only two-thirds of the way through do you find out his wife's been along the whole time . . . and that, [only] when she suddenly gets ill enough to force herself into the narrative.

— Peter Redfield, commenting on rereading Levi-Strauss' Tristes tropiques (letter of 14 November 1991)

SUNDAY 12/VIII/90

Early morning, we talk again and decide not only that we would like to leave sooner than planned, but that it's feasible since we're finding much more, and more easily and quickly, than any of us had imagined at the beginning. Agreed to find out what Ken would really like to do, if he had his druthers. Spent the second part of the morning with Ken, logging the large number of items collected in Loka onto fiches. We see once again that we're doing fine on calabashes and cloth and that it's largely wood and miscellaneous ethnographica that remain to be completed.

For lunch, packaged noodle soup again, but this time complemented by delicious avocados from the tree near our back door. We have a long discussion with Ken about what he wants to do for the rest of the stay. He says he'd like to remain upriver for the full time as planned, partly to do some catch-up ethnography about the past several years. So we agree that, if La Directrice approves, the two of us will fly back in a week or so, meeting with La Directrice to discuss plans for the museum more generally (which we're very eager to do, after all this relatively mindless collecting), and Ken will finish up here. All three of us have been having stomach problems.

Ken and Rich go up to the "Mountain" and buy several items: a basket, a child's broom, a stool, a winnowing tray, and some textiles, while Sally pores over the Dutch translation of her "primitive art" book. The nearest Dutch-English dictionary must be several hundred miles away in Paramaribo.

Pleasant dinner at Mme Jeanne's. As we're leaving, Sally says she feels nauseous and almost instantly loses consciousness, collapsing on the floor. Eyes open but completely gone. Dead weight. Comes to after a long thirty seconds of cajoling and gentle slapping. "Where am I? What happened?" Rich, with Ken's help, pulls her to her feet, but in a few seconds she's leaning over Mme Jeanne's balcony, retching and vomiting onto the mud below the house. Blue jeans soaked

It was a typical morning. . . . Peering out from under my plaid hammock . . . I saw a bare-breasted [Wayana Indian] maiden in red loincloth with matching red elastic garters, her body tinted red with vegetable dye, stoking the breakfast campfire. Meanwhile, one of the boatmen shot a green parrot for lunch. . . . Merenge [an Aluku] was intoning his morning prayer to Massa Gadu in melodious, English-flecked Taki-taki. Stomach growling from the previous evening's peccary stew, I charged into the jungle, grabbing a banana leaf in lieu of toilet paper. I took one step into the forest, tripped on a liana, but I did not fall. The dense wall of undergrowth smacked me in the face and held me upright. I had, I realized, just confronted the fabled Green Hell of French Guiana.

— Raymond A. Sokolov, "A Greenhorn's Tour" (1974), p. 1

Kenneth Brecher . . . directs the Boston Children's Museum outside of which is a large milk bottle. His chairman of the board once remarked how wonderful it was to have such a marker so all could remember the museum. Kenneth suggested that maybe kids no longer knew what a milk bottle was. She thought it impossible. So he went outside and asked an eight-year-old: what's that? The kid replied: "I don't know." "Well, what do you think it is?" After some reflection, the kid hazarded: "it must be the smokestack of a nuclear power plant."

— Michael M. J. Fischer, "Museums and Festivals" (1989), p. 220

with urine. Ken visibly agitated. After a couple of minutes, more embarrassed than damaged, she's able to walk the fifty yards to our place. Rich and Ken agree that the two of them will proceed as planned with the Papai Siton trip the next day. Sally starts a course of antibiotics and climbs into bed.

MONDAY 13/VIII/90

Sally's a bit weak but otherwise chipper. Ken and Rich set off early for a day of collecting.

On arrival in Papai Siton, Ken goes off to his friend Captain Tobu and Rich, accompanied by Nyolu, goes to talk with old Captain Tafanye. Tafanye asks Nyolu to haul out a small metal trunk from under his bed and place it on the table and then tells Rich he can select five pieces for the museum (much as Saramaka Chief Agbagó had told us, in 1978, that he wanted to give us four old patchwork textiles, which we were to choose from his trunks and use for the exhibit, "Afro-American Arts from the Suriname Rain Forest"). Rich and Nyolu unfold some twenty or thirty textiles: breechcloths of various lengths and breadths (and epochs); the special rectangular cloths made to be tied around men's necks for *awasa* dancing (an item that Nyolu, who's in his twenties, had never seen or heard of); sacks of different dimensions—for hammocks, cartridges, cassava cereal; bonnets that men once wore for "sport"; a "soldier's hat" featuring a red button embossed with a scotch terrier; various items of sartorial elegance that were modish at particular moments; several cloths intended to be draped over the captain's coffin when he died; and so on.

Rich selected a half dozen: a couple of finely embroidered breechcloths, the modish soldier's hat, a doll's-size "handbag," stuffed like a miniature pillow, that Tafanye had used years ago as a vanity garment when he went to village "plays," a complex cushion hung all

Each of them opened his travel-basket, and in it were the different pieces of apparel which they wear when in Paramaribo or for ceremonial occasions. And they dressed themselves in the best manner they could. Our proud commodore, *Akra*, was particularly distinguished in the strange manner in which he dressed. By his bartering in Paramaribo, he had gotten a splendid colored night-shirt that had been made at Zitz, and for which he had been charged fifty guilders. He wore it tied together with a dagger, and he had a hat with tresses on it. In this ridiculous attire he ordered his comrades about, and I had a difficult time suppressing my laughter.

— Johann Andreus Riemer, *Missions-Reise nach Suriname und Barbice* (1801), pp. 201–202

Captain Tafanye's soldier's hat and tiny handbag

over with smaller patchwork cloths that was made as a decoration to hang on the large end of the captain's coffin (but which he showed no special reluctance to part with, since he had a couple of others), and an *awasa* cloth. Tafanye had much the same attitude toward these cloths as Saramaka Chief Agbagó had had when he opened his many trunks for our inspection in 1978. "Each cloth," Tafanye repeatedly told Rich, "means a woman. One cloth, one woman." Each—including those destined someday for his coffin—had been a present from a lover. Reminiscing on the romances of many decades past, with the cloths to prompt him, he smiled and chuckled much as Agbagó had done upon discovering a bundle of adolescent girls' aprons, each representing a nubile lover of his own youth. For both Agbagó and Tafanye, rummaging through their textile trunks was a special trip down memory lane.

Once the choices were made, Rich asked how much we should pay. The captain wanted to know what we'd paid others and Rich said 100F per cloth. "All right, but let's make it 700F for the six, since they're old." As Rich paid, Nyolu grabbed an old bonnet from the trunk, stuck it on his head, and told the captain it was now his. Tafanye shrugged and laughed. Later, Rich told Nyolu he could sport it for the day (which he did), but that it would end up in the museum collection (which it did). Rich and Nyolu found Ken in Tobu's house where the captain offered them a meal.

Tobu brought out an eighty-year-old hammock that he'd been keeping for decades. First time either Ken or Rich had actually seen a Maroon-made hammock; imported Brazilian ones have been standard among Maroons for years. Tightly-woven from hand-spun, home-grown cotton. Tobu said the last Aluku who knew how to make hammocks died two decades ago. Ken had set up the purchase of various other ethnographic objects—a fishing arrow, a Creole-style woven hat, a pestle, a rice-husk broom, and a gourd container—which Rich paid for, as well as some other items to be picked up on later visits. Then back to Tafanye for the promised trip to the vil-

Turn-of-the-century stool with "kissing" birds

lage of Old Papai Siton, five minutes downstream, which had been abandoned when the commune was set up two decades ago.

Tafanye took Rich and Ken up onto the porch of his decaying house-on-stilts and brought out a dust-covered bottle of rum. Libations, asking the ancestors' permission for selling what he was about to. He then went inside and brought out a single stool. "This is what I have for the museum," he announced. (Note that some of our major acquisitions fall, from the point of view of the individual Aluku owner, somewhere between gift and sale; they represent gestures of good-will and generosity, not just passive acquiescence to our project.) It was a three-piece, pierced stool in turn-of-the-century style, partly broken on one side but with two "kissing" birds at either end. "Ducks," he said, but without much conviction. Made our usual speech and took down the necessary data. Agreed on a price of 800F, the most we've paid for a (non-commissioned) object to date.

Then a tour through the old village, where several houses have had their painted facades "awakened" (that is repainted) recently by the members of an official *association* called Kawina. Ken, in his dissertation, described how such Aluku *associations* (a kind of not-for-profit organization), duly registered with the Prefecture in Cayenne according to a French law of 1901, have been in operation since the early 1980s. Founded by young, educated Alukus who live mainly in Cayenne, they have focused on a mix of cultural revitalization and touristic development—thus far without much effect. The most active of these groups at present, the "Association 'Mi Wani Sabi' " is particularly involved in the preservation of Aluku art and has ties with the socialist party, which holds the purse strings in today's Guyane. They have cooperated with the BPE in staging a couple of small exhibits in Cayenne and have lent the BPE the several Aluku objects we saw in their storerooms. When we first arrived in Maripasoula, Ken tried to contact their officers so we could have a meeting and work out collaboration about both collecting and eventual

Where things cross a cultural boundary we re-invent their meanings. The Hawaiians and the *Daedalus*'s crew exchanged curiosities across their different cultural boundaries. The *Daedalus*'s crew re-invented what they received, made icons and weapons into saleable collector's pieces. Collectors and museum visitors would read these goods as signs of savage Otherness. How could they read them for what they were — things that bound men to gods, separated men from women, chiefs from commoners? And how could their readings be sacramental of their meaning, *actually* binding men to gods, separating men from women, chiefs from commoners? The new readings were sacramental of other meanings, of the class and status of collectors, of the superiority of the civilized over savages. The Hawaiians were as inventive. Re-shaping the strangers' goods to their own functions, they were also re-shaped a little by things over whose production and introduction they had little or no control.

— Dening, *History's Anthropology*, pp. 8–9

plans for the museum. But no one was available upriver, everyone was away on the coast. Rich now gets the idea that a painted house facade would be worth commissioning, and that perhaps Manku's father—who Ken says owns the nicest of the newly-redone houses—might be the man to ask.

Back in Komontibo and Papai Siton, Ken and Rich make various purchases—some textiles from Captain Tobu, a mortar and pestle and a tray in another part of the village, and others. Ken discusses drums with several people. Rich sees a transaction he doesn't know how to write up without falling into the caricatural style of that pernicious South African film, "The Gods Must be Crazy." An old woman, the medium of a snake god, bare-breasted and wearing a wrap-skirt—one of the most "traditional" women we've met in Aluku—has made an agreement with Ken to sell two rattles used in rituals. They're speckled with kaolin. Ken goes off to do something else, telling Rich to buy them. Meanwhile, a young (possibly Ndjuka) woman dressed in fashionable city clothes, a traveling peddler, has come over with some Tupperware-type refrigerator containers and hawks them to the old woman. She also sells her a lacy pink bra many sizes too small. Total, 300F. When she leaves, Rich asks the woman how much she wants for the rattles. She says "three hundred francs." It's steep, and would have seemed arbitrary, but it all makes sense and Rich pays. Much of the day's take has been due to Ken's personal relations in Komontibo/Papai Siton, dating from his fieldwork. This is very much his "home territory."

Rich and Ken head back upriver to see how Sally is feeling and what news she has from Cayenne. She's spoken on the phone with La Directrice, who likes the idea of our flying to Cayenne early and meeting for discussions about museum plans while Ken finishes up the field collecting. Friday the 18th is, however, a busy day for her; she'd like us to take the plane on the 20th instead. After her phone call with La Directrice, Sally had trudged off to the crude plank structure that serves as an office for Air Guyane and addressed the person

The bonnet Nyolu appropriated from Captain Tafanye [See page 207]

in charge, a peroxide-blond gendarme's wife working with a ledger book, a pencil, and a well-worn eraser. Absolutely impossible to make a reservation for the next ten days, she tells her. Not that there wouldn't be plenty of places. But "these people" have no sense of time or responsibility. "They make reservations, but half the time they just don't show up, so you can't give the place to anyone else and the planes fly off half empty. I can't possibly make a reservation for you until the 24th." Sally leans over the counter to read her notebook upside-down; the first name listed for the date we want is Topo, slated for two seats. Topo, an Aluku, is the mechanic who's been issuing us one of the government-owned outboard motors each morning for our collecting mission; having talked with him recently, Sally has reason to believe that he's staying in the interior for the foreseeable future. Perhaps, she offers, she could ask him his plans and, if he's not flying, we could take his place. "Chère Madame," the woman replies with a thin veneer of patience, "there's no reason to believe that your Mr. Topo is the person on my list. They all have the same names: Topo, Popo, Bubu, Tupu. There's no way to tell them apart. The only thing you can do is just to show up an hour before and wait to see if there's room on the plane." Sally makes her most valiant attempt to continue the conversation smilingly, à la française, and in the end the woman agrees to let her know if anything opens up. Walking away, Sally thinks about refiguring her as a character in the pseudonymous academic novel she's been working on.

Then back to the mairie, where she was received by the mayor. He was all smiles, entertaining this white woman who spoke in Saramaccan. And delighted to receive a copy of our edition of Stedman's Narrative as a gift. He'd seen the book, he said, but hadn't been able to afford the $100 price tag. He invited us to dinner on Thursday.

Then, on to an interview with DM, in his office in the same modern building, to see whether he could pull some strings to get us seats on the plane to Cayenne. The framed photo-portrait of a

By the mid-1980s, the Kotika *hoofdkapitein* was being treated by the coastal Surinamese authorities as an important dignitary, receiving invitations to all the major functions and meetings in Paramaribo to which the paramount chiefs of all the other [Suriname] Maroon tribes were invited. Such invitations were of course never extended to Gaanman [Aluku Paramount Chief] Tolinga, who was, after all, a French subject.

— Bilby, *The Remaking of the Aluku,* pp. 264–65

broadly smiling DM, an exact replica of those we'd seen at his house in Cayenne, beams down from the wall behind his desk, complete with florid autograph. He treated the request as though the idea of a full plane was pure fantasy; of course he'd get us out and had only to know what date we preferred. Sally'll check back tomorrow to see what he's been able to work out.

Once Ken and Rich get back, the three of us log in the day's haul, which we're pleased with. One more good day of finding wooden objects and we'll have a balanced collection. Dinner, this time uneventful, at Mme Jeanne's. We get ready for the next day's collecting at Kotika, the only Aluku village on the Suriname side of the river, the oldest still-inhabited Aluku village. It's reputed to have "many old things."

Manku and Nyolu show up in the evening and point out that on other expeditions their food has been included. Wouldn't it be better, they argue, to take a butane burner, a pot, and some rice and cook a meal each day when we're away? Rich asks about meat and is told not to worry. We say we'll bring rice and the burner.

TUESDAY 14/VIII/90

At 8 AM, Rich and Sally meet briefly in the *mairie* with DM, who's unable to get through to Cayenne by phone. But he's leaving on the flight today and will arrange things for us with La Directrice in the city. We should check in tomorrow with the local Air Guyane woman, who will have received orders from Cayenne.

An hour and a half downriver to Kotika. Both captains are away. Because of the importance of this visit, the three of us decide to go back up to Agoode, where the Headcaptain is cutting a garden for his wife, to speak with him. But first, Nyolu gives a young woman the rice we've brought plus a frozen chicken he and Manku have bought, saying we'd be back to eat later. Before leaving we visit in

The approach to Boniville [Agoode] is totally unreminiscent of our arrival in Indian villages. We almost get by without being noticed. At the landing place, a number of Boni women are busy washing dishes of shiny aluminum in the river and glance at us casually as they keep working. Big frying pans, pots of every size, ladles, spoons, plates, cups. . . . The utensils of the perfect "civilized" kitchen seem strangely anomalous next to the long wraps in multicolored squares, belted at the waist, that reach to their ankles; generally large in size, most of them have their hair pulled into a bun, big rings in their ears, and no bra.

— Resse, *Guyane française*, p. 105

The Rebels . . . were commanded by one *bony*, a relentless Mullatto, who was born in the forest. . . . The *White Men* taken alive at the engagement as I have related . . . had one by one been Stript by the Negroes so soon as they arrived in the rebel Village . . . where they had by bonys orders been flog'd to death, for the recreation of theyr Wives and their Children.

— Stedman, *Narrative* (1790/1988), pp. 188–89

the house of an old woman. We ask about a *ketebe* — a rolled woven mat — we see against one wall. She says matter-of-factly she can't sell it, it's for her burial. If she didn't have it, she explains, they'd have to bury her in plastic and she'd rot much faster. We're momentarily horrified, completely taken aback.

Across the broad Lawa from the Kotika landing place, on the French side, we see the houses of Tabiki, one of the seven "traditional" villages of the pre-commune era. Today, we're told, its only permanent resident is an old woman — everyone else has moved to Maripasoula, Papai Siton, or the coast. If there isn't time before the two of us leave, Ken will try to visit on his own.

Upstream again to Agoode, where eventually we were able to call the Kotika Headcaptain from his nearby garden, and he invited us into his wife's sitting room. We explained how we'd gone to Kotika but didn't feel it would be respectful to begin our work in his absence. Ken, who knew the Headcaptain from his days of fieldwork, explained at some length the nature of our Mission. The Headcaptain listened impassively, giving no signs of approval of the enterprise. At the end, he said he couldn't really give us an answer, since the other captain of Kotika was absent in Loka and would need to be consulted. We proposed Ken's going to fetch him, and eventually Nyolu drove him upriver to that village.

The two of us stayed behind, with Manku, to chat with the Headcaptain and present him with the gift we had brought for him — a copy of Stedman's *Narrative*. Together we turned the pages, examining the engravings of eighteenth-century slave tortures, Maroon warriors, and colonial soldiers. When we came to the William Blake engraving of "The celebrated Graman Quacy," Rich related at length the Saramaka and whitefolks' versions of his story, singing the óbia-song of Wámba's forest-spirit at the appropriate point in the Saramaka version. The captain was visibly moved; so was Manku, who admonished him in a hushed whisper, "Never show this to any one else. Take it to your inner room and turn each page carefully, one

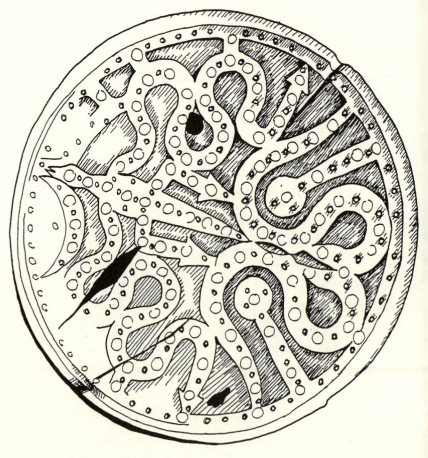

The Kotika captain's tray

by one. This is not for young people to see." Libations and thanks. We asked about a handsome tray — 1940s style — propped up against a wall. The Headcaptain's wife said she couldn't sell it. The husband who'd made it had died; she didn't have the man any more but she had the memory through the tray. (Ken later tells us that in Loka a woman said the same thing about a stool that her dead grandfather had made.) Out in the yard, an Aluku woman sold us a stool made by a former husband from Ndjuka.

Sally asked about Ma Do, a woman whose name she'd been given by Captain Tobu in Papai Siton as a well-known local calabash carver. She was taken off to her house. By coincidence, the woman had once had a husband from Dángogó and spent time there some years back. Warm reception. Catch-up news on lots of mutual Saramaka friends. Viewing and buying of half a dozen beautifully carved calabashes, with her signature carefully etched on the outside rim. In passing, the woman mentioned that when she was in Saramaka, the women there asked her if she knew how to carve calabashes; she, feeling like an outsider (and behaving with the exaggerated politesse appropriate in a husband's village), claimed never to have learned the art.

Ken and Nyolu return with the other captain and we go through the whole museum speech again, in the house of the Headcaptain's wife. By now, there's more of a spirit of cooperation. In the end, they agree to come with us to their village and we set off downstream once more, having bought a winnowing tray we happened to see on our way out of Agoode. It was sold to us by a wife of old Captain Adiso from Asisi, who'd carved it for her several decades ago.

It's 1 PM when we finally go ashore in Kotika, leave our things in the captain's house, and head off with Manku and Nyolu to eat the chicken and rice that've been prepared in our absence and set out in bowls on a low table. Delicious. Then back to the captain's house, where he pulls out a beautiful, old round tray decorated with car-tridge burns and brass tacks, saying this is for you to view and photo

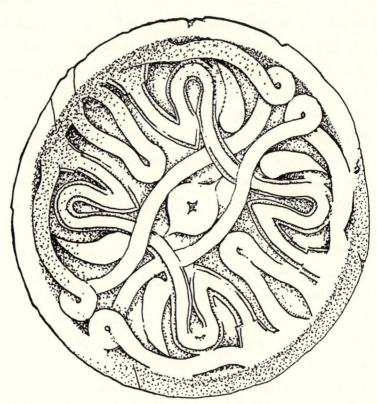

Headcaptain Peeti's tray from Kotika

but we can't sell it. We admire it and take its history. The Headcaptain brings out a tray of similar vintage which he says he will sell, but it's very worn by decades of washing and the designs have been almost obliterated. Soon, other men appear with wooden objects — stools, food stirrers, hammock threaders, and combs. And women begin crowding the doorway with calabashes. We tell them we'll deal with each in turn. Starting with a couple of food stirrers and combs, we eventually work our way up to the Headcaptain's tray and agree on 900F.

The captain who'd said he couldn't sell his tray begins to have second thoughts. Would we buy it for the museum even if it was very expensive? We say we could pay whatever is fitting. He proposes 1,200F and we agree. When he expresses concern about its being treated well, Sally promises him she'll wash it personally when we get to Cayenne, rather than entrusting it to a curator. As the afternoon progresses the pace quickens until the three of us are having real difficulties fielding all the offers, peeling off the bills, scribbling down the documentation.

Long session with Paramount Chief Difou's widow, mediated by her Paramaribo-educated granddaughter who makes a point of speaking some English and Dutch. We buy several of the deceased Chief's objects, more for historical than aesthetic reasons, that is, simply because they were made by him. Interrupted frequently by others who've brought out things for sale. The woman who had said she couldn't sell the burial mat has apparently changed her mind and wants to sell; we don't take her up on it and let the matter drop. Truly, it's hard to keep up with all the offers.

We buy all kinds of things, largely in wood — broken off canoe prows, a two-headed comb, and table tops. As we're saying our goodbyes, the captain discreetly indicates that he needs a moment with Rich in private. He has been thinking about the sale of the tray, he says; clearly he has also been watching the course of our other purchases. "Mi twompé" ("I made a mistake"), he whispers in mixed

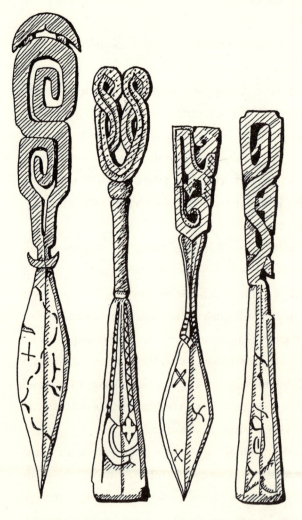

Food stirrers from our day in Kotika; the two on the right were carved by the late Papa Kodjo

Aluku and French Creole, "I realize I should have asked a higher price." We propose an extra 200F, and he seems pleased. By the time we finally board the canoe, knowing it's already close to nightfall and that we'll have to negotiate the final part of the upriver trip in darkness, we feel elated. We've topped off our collection with enough good quality wood to feel we have a balanced collection at last. From here on out it should be, as they say, gravy. In a burst of shared enthusiasm, Manku lets Nyolu take over at the motor, and he almost capsizes us hotrodding it into the dock at Maripasoula.

During dinner at Mme Jeanne's, two men—friends of Ken's—approached us with a stool that one of them said he found in his mother's house when she died. We bought it. Back in our place, the three of us huddled around the radio to hear the latest news of the Middle East as well as the civil war in Suriname.

WEDNESDAY 15/VIII/90

The two of us meet briefly with the mayor, leaving an envelope with cash in his safekeeping, to be paid to Obentié (2,000F) for the stereobox and Daniel Ateni (6,000F) for the canoe, once they're completed and he has taken possession on behalf of the BPE; he'll then contact La Directrice to arrange transport to the coast. The rest of the morning spent à trois logging in the finds from Kotika. We check in with the Air Guyane lady who says that, according to her information from Cayenne, there's no way we can leave any day in the next two weeks—except tomorrow. We decide to go for it. Intense packing. Ken and Rich hire a truck to take them to Ken's rooms, and move the whole collection down to where we've been staying, which will become Ken's after tomorrow. Sally and Rich empty the trunks of their expedition gear and Sally uses them to pack up the collection, cushioning the delicate wood with cloths. We select fifty-some-odd

Sometimes I fell on [Parisian] shopkeepers who were delighted by the challenge of my mission and ready to adapt their specialized knowledge to its exoticism. A fish-hook maker near the Canal Saint-Martin let me have all his left-overs at a bargain price: for a whole year I tramped the bush with several kilos of these hooks, but nobody wanted them, since they were too small for any fish worthy of the Amazon fisherman. In the end, I got rid of them at the Bolivian frontier.

— Lévi-Strauss, *Tristes tropiques*, pp. 288–89

objects and pack them in a small trunk to take with us on the plane; the rest will go by boat with Ken.

Ken continues commissioning ethnographica up on the Mountain and eventually shows up with several previously commissioned *pakibas*—calabashes with covers, carved on the interior. They're neat; we've never seen anything like them in Saramaka. He's also bought a drum for himself, and plans to have a man teach him *apinti* language on it during the coming ten days, after our departure. And he's found several other items: a gourd container, a kitchen whisk, and a stool. We log them all in, ending with object No. 188.

The three of us wander over to the little store run by Mme Duplessis, the Creole ex-wife of the former mayor of Maripasoula. We buy softdrinks and then ask if she might be interested in buying, for her store, the Brazilian earrings we had bought in Cayenne; Sally is sporting a pair and has the others in a plastic sack, hoping to unload them at half-price since Aluku women haven't shown the slightest interest in them. Mme Duplessis glances at the colorful array and makes a face. "Chérie," she tells Sally, "If they're not made of gold, there's not a person in Maripasoula who would even look at them."

When Manku and Nyolu show up at dusk, Rich offers what's left of our Johnny Walker bottle all around and announces the expedition's new plans. As of tomorrow, Ken's their boss. He'll want to make at least three overnight trips downriver before they make their final descent to St. Laurent. We discuss the fragility of the collection and ask their help in making sure it gets back in good condition. They're reassuring and make clear they've come to feel a real commitment to the project. They agree to stop by the next morning and help carry our luggage to Air Guyane. Final dinner with Ken at Mme Jeanne's. We agree to phone him there on Monday evening from Cayenne. We then transfer the remaining collecting money and blank *fiches* to Ken, and he traipses back to his now bare hotel room to sleep for a final night.

The [newly-formed] *commune* of Maripasoula . . . lost no time.

At its very first meeting in May 1969, the municipal council requested that all state-owned buildings in its territory (the former gendarmerie, and so forth, which had cost tens of millions of old francs) would become its own property. At its second meeting, it decided that Maripasoula would henceforth become a tourist destination. And using a state subvention of 16 million old francs . . . the *commune* immediately began the transformation of the former gendarmerie into a hotel, setting up ten or so rooms with running water and the basic conveniences required for tourists.

Benefitting from laws that permit a French *commune* to rent out the buildings which belong to it, the *commune* of Maripasoula now offers special week-end excursions for tourists who arrive in chartered airplanes to visit the Wayana Indians.

— Hurault, *Français et Indiens*, p. 303

During the mid-1980s, an irregular trickle of international drifters and misfits continued to pass through the Aluku territory. A few of them crossed my own path: a French seminary dropout; a con artist from the United States; a British fortune hunter; a Canadian retiree launching a new career; a French former computer programmer; a Guyanese novelist; a Franco-Vietnamese artist. In the interior of French Guiana, even with its overadministered communes, the myth of the "open frontier," holding out the promise of individual freedom, remains vigorous.

— Bilby, *The Remaking of the Aluku*, pp. 229–30

Douglas Newton recounts how he paid Kwoma artists in New Guinea one dollar for each of the bark cloth panels that are displayed in the $18.3 million Rockefeller Wing of the Metropolitan Museum of Art.

— S. Price, *Primitive Art*, p. 97

THURSDAY 16/VIII/90

Last-minute packing. 7:30 AM: Ken shows up for tea, Manku and Nyolu arrive soon after. Sally goes off to the *mairie* to call La Directrice so she can have us met at the airport, but is told that the phone lines are down until 2 PM, so she can't get through. She leaves a note for the absent mayor, expressing our regrets for the dinner tonight. We all help carry the luggage to the Air Guyane office, get weighed in, and are told we'll be picked up at 10 at the hotel up the road known as Chez Dédé, to be driven to the airstrip. We say an affectionate goodbye to Nyolu and Manku, exchange promises to stay in touch, and trudge up the hill with Ken.

Beers and sandwiches, talk of anthropology amidst a motley collection of European tourists, dusty Aluku carvings hung on the walls, large stocks of convenience items for sale. Eventually we're taken off to the airstrip in a van driven by one of Captain Tobu's sons, and we squeeze into the two-engine plane, trying to protect the several delicate items that we're hand-carrying, wrapped with care in garbage bags, back to La Directrice—Obentié's two carved paddles and the captain's round tray from Kotika. (We reflect that the tray, which we bought for $280, might fetch up to $10,000 on the art market.) Smooth flight over the rippling, dark green forest floor, cut by winding brown ribbons of water.

"Let's go on to Cayenne," said *Cacambo.* "There we'll find Frenchmen."
— Voltaire, *Candide*, Ch. XVII

4

From Rochambeau airport, Sally calls La Directrice, who's audibly cold and points out sternly that she's planned everything (lodging, car, etc., etc.) for our arrival, not today but on the 20th, and that she left a message to that effect with the mayor's office in Maripasoula. The message was never delivered, Sally explains. La Directrice is displeased, busy, not inclined to discuss it. But here we are. So we're told to take a taxi and to check in with Mme C, the secretary, since La Directrice is busy all afternoon and will not be able to see us.

As we pull up in front of the BPE in Cayenne, La Directrice is just emerging, on her way to one of the meetings that were keeping her occupied for the day. Cool but correct greetings. She accompanies us back into the building, in a perfunctory acknowledgment that we'd returned from our Mission. We're given instructions for getting to the little guest house where we'll be staying tonight until she can find us an apartment for the rest of our stay. And there's no visible dissent when we suggest that she have a quick look at some of the stuff we've collected.

When we open the packages and trunk, and unveil the first several objects, the air begins to change; and as one piece after another is unwrapped, La Directrice's expression shifts from annoyance to mild interest, then to approval, and finally to something approaching real excitement. She'll just have to be late for her meeting, she decides; then she phones to say that she won't be coming at all. It

A newsroom memo: "One Englishmen is a story. Ten Frenchmen is a story. One hundred Germans is a story. And nothing ever happens in Chile." . . . A hundred Pakistanis going off a mountain in a bus make less of a story than three Englishmen drowning in the Thames.

— Mort Rosenblum, *Coups and Earthquakes* (1979), p. 124

seems that this is the collection that she never imagined being able to have for the museum—old pieces, varied media, solid documentation. When we finally leave to drop off our bags, we're given a *bon de commande*—not for the little guest house she had assigned us just a half hour earlier, but for an air-conditioned room, breakfast included, in Cayenne's finest hotel. She suggests we meet at 8:30 the next morning.

In our hotel room, we watch the TV news and confirm a rumor that the Paramaka capital of Langatabiki has been fired on with air-to-ground rockets by the Suriname army's Alouette 3 helicopter-gunship. One dead and four seriously wounded, taken to the hospital in St. Laurent, according to the report. Phone discussion with AM, the Reuters correspondent. He pulls up on his computer screen various stories he's filed during the past few weeks and reads them to Rich, but there's nothing we haven't already heard from people on the river. AM complains about how hard it is to get anything about this part of the world, other than Ariane news, printed in the international press. Chinese dinner. Blissful sleep.

FRIDAY 17 / VIII / 90

8:30 meeting with La Directrice. Oral report on our mission. Broad smiles all around. We go over accounting, return some 3,600F of unused field assistant money, and submit invoices for various advances we've made from our own resources. La Directrice accompanies us to Avis, where we pick up a car for the duration of our stay. She shows us the pleasant apartment that she's retained for the same period. She's also pulled strings to get us an Air France departure in a week, as we had asked (but not thought possible during this busiest of all months for French airlines). We decided to head off right away for a couple of days in St. Laurent. This time La Directrice has put us in the Star Hotel; no more summer camp.

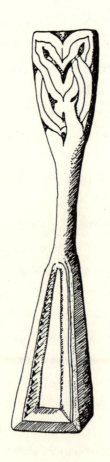

Captain Dooi's laundry beater

On our way out of Cayenne, we stop at Mandó's woodcarving atelier; neither he nor his colleagues has begun the commissions that we'd arranged before going upriver, but — now that we're back — they'll get to them immediately. Three-hour, uneventful drive along the coast, through heat and occasional downpours. Outside of St. Laurent, stopped to visit with the carvers from Bótopási, who hadn't worked on their commissions either. But they were ready to get started now.

First stop in St. Laurent: Dr. J's, where we retrieve some things left in his house when we went upriver and pick up the two cases of rum, which somehow never got put on a government boat; we'll leave a third of them for Ken and put our share in a BPE closet, to use in the Ndjuka mission next summer. Beers and a pleasant chat with the doctor and his wife, who serve as a nerve center for anthropological and other comings and goings. On to the Star Hotel, where we present our purchase order and are given their finest room. Greeted Diane Vernon, who's finished housesitting and is now staying at the Star too, and arranged to eat dinner together at 7.

Then off to Sabonyé, where we followed up on the commissions that we'd initiated several weeks earlier. Old man Kóbi, the Saramaka healer, had been having stomach problems, and the reeds for our two baskets lay unstripped under his house. But he promised to produce the baskets by the end of the month, when we said Ken would be by to pick them up. Then on to Dakan's, where we asked about the Aluku stool we'd left for repair, addressing ourselves to a young woman in his house. She replied that he was away and that she couldn't help us with the stool since it was in the house of "a certain woman" — an unambiguous reference to a co-wife who lived next door. We found Dakan's other wife, whom we'd met before, and picked up the stool, now repaired. Then to Captain Dooi, who was working on a long canoe by the river, and who took us to his house to show us a laundry beater he'd mentioned before our trip

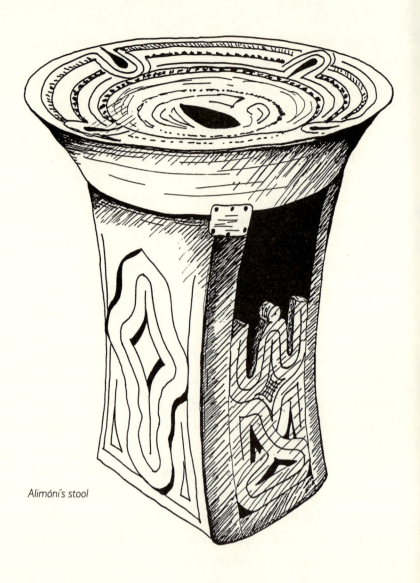

Alimóni's stool

to Aluku. Saramaka-style handle and Aluku-style shaft, reflecting his mixed parentage. It was nice, but quite dirty, so he offered to have a wife soak it in lime juice overnight and told us it would be ready to pick up tomorrow morning. Then into town to the house of some Paramakas we'd met several weeks earlier; they hadn't been able to come up with the textiles they'd hoped to retrieve from their upriver garden camps, but we had a friendly visit and told them we'd be back again next year.

Final collecting stop: on the road to St. Jean, our Saramaka friends Alimóni and his wife. We arrived in the heat of a conjugal spiff of the sort we've seen many times; he was accusing her of churning up gossip about an old girlfriend of his, and was upset enough so that he had trouble dealing with us. She finally went off to a neighbor while he carped for a few minutes about the pettiness of women's behavior. Eventually he brought out the round stool—a real beauty for which we gladly paid the 500F he asked. We also bought the purpleheart pestle that his wife had offered us before we went upriver. Dinner with Diane and Benji at a Chinese restaurant, discussing next year's joint collecting expedition. Nine PM: Voice of America, BBC, and Radio Nederland, to listen to news of two wars—the continuing build-up in the Gulf and the latest developments along the Maroni.

SATURDAY 18/VIII/90

We wake up not knowing where we are; we've been sleeping in too many beds. Breakfast with Diane, where we worked on details of next year's collecting mission. Checked out of the hotel a day ahead of schedule, loaded the car, and went off to pick up the laundry beater from Captain Dooi. Drove out to Kilometer 10 on the road to Mana, where we'd left young Baala, the psychiatrist's Saramaka "mental patient," some weeks ago. He was off fishing with some friends, but the people we saw told us that he was doing just fine—

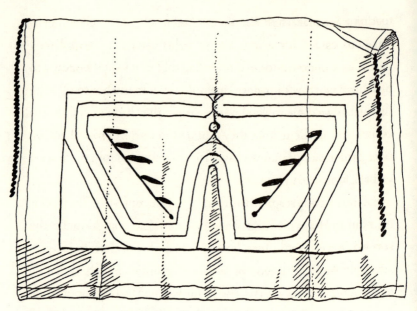

One of the textiles we bought from Tjodj's sister-in-law, a man's cape sewn by Anate Bakatia

that he was normal and happy and pleased to be back. Then on to our Bótopási friends where we set prices for four commissioned pieces — a woman's paddle, a winnowing tray, and two combs — to be picked up in a few weeks by Ken. Returned with Tjodj and his sister-in-law to St. Laurent where he was hoping to find a patchwork breechcloth in a trunk in his son's rented room. The breechcloth wasn't there, but the sister-in-law took us to another house in town and showed us some recent textiles; we bought three — including two kinds of sewing we hadn't known before. Before leaving St. Laurent, Tjodj asked whether we could fill up a five-liter container with gas for his chainsaw so that he could cut the tree buttress out of which he would fashion a paddle for us. He had only a few francs in change so we bought the gas and a liter of oil to mix with it. Back to the Star Hotel, where we gave Diane a list of six commissions and 1,280F, plus instructions, to hold for Ken's arrival. Dropped Tjodj and his sister-in-law off at their place and continued on for the three-hour drive to Cayenne. Between Iracoubo and Sinnamary, we notice three road signs warning "RECHTS HOUDEN" (keep right), fading reminders of the days when pre-civil-war Surinamers could take the ferry across the Marowijne with their left-side-of-the-road-drive cars. We were so exhausted as we passed Kourou that we decided not to stop. Forced ourselves to buy some groceries before dropping off for a deep nap. Woke up and logged in the rest of the Saramaka collection, cooked dinner, and listened to war news. Deep sleep despite an Amerindian ceremony in the neighborhood, with drumming and singing, which lasted till after dawn.

SUNDAY 19/VIII/90

Spent the whole morning figuring out (and then writing out in correct French categories for presentation to La Directrice) the specifics of next year's mission — on the chance that we'll want to do

For instance, I have known it to happen that such a brute [of an Over-seer], being tired of an old Negro, and only wishing to get rid of him, took him out a-fowling when, desiring him to discover the game, the first bird that started he shot the poor man dead upon the spot, which is called an *accident* without any further enquiry is made about it. Others have been killed in the following manner to get rid of them: a strong stake being fas-tened in the ground, the slave was chained to it in the middle of an open plain and under burning sunshine, where one gill of water, with one single plantain, was brought every day till he was starved to death. But this is not called dying with famine by his master who, declaring he had wanted neither meat or drink till he expired, is honourably acquitted. Still another method of murdering with impunity has often been put in practice. This is to tie them stark naked to a tree in the forest, with arms and legs ex-panded, under pretence of stretching their limbs, but where they remain (being regularly fed) till they are absolutely stung to death by the gnats or mosquitoes, which is, to be sure a most infernal punishment and a child of the most diabolical invention. Nay, kicking them overboard, with a weight chained to their heels by which they are inevitably drowned, is called acci-dental death, while even by the orders of a woman, Negro slaves have been privately burned to death, miserably chained in a surrounding pile of flaming faggots. As to the breaking out of their teeth for tasting the sugar cane cultivated by themselves, or slitting up their nose and cutting off their ears from private peek, these are looked upon as laughable trifles, not worth so much as to be mentioned or to come into consideration.

In short, to such a pitch of desperation has this unhappy race of men sometimes been driven, that from spite to end their days and to be re-

it. Our dates, Diane's dates, the complete budget information, and so on. Tedious, but our experience this year allows us to put it all together much more realistically. Packaged soup for lunch again. Afternoon spent writing up back notes and thinking about museums as strange beasts. Before dark we stroll through the eery Sunday silence of Cayenne to the nearly-deserted Place des Palmistes. Phone the U.S. from a urine-stinking phone booth and learn that all is well with our kids, one in New York, one in Chile. Leftovers for dinner, more war news, and to bed. We're both feeling low, with sore throats. Rich spends part of the night, wakeful, stringing together interminable dark memories from Stedman, some of the horrors of the world experienced by the ancestors of the Aluku.

MONDAY 20/VIII/90

6:30 AM, awakened by the grinding sound of motor bikes; it reminds us of the old days in Paramaribo. We passed a damp, sweaty night under a sheet to escape the hordes of mosquitoes which seem oblivious to the marijuana-like aroma of our two Chinese mosquito spirals. Even in an airy apartment, open on two sides, the night air in Cayenne hangs heavy and still.

Leading off the RFO-radio local news this morning, two murders (personal accounts being settled by shotgun) and a burglary. A recently retired member of the French Foreign Legion, who had come back to Guyane to "live out his days in peace," held up a Chinese store with "a pointed object" for the day's receipts (ca. 1,000F) and was apprehended "by the forces of order" fifty meters down the road where, wielding a large rock in his hand, he was in the process of holding up another store. And then much hoopla about the Tour de la Guyane, a bike race involving foreign competitors that was doing the Sinnamary-St. Laurent stretch today.

lieved from bondage, they have even leaped into a cauldron of boiling sugar, thus at one blow depriving the tyrant of his crop and his servant. . . .

The pious mother of the charity-house nefariously kept flogging the poor slaves daily because they were, she said, unbelievers. To one black woman, in particular, she wantonly gave four hundred lashes, who bore them without a complaint, while the men she always stripped *perfectly* naked, that not a *single* part of their body might escape her attention. . . .

A Mrs. Stolker, going to her estate in a tent-barge, a Negro woman with her sucking infant happened to be passengers and seated on the bow or fore-part of the boat, but where the child crying (without it could possibly be hushed) and Mrs. Stolker not delighting in such music, she ordered the mother to bring it aft and deliver it into her own hands, with which, forthwith, in the presence of the distracted parent, she thrust it out one of the tilt-windows and held it underwater till it *was drowned.* The fond mother (being desperate from the loss of her helpless baby) instantly leaped overboard in the same stream where floated her beloved offspring, and in conjunction with which she was determined to end her miserable existence. However, in this she was prevented by the care of the Negro slaves that rowed the barge, and was corrected by her mistress for her unnatural temerity with three or four hundred lashes. . . .

Arriving one day at her estate to view some newly purchased Negroes, her eye chanced to fall on a fine Negro girl about fifteen years of age, who could not so much as speak the language of the country. Still observing her to have such a remarkably fine figure, and such a sweet face, her diabolical jealousy instantly prompted her to burn the girl all over the cheeks, mouth, and forehead with a red hot iron, and cut off the Achilles tendon of one of her limbs, which not only rendered her a monster, but miserably lame so long as she lived, without the victim knowing what she had done to deserve such a punishment. Some of the Negroes one day representing to this lady the many severities she daily inflicted, and supplicating her to be of a milder disposition, she instantly knocked out the brains of a Quadroon child, and caused two of the heads of its relations to be chopped off, being young Negro men who had endeavoured to oppose it. . . .

This child's father, whose name is Jolicoeur, is one of them [the Aluku Rebels], the first captain belonging to Baron's men, and not without cause one of the fiercest Rebels in the forest, which he has lately shown on the neighbouring estate Nieuw-Rosenbeek, where now our colonel commands.

Here one Mr. Schults, a Jew, was the manager at that time (who formerly was the manager of Faukenberg), when the Rebels suddenly appeared

Arrived at La Directrice's office at 8:30, two canvas duffle bags with the Saramaka and Paramaka objects we'd collected in St. Laurent in hand. Brief display and then presentation of the *fiches* as well as an invoice for the money we'd advanced. Everything going swimmingly. We discuss DM's proposition to have the "Sur les Traces de Boni" committee of the Conseil Régional subsidize a French translation/ edition of our art book, with a new chapter which we'd write on the Aluku collection in the museum. La Directrice is enthusiastic and promises to support it, partly by helping to set up a meeting with the elusive bureaucrat who's responsible for the committee. La Directrice and Le Conseiller need to go to a meeting, but she would like the four of us to start serious discussions about the museum at 3:30.

Downstairs with Mlle Z, for Sally's demonstration-washing of the old tray from Kotika, about which there has been much preliminary discussion. Should it be left untouched? Treated according to museological textbooks? We convince them that it should be washed with limes and then rinsed with water, as it would be in a Maroon village. Sally cites her promise to the captain who sold it that she and no one else would take care of the washing, and that vow is respected. Mlle Z offers Sally a pair of surgical gloves of the kind that she dons whenever she touches a museum object. Sally declines. All this in the context of the fact that calabashes collected some months back have been developing mold because the room in which they are kept is dank, musty, and un-ventilated. Mlle Z alludes to sophisticated methods, weekly washings in chemicals, etc. We propose a little air circulation and common sense. It's a touchy discussion. Mlle Z, who was apparently chosen for her position because she had gone through a course in computer skills, is inexperienced in other domains. Rich checks in with Mme C about when we will be reimbursed for the moneys we've advanced and learns that La Directrice, following the rules to the letter, has instructed her to reduce our "living expenses" from fifty to thirty-six

and took possession of the whole plantation. Having tied his hands and plundered the house, they next began feasting and dancing, before they thought it proper to end his miserable existence.

In this deplorable situation now lay the victim, only awaiting Baron's signal for death, when his eyes chancing to fall on the above captain, he addressed him nearly in the following words. "O Jolicoeur, now remember Mr. Schults who was once your deputy-master. Remember the dainties I gave you from my own table, when you were but a child and my favourite, my darling among so many others. Remember this and now spare my life, by your powerful intercession." To which Jolicoeur replied, "I remember it perfectly well, but you, O Tyrant, should recollect how you ravished my poor mother, and flogged my father for coming to her assistance. Recollect that the shameful act was perpetrated in my infant presence, recollect this and then die by my hands, and next be damned," saying which, he severed his head from his body with a hatchet at one blow, and with which having played at bowls upon the beach, he next with a knife cut the skin from his back, which he spread over one of the cannon to stop the firing.

— Stedman, *Narrative* (1790/1992), pp. 271–72, 246, 148,
176–77, 149–50

The National Open Air and Cultural History Museum in Pretoria hires native women in "traditional" garb to grind corn outside grass and mud huts for the edification of white museumgoers, who are apparently un-interested in real scenes of native women living in houses of corrugated metal in squatter settlements nearby.

— Chappell, "Museums," p. 655

You can visit Den Haag (*deux étoiles*), enter the Mauritshuis Museum (*trois étoiles*), sit devotionally before Vermeer's *Delft,* and hear French passers-by reciting, as if by memory, not Proust or Vermeer but the *Guide Miche*'s quotation of Proust's narrator on Vermeer, which may be precisely what is proper to recite in this kind of going-viewing. That fitting caption from a not-so-prosy guidebook was repeatedly intoned by travelers, as I over-heard them: "le plus beau tableau du monde."

— James Boon, "Why Museums Make me Sad" (1991), p. 267

days, keeping for the BPE the only extra money we might have left Guyane with, after all our work.

Lunch *à deux* in a Vietnamese restaurant. Then, intense preparation of the 1991 collecting schedule and budget, for presentation to La Directrice in the afternoon. At 3:30, back to the BPE where we learn that Jean Michotte, Director of ORSTOM Cayenne, who we'd met a couple of times in earlier visits, has died suddenly. Michotte was a family friend and colleague of La Directrice's and one of AO's closest buddies; his death will halt business-as-usual for all the people we deal with here (except, perhaps, Le Conseiller) for the next day or two. Sally takes her datebook and crosses out our own meeting with Michotte, which we'd scheduled for tomorrow morning, in part to present ORSTOM with a copy of *Alabi's World*. Le Conseiller walks in and proposes that the three of us meet anyway, and we spend a couple of hours discussing various aspects of the plans for the museum.

In our absence upriver, Le Conseiller and La Directrice have re-thought the space allotted for exhibitions, taking into account our alarm at the limitations of the original plan. The eco-system materials will therefore be moved outside the building (possibly next to the proposed *restaurant gastronomique*, concessions selling ornamental and medicinal plants, and the *maison de l'artisanat* for local craftsmen), freeing up space for cultural exhibits. He asks whether we have a plan for the Maroon area, however tentative. Feeling physically exhausted and, in the wake of too much collecting in too short a time, intellectually enervated, we fall back on our 1980-vintage didactic concerns — cultural distinctions among the different groups, the (art) historical dimension, and ethno-aesthetics. He immediately expresses concern, having spent a lot of time talking with the Grenands, about the danger of our "over-aestheticizing" the Maroons (especially in relation to the Amerindian groups). We counter by arguing that it is the Maroons, and not we, who lay emphasis on the aesthetic dimension of their material life. If the Amerindian ex-

[A young woman named Shallini Venturelli had recently arrived in the United States from India, when she was invited to speak to a ladies club. She reports:]

The club secretary had advised me that perhaps a dose of history with a pinch of politics and culture would be wonderfully suited to their taste. I obliged. After an excellent tea served on fine silver, I started to talk. I talked of the past, of struggles, of despair and poverty on the subcontinent; I talked of the present, of political battles and world maneuvers, of challenges that lay ahead; I spoke of the right to learn, the right to self-awareness, of the chains of tradition and the poverty of women.

I did not notice for a long time that the faces around me had begun to twitch, that the women were shifting restlessly. When I suddenly became aware of the growing discomfort, I stopped. "Does someone have a question?" I asked.

The club secretary rose and drew me to the window.

"My dear," she said in a low voice, "it is history and culture they wish to hear about, not misfortunes." "But the truth is not misfortune; it is truth," I replied in a whisper, thoroughly confused. "Of course. But can't you leave out the bad parts? Talk about maharajas. And there are elephants and tigers, and you can even tell us about your beautiful sari, and show us how you put it on."

I looked down at the floor. There was an exquisite Persian carpet under my feet; I hadn't noticed. I remained by the window for a few minutes. The secretary had returned to her seat, and there were smiles and expectation on a few faces. "Ladies," I said, "my deepest apologies for meddling with your fantasies. Since I do not share them, and India is not a fairy tale or a novel by Rudyard Kipling, I must say goodby. Thank you."

— Cited in Rosenblum, *Coups and Earthquakes*, pp. 164–65

During the twenties [in Paris] the term *nègre* could embrace modern American jazz, African tribal masks, voodoo ritual, Oceanian sculpture, and even pre-Columbian artifacts. . . . A mask or statue or any shred of black culture could effectively summon a complete world of dreams and possibilities — passionate, rhythmic, concrete, mystical, unchained: an "Africa." . . . By the time of the Mission Dakar-Djibouti this interest in Africa had become a fully developed *exotisme*. The public and the museums were eager for more of an aestheticized commodity.

— Clifford, *The Predicament of Culture*, pp. 136–37

hibit stresses ties with the eco-system and mythology, we suggest, that doesn't mean that the same emphases are appropriate for Maroons. Le Conseiller says we'll have to hash this out with him and the Grenands in meetings over the coming year or two.

We imagine it will be interesting, since the general debate has been so lively during the past decade—with museums like the Tropenmuseum in Amsterdam or the Übersee-Museum in Bremen championing a 1960s-style focus on "the plight" of Third World peoples or the workings of internal colonialism in certain countries, while others like the Rockefeller Wing of the Met waffle between limited "anthropological" label texts and encouragement for the visitor to experience a direct, universal-aesthetic encounter with the objects. Our own past experiences as occasional curators have tended to strand us awkwardly in the middle of all this: we've argued that acknowledging the legitimacy of art from other cultures, and of aesthetic ideas that may be at odds with our own culturally-learned notions, is an inherently political act. But the experiences of this summer, once digested with a bit of distance, are sure to suggest further ideas and modifications of what we'd really like to see done. So, this is a debate we very much look forward to.

We then raised two more delicate, quasi-personal issues, content that La Directrice was temporarily absent, since we thought it best to start by feeling them out with Le Conseiller. First the problem of the Saramaka collection. Given that the civil war shows no sign of ending, we said, and given our own hesitations about collecting in Saramaka villages (which we didn't go into), the only viable solution would seem to be for us to lend (for an initial period of ten or fifteen years?) part of our personal collection, acquired in the sixties and seventies largely as gifts, adding only enough newly-collected material to fill in for styles and kinds of objects that have been introduced over the past decade and a half, which we could get in St. Laurent and Cayenne. (We've always felt that the Saramaka things we own should end up in a museum, preferably in Suriname,

SP: You once told me that during the 1930s there was a strong concern in the Musée de l'Homme about proving that anthropology was a true "science."

ML: As anthropologists, we were supposed to deny being literary. . . . Rivière is the one who decided to get rid of the wooden cases and install metal ones, in order to make them look more sober and austere and severe. And then there was the anti-aestheticism of Rivière and his peers at the time. They didn't want to hear any talk of "*art nègre*"; it had become too fashionable. Besides, anthropology couldn't be reduced to what was called "*art nègre*" or to the study of exotic arts.

> — S. Price and Jean Jamin, "A Conversation with Michel Leiris" (1988), p. 164

The final space, and the most extensive, is the "Art Museum." This is the familiar insect-in-amber approach — African cultural products set on pedestals, covered with Plexiglas, and highlighted, with their labels the common limited functional statements . . . and "aesthetic" glosses (usually descriptions of what can already be seen, e.g., . . . "the horizontal oval of the head exactly duplicates the lozenges of the eyes and mouth"). This is certainly the customary way in which African objects are seen today and represents a dual failure — an attempt to embrace a form of (phony) legitimacy (the anthropological information) while disguising an impotent aesthetic commentary whose only purpose is to sanction the piece as commodity. . . . The design style bears the same relationship to the "Curiosity Room" as contemporary zoos bear to earlier ones — as if with the removal of bars and their substitution with moats, *faux* natural settings, and the like the bitter facts of captivity will be less obvious and the animals happier, grateful.

> — James C. Faris, commenting on an exhibition at the Center for African Art in New York, in "'ART/artifact'," pp. 778–79

There was joking behavior about the tension over the "art" versus "ethnography" division in the art world: this is an art museum, not an ethnography museum. How much context can you supply before it is perceived as not art, but ethnography? How important is it to not color code the walls with earth tones as African material culture is usually displayed (for then it would be ethnography, not art)? The discussion seemed bizarre to nonmuseum types.

> — Fischer, "Museums and Festivals," p. 212

but have never made a commitment. Given the uncertain state of things in that country, this seems like an appropriate alternative.) Le Conseiller is supportive, and we even talk a little about eventual modalities—bringing our catalogue cards and photos to Cayenne next year, making a trip to New York to assemble the objects, etc.

Second delicate issue, and the one we'd rather not bring up directly with La Directrice—our own slightly irritated feelings about not receiving any compensation for our work on this project. The Grenands and their co-workers among the Amerindians, and Le Conseiller, are paid salaries for this work by ORSTOM or CNRS, and local employees (from La Directrice and Mlle Z to Nyolu and Manku) are paid by the Conseil Régional. We fall into neither category and are devoting our time and expertise gratis; the same is true for Ken. Might there be, we ask, any way of placing our future contributions to the project into some salaried/contracted/honorarium'd niche? Le Conseiller says he understands fully and will try to take it up with La Directrice on our behalf. He suspects something can be worked out, but only by finding a little here and a little there, over the next couple of years. We *are* in an anomalous position, relative to all the others on the museum's Comité Scientifique, and he'll do his best to see what might be done.

Around 6, we go off with Le Conseiller to the Annex, carrying the lime-drenched tray, since the Bureau has no sink where it could be rinsed off. Sally places it in the Annex's bathtub, cleans it of the last trace of lime pulp, and sets it next to a window to dry. We take the unauthorized step of opening two high glass jalousies to allow a little air into the place, anticipating Mlle Z's protests. The last item on our day's list of things to do was to buy an electric fan, since we'd hardly slept the night before in the still Cayenne heat. We mention it to Le Conseiller, who suggests that we pass the bill on to La Directrice and place the fan in the Bureau's storeroom for ventilation when we leave on Saturday, thus solving two problems with one purchase.

The modern division of art and ethnography into distinct institutions has restricted the former's analytic power and the latter's subversive vocation.

— Clifford, *The Predicament of Culture*, p. 12

The *Guava-Tree* grows to about 24 Feet, with Leafs like those of a Plumb-tree it is Light-Coloured . . . but the Fruit which is Yellow Oval, and the Size of a Small Apple Incloses a Reddish Pulp, full of Small seeds, that is Very sweet, And may be Eaten raw or made in Marmalades, Jelly's &c when it is Delicious. . . .

The Sour-Sap Grows on a Tree of a moderate Size. . . . This fruit is of a Pyramidical Form heavier than the Largest Pear Perfectly green and all Covered over with inoffensive Prickles, the Skin is Extremely Thin the pulp a Soft pithy Substance as white as milk, and of a sweet taste mix'd with a most Agreeable Acid, in which are Seeds like large kernels of an Apple.

Their Joice Combin'd emits a Grateful Stream
Like Hibla's Honey mixts with Devons Cream.

— Stedman, *Narrative* (1790/1988), pp. 322, 506–507

The objective will be to provide interested visitors the means to make a critical reading and to decode the museological enterprise itself; in some sense to demystify it, by giving it back its historicity, and in this way to achieve a more effective transmission of anthropological knowledge.

— Gérard Collomb, "La transmission d'un savoir anthropologique" (1989), p. 10

Just after 8, we phone Ken at Mme Jeanne's in Maripasoula, as promised. He can hear fine, but Rich, in a payphone on a street-corner, can hardly make out what Ken says, even after three calls are made in an attempt to get a better connection through the satellite-linkup. We think he says all is going well, that he's up to object number 241, and that he intends to stay upriver to the end, since he has various ethnographic plans. We arrange things so that Bwino, the Aluku driver who'd originally taken us to St. Laurent, will pick him up at 1 PM on 28 August, to transfer the rest of the collection directly from the canoe to Cayenne. Everything seems to be going as planned.

We get guava and soursop ice cream cones near the Place des Palmistes and wander through the quiet streets toward our apartment, and bed. On the Rue Christophe Colomb, pass a row of dilapidated colonial houses, with ornately carved verandahs, that the Conseil Général is helping to renovate; Guyane is discovering its "historical" heritage just as it's disappearing, after that same Conseil Général has dispensed tens of millions of francs over the past three decades to transform Cayenne into a city of faceless reinforced concrete. We're struck by the complexity of the city's smells: urine, rotting garbage, dog shit, bleach and perfumed disinfectants, motorbike fumes. . . .

TUESDAY 21/VIII/90

Slept much better last night, with our new fan nearby, though we're both still feeling sick. Early morning discussion about the current state of anthropology and the idea of museums. The more we think about it, the more we're coming to believe that, given what we've seen of Aluku life this summer, a permanent exhibition that centers on Aluku art would be a political and intellectual cop-out; art is simply not something they care very much about any more. But how

Modern ethnographic histories are perhaps condemned to oscillate between two metanarratives: one of homogenization, the other of emergence; one of loss, the other of invention. In most specific conjunctures both narratives are relevant, each undermining the other's claim to tell "the whole story."

> — Clifford, *The Predicament of Culture*, p. 17

Anthropology is not a dispassionate science like astronomy, which springs from the contemplation of things at a distance. It is the outcome of a historical process which has made the larger part of mankind subservient to the other, and during which millions of innocent human beings have had their resources plundered and their institutions and beliefs destroyed, whilst they themselves were ruthlessly killed, thrown into bondage, and contaminated by diseases they were unable to resist. Anthropology is the daughter to this era of violence . . . a state of affairs in which I part of mankind treated the other as an object.

> — Claude Lévi-Strauss, "Anthropology: Its Achievement and
> Future" (1966), p. 126

Soft-shell crab, the meat and milk of the coconut, curry, hot peppers, and the ground green leaf of the tropical dasheen plant combine to make Callaloo . . . a metaphor for the racial diversity of their [Caribbean] nations, containing "every little piece of difference." The more diverse the ingredients, the sweeter the soup.

> — Judith Bettelheim, John Nunley, and Barbara Bridges,
> "Caribbean Festival Arts: An Introduction" (1988), p. 31

To repeat: [in Brooklyn, Toronto, and London] a whole lot of shaking, drumming, chanting, feathering, beading, multi-lappeting, and sequinning is going on. How did it happen? Immigration, mon. . . . Several art histories, not one, flourish today upon our planet. The creole thing to do is to mix them. Gone is the notion of a single canon. Bring on the Callaloo.

> — Robert Farris Thompson, "Recapturing Heaven's Glamour"
> (1988), pp. 17, 29

More precisely, a major question for anthropologists concerned with the West's Other *in* the West is this: How do discursive interventions by anthropologists articulate the politics of difference in the spaces defined by the modern state?

> — Talal Asad, "Ethnography, Literature, and Politics" (1990),
> p. 260

might we depict Aluku life—where it's been, where it seems to be going, what choices lie ahead—in the context of the new museum, and in a way that would be politically acceptable to La Directrice and the Conseil Régional? We realize that part of our malaise this summer has to do with carrying the metaphorical weight of, say, the Musée de l'Homme or the American Museum of Natural History on our backs as we went about "collecting." The possibility that the exhibits we help plan might not have to look like Boas ca. 1903 or Griaule ca. 1935, which we haven't spent enough time considering, is suddenly liberating. Looking back over some of the unpublished reports/essays/proposals that Le Conseiller has shared with us, we now suspect that he would be supportive of any innovative conceptualizations we manage to come up with. The idea of a master narrative that's neither a requiem for "vanishing races" nor a mindless celebration of "Callalou Culture" is something to conjure with.

Painting a more balanced picture, by whatever technique (whether postmodern pastiche or something else), is hard enough in the medium of writing. How much more difficult, for us at least, to figure out how to do it in the medium of museum display. In his dissertation, Ken labored mightily to depict the Aluku in the round, to balance the story of their apparent and undeniable francisation with accounts of resistance, of the ways that, underneath it all, the Aluku have been able to maintain (or continually recreate) a sense of themselves as a people, to cherish their links with a heroic past. We think of his description of one late-night mock beauty pageant, a wonderful burlesque of the modernization process (the kind of scene that Roger Abrahams has so often picked up on elsewhere in the Afro-Caribbean). Given the briefness of our own stay in Aluku—the fact that we were travel-logging more than ethnographizing—as well as our inevitable "view from Saramaka" (where state penetration has been more sporadic and circumscribed), it's not surprising that we've been struck more by change and loss than by subtle forms of creative resistance, including parody. Intellectually, we're well

What is possible in this space of contact, crossing over, assimilation, appropriation, juxtaposition, and fusion has not been adequately explored; indeed, this space has no real name. What we know is that there are numerous ragged zones of contact between peoples who hold incommensurable values and beliefs, traditions, and philosophies.

— Rose, *Living the Ethnographic Life*, p. 44

PAPAI SITON, September, 1985: *La Fête de Papaïchton* is in its third year. Every commune with a decent sense of civic pride must have its *fête communale* . . . its four nights of state-sponsored merrymaking. . . . The large lawn in front of the gendarmerie is strung with multi-colored lights and streamers, and both sides are lined with hastily constructed booths selling snacks: armadillo morsels, monkey and rice, Vienna sausages on toothpicks, vanilla yogurt. . . . In the center of the lawn a platform with spotlights has been set up. At one end of the stage is a long banquet table covered in white cloth. Seated behind the table and the bottles of champagne are the mayor, his assistants, a high-ranking Creole politician belonging to the RPR, and a few other dignitaries, all wearing formal attire. They have narrowed the contenders for the title of "Miss Papaïchton" down to two finalists. . . . The two contestants are escorted onstage by their "cavaliers," two young Creole gentlemen in tuxedos from Maripasoula, who guide them through the motions of a waltz. . . . When the winner is announced and presented with her bouquet, a voice comes over the PA system, speaking in French: "Let's give her a hand!" There is light, scattered applause, and the slow dance music is restored.

. . . During the 1980s, as the first post-commune generation came of age, the issue of identity became for the Aluku, as it was for the rest of French Guiana, something of an enigma. . . . Seldom did I witness a more dramatic manifestation of [their] awareness of themselves as active agents in their own remaking than on one night in 1985 when the Aluku staged their own pageant. Earlier in the day, the elders had gathered at the Komontibo mortuary hut, where they had lovingly heaped mounds of cooked rice on a plantain leaf stretched atop the earth, as a sacramental offering to the ancestors.

. . . Shortly before midnight the fun began. Next to the mortuary hut was the table of honor, set with bottles of beer and rum. Behind it sat the chiefs of several villages. On the right was a turntable with an emcee with microphone . . . [who], mixing French and Aluku, announced the debut of Mademoiselle Anisette. Out of the dressing room sauntered an eighteen-year-old ingenue, decked out in a crazy quilt of mail-order chic,

aware of the dangers of viewing Alukus as passive victims, of blurring their individual life experiences in a rapidly changing world. Nevertheless, on the basis of what Stedman liked to call "occular demonstration"—what we think we saw with our own eyes—we cannot deny having felt overwhelmed much of the time we spent in their territory by the massive steamroller of French colonialism, with its destructive bending of consciousness and identity. With Ken's help, we'll try to figure out how to register emerging modes of Alukuness for the museum, how to tell a story that's not cartoonish. But in a sense (and not surprisingly) we stand before the same dilemma as anthropology itself, wondering how to position ourselves to make sense of processes that at once homogenize and create new forms of difference, how to perform the impossible task of reconciling what Jim Clifford, in his lit-crit way, refers to as the tragic and comic plots of global cultural history.

Mid-morning meeting with La Directrice, who looked unslept and deeply upset in the wake of Michotte's death, which she said really knocked her out. It was clearly not the time for us to begin raising our growing doubts about the whole museum enterprise. So, instead, we went over our plans and budgets for next year's collecting mission. Le Conseiller joined us halfway through. Some discussion of conservation problems; Le Conseiller seems particularly exasperated by Mlle Z's lackadaisical approach to the care of the objects entrusted to her. Returned a phone call from MC, organizer of a future conference on the family in Guyane, but only after the secretaries at both the BPE and MC's office botched the transfer of the call several times (not pushing the right buttons on their state-of-the-art phones). High tech, as often happens in the U.S. these days as well, is running ahead of human competence. Finally convinced Mlle Z that protecting the objects we collected from mold (by opening windows) was more important than keeping them dust-free, and she agreed (in principle) to move them to the Annex this week, and allow some circulation of air.

her delicately arranged coiffure radiant from hours of preening. In one hand was her "kabalye" (cavalier), her escort, himself an image of freshly pressed perfection, in the other a coyly fluttering fan. The couple made a stately circuit around the clearing . . . the young man occasionally twirled his partner on her tiptoes for all to admire, sending gusts of perfume into the audience. . . . As the [phonographic] chanteuse milked her little-girl voice to the last emotional drop, the couple whirled out to the center of the clearing and broke into a torrid ballroom dance, tightly clasping one another in a parody of passion. The spectators . . . finally let their laughter come freely. Four other couples repeated the performance . . . but in the end it was Anisette, with 28 votes, who became the first "Miss Komontibo."

Just as the evening seemed to be winding down to a close, two of the elderly *kapiten* [village headmen] leapt from behind their table, each seizing an older woman by the hand. Out in the central clearing, the two senior couples embraced in their own dance of passion, besting their juniors with a parody of a parody. As one of the men swept his dumbfounded partner off her feet, tossing her back and holding her in a clumsy tango pose, the audience became convulsed with laughter.

This was one spectacle of *francisation* to which the French were not invited. But when the participants held up a mirror, the French were there nonetheless. In burlesquing the "other," the Aluku performers had also burlesqued what they saw themselves becoming.

    — Bilby, *The Remaking of the Aluku*, pp. 216–21

. . . the rapid adaptation by the Tlingit to the new demand for their goods. [In 1791,] as soon as Malaspina's officers had "found much that was worth obtaining for the Royal Museum" from among the domestic utensils and weapons of the Yakutat, "the women were observed much occupied making [baskets] and the men in making dolls, spoons and other articles of wood which the men and even the officers purchased eagerly." The production of artifacts for the European market commenced very early.

    — Cole, *Captured Heritage*, p. 5

Lunch at a Creole restaurant with Le Conseiller and a young anthropologist who's doing research on the Hmong here in Guyane and elsewhere; he had spent some time in Minneapolis, so we had tales to trade about the cold. Otherwise, over lunch, the usual kind of comparative remarks about academic life in France vs. the U.S., salaries, research perks, publishing, etc.

We are both now quite sick with bad sore throats. Half-hour rest and then off to Mandó's woodcarving stand, partly to check on how our commissions were coming along, partly because La Directrice had given us the go-ahead, following Le Conseiller's prompting, to put together a little collection of Saramaka tourist carvings. Long visit. Mandó told us that he settled at his place on the road outside of Cayenne in 1978 and has made his living carving there ever since. There are now four or five houses, with wives, children (including several teenage sons who work in his atelier), and others. During the mid-seventies, when Mandó was carving for the tourist trade in Paramaribo, he made several trips to Cayenne to hawk his wares, and because of his success, he decided to move here permanently.

The round tray looks like it will be handsome; we commissioned a standard Saramaka (paddle-) canoe for 1991 delivery, discussed the museum, bought four tourist carvings (a folding stool, two armadillos, and an owl) and commissioned Rich's favorite piece — a map of Guyane surmounted by a phallic Ariane rocket. When we asked Mandó who had first had the idea of carving an owl, he credited it to one of his former co-workers, Betjé, from his home village of Kambalóa, who did it in imitation of a Western-manufactured owl figure he'd seen in a store window in Cayenne. As for the armadillo, Mandó smiled shyly and told us that he'd have to "nyán búka" ("modestly take credit") on that one, that he was the one to have popularized them, making the wooden models after the taxidermist-mounted souvenir armadillos that used to be omnipresent in Paramaribo shops.

Following some comments by us on Aluku "westernization," Mandó and his co-workers engaged in an interesting exchange about

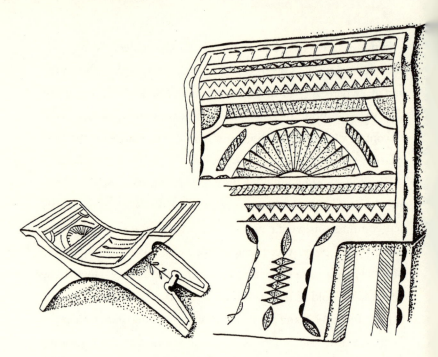

A folding stool carved for the tourist trade by Mandó's son, Gosí

recent changes in Saramaka life. Girls have now completely abandoned koyós (adolescent aprons), they say, but kammbás (body cicatrizations) are still going strong. Remarks about how they don't know too much about the details, but they see women going off behind houses in small groups and know that that's what they're doing. Giggles. Young women no longer cut them on the face, only under their skirts. They commented that men have westernized more than women. From the village of Yáuyáu on upstream, things haven't changed much. But from there on downriver, while men still have breechcloths in their trunks, they wear them only on special occasions—to install a new captain, at New Year's, etc. Women have not stopped wearing wrap-skirts and going bare-breasted on an everyday basis anywhere in Saramaka.

Mandó said he was planning a brief trip back to Saramaka to look after a wife there, maybe staying for a month. On the spur of the moment, we proposed that he keep his eyes out for handsome fési-tén objects, suitable for purchase by the Bureau du Patrimoine. He was quite enthusiastic, as were the others. An interesting money-making opportunity.

Driving off, we discuss the implications of what we've just opened up. Could it turn into a Pandora's Box of Saramaka "runners" along the lines of those in Africa, pillaging their grandmothers' storerooms and getting fat on the proceeds? Hard to imagine since there's not really a market. But we're not sure.

Stopped at Kalusé's, where we're told that he got out of the hospital only two days ago, after a week's stay for an accidental machete wound on his leg. He'd gone off to Kourou, so we'll check back tomorrow. Cooked dinner in our apartment. For the third straight night listened to two hours of short-wave war news from the Middle East. We feel very far away.

"Have you seen this ad for a book of folktales from Suriname? Whatever has gotten into the Prices?" asked Professor Goodfellow, the noted anthropologist. "After all those books on history and ethnography," he mused, "why are they now turning to childrens' stories and nonsense songs — mere folklore? Must be their move to Martinique. A touch of that Caribbean sun or too much rum, I dare say!"

> — R. and S. Price, *Two Evenings in Saramaka* (1991), p. xi

The ride back to Sefrou, down the curving empty highway, was glorious. We sang and joked all the way. Ali teased me, asking the Berber girl I had spent the night with if Monsieur Paul was *shih*, which is the opposite of *'ayyan* and means strong, energetic, full of life. *Numero wahed*, first class, she kindly replied, and then both Soussi's portly cousin and Ali demanded to know the most insistent and central of Moroccan questions: *shal*? In most cases, this means "how much," but in this case it meant "how many times?" — the clearest gauge of how *shih* I was. I teasingly answered *bezzef*, many times.

> — Paul Rabinow, *Reflections on Fieldwork in Morocco* (1977),
> p. 69

At breakfast, noticed that the vaguely tropical-tasting camembert we've been eating for the past few mornings is marked "à consommer de préférence avant 1 janvier 1990."

Morning: writing notes. Looking back over our computer diary, Rich notices a consistent omission and imagines our friend Professor Goodfellow closing the final page of "Collecting Guyane" with a scowl, placing it on his nighttable, and muttering "But where's the sex?" We have tried, like Leiris in L'Afrique Fantôme, to record maximally, but as Leiris himself told Sally regarding that book, "One never tells all, of course."

We discuss the apparent depth of angst in Leiris' diary compared to our own. He embarked, Sally remarks, at a particularly formative moment in his life, on a two-year voyage of (self) discovery; for us, the equivalent was our long-term fieldwork of the 1960s in Saramaka. This summer we'd been on a month-and-a-half-long project, one that involved a very different level of commitment. But is it also possible, we wonder, that our relative coolness above the fray, at least in our own minds and as we've expressed it through this diary, reflects a difference between postmodernist and modernist sensibilities? More unanswered questions.

10:30: to the BPE to deliver the rum, film, file cards, and other field supplies that are to be held there for our 1991 mission. Mme C gives Rich an envelope with 16,000-some-odd francs to reimburse us for money we'd advanced for Saramaka objects, gasoline, and various other mission expenses. Our Air France tickets have been changed from Saturday afternoon to early morning with no explanation. We phone Martinique to arrange to be picked up at the airport.

Brief meeting with La Directrice, who asks us to come by the BPE tomorrow morning so we can walk together to the meeting with the bureaucrat about translating subsidies. Le Conseiller takes us aside to say that he's talked with La Directrice about our non-salaried

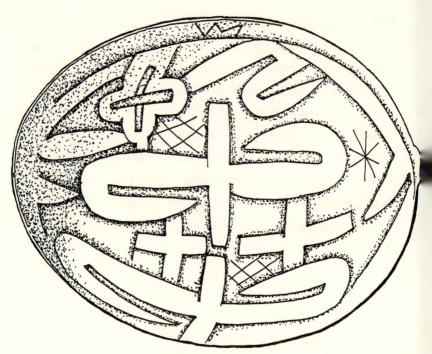

Calabash bowl carved by the late Ma Alelia, bought August 14 in Kotika

status, and that she was very surprised; she had not known what our situation was, she told him. Presumably, she'll bring it up with us before we leave. Said good-bye to Le Conseiller, who's taking off for Paris this afternoon; exchange promises to see each other in Paris during our visit there in October/November. La Directrice tells us to plan on spending the morning with her on Friday. Then off to a half-hour meeting with MC, *économiste de la santé*, who's a real enthusiast about research in Guyane and would like to involve more outsiders. He gave us, and our students, an open invitation to apply for small research grants, several thousand dollars each, on almost any subject. Says he'll visit us in Martinique, where he goes often to see relatives.

Lunch in the Sranan Mini-Restaurant, our favorite place to eat in all Cayenne. A hole-in-the-wall near the market, owned by a Paramaribo Javanese woman who employs young Saramaka men as cooks-cum-waiters. Meals are Suriname-style, with lots of hot-pepper paste on the side. The clientele is varied but there are usually urban Surinamers around, who listen in on our Saramaccan interactions with the staff in amusement or suspicion. We avoid talking about the civil war until we're alone with the head cook, who takes us down an adjoining alley into the cramped room he shares with his teenage Saramaka wife and newborn baby.

Walked through the market, feeling too tired and sick to make a positive decision about cooking for dinner. Back to the apartment for a change of clothes and then off to Kourou to see our friends there. As we drove in, some young men and women loudly called out Rich's name: "Lisáti!" and surrounded the car. Turned out to be people who were little kids in Dángogó when we made our first trip to Saramaka. Lots of excitement. Amômbebúka had gone to Para-maribo, so we went directly to the area where the men who helped us with our folktale book live. Long and extremely warm visit with Antonísi, who offered us beers from his refrigerator, thanked us profusely for the record we had left for him on our last visit to Kourou

Not long ago, we had the occasion to visit some old friends in the so-called "Village Saramaka" at Kourou. Living in mean little shacks almost in the shadow of the Ariane rocket, these immigrant workers continue to supply much of the manual labor at the missile base. We accompanied a woman (who had been our neighbor twenty years earlier in Dángogó) on what she called "a little trip to her provision-ground"; entering the small supermarket nearby, barefoot and barebreasted, she selected her groceries — a frozen chicken from Brittany (with labels in French and Arabic), a tin of sardines from Nantes, some Parisian candies for the kids. The next day, back in Cayenne, we were invited by colleagues from ORSTOM [the major French scientific research organization in Guyane] to a posh restaurant where, under a set-piece "tropical" thatch roof, we drank fine wines from the metropole and ate delicious stews of monkey, armadillo, and tapir — all everyday foods of Saramakas back home in Suriname.

— R. and S. Price, "Working for The Man," p. 199

(when he was absent), and called his new young wife into the house, telling her not to be distant or taciturn, these were close friends. Her demeanor—shy, coy, knees modestly covered with a cloth—reminded us of women in villages on the Pikílio decades ago. Antonísi mentioned that he would soon leave for his vacation, spending a month in Suriname to visit his mother and other relatives.

We told him in detail about the museum project, our collecting in Aluku, and the trip coming up next summer in Ndjuka. We talked about how the war in Suriname posed problems for our collecting in Saramaka. Reminded him that we'd seen three beautiful objects carved by Sêkêtima (arguably, the greatest twentieth-century carver in Saramaka) as presents for Antonísi's grandmother, Ansebúka. We knew that Antonísi's mother, Kabuési, a close friend of ours in Dángogó, had inherited these things when Ansebúka died in 1968. We said we didn't know whether she still had them and whether she might be willing to part with one or more of them for the museum. If she wanted to keep them, we certainly wouldn't press. But if she'd like to sell under those circumstances, the museum would be able to pay a price appropriate to their special beauty.

Antonísi asked whether we wanted one or all of them. We told him we imagined a price of 2,500F for the round tray, and perhaps 6,000F if she wanted to sell all three. But that she should do exactly what she wanted, including giving a blanket no to the whole idea of selling. Knowing Kabuési, we have confidence that she won't do anything she doesn't want to do. Antonísi reminded us that he and his brother Sinêli are Kabuési's only heirs, and volunteered that for his part, he thought it might be better for the objects to be on display in a museum than for them to sit in a closed house in Saramaka. We also mentioned our interest in textiles, other kinds of wooden objects, and so on, and he said he'd see if he could come back with several things from which we could choose.

For the second time in two days, we worry about delegating responsibility, and perhaps losing control of the collecting encounter.

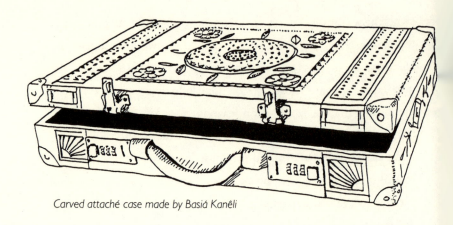

Carved attaché case made by Basiá Kanêli

We tend to think that our long-term relationship with Antonísi (and with Kabuési) makes a difference; this isn't just another transaction between collector and native. In 1968, Antonísi's four-year-old brother, a child weakened by sickle-cell anemia, died in our arms of multiple bee-bites while Kabuési was cutting rice in her garden. We've been through a lot together. We believe that our dealings with Kabuési—including this incipient one that would pass through Antonísi—are those of real friends.

Antonísi told us that he'd heard, from a recent traveler, that Boiko was in Paramaribo. After having been stuck in Saramaka for months, he was apparently on his way toward Ndjuka with some others when government soldiers ran into them and fired on them. Boiko managed to get away and escape to Paramaribo—the very city he'd been afraid of setting foot in—but he lost everything he owned and arrived with only the clothes on his back. He's now visiting embassies, slipping through the streets under cover of darkness, trying to replace his passport, air tickets, and other missing documents, as well as some money, so he can travel back to Baltimore.

Leaving Antonísi, we stopped by at the Village Saramaka's main woodcarving atelier, a large open shed crammed and hung all over with armadillos, umbrellas, maps of French Guiana, carafes, plaques, and paddles—all in hastily incised cedar and, to our eyes, rather ugly. Talked with the men and boys sitting there. Sally was hauled off as a Saramaccan-speaking curiosity by a bunch of women, but managed to return after ten minutes or so. In the jumble of tourist carvings, our eyes were caught by something we'd never seen—a handsome, cedar attaché case, sculpted à la Saramaka, varnished, and fitted with two combination locks in brass. A second, less spectacular one, hung nearby. We bought the nicer one, bargaining like tourists (except that we were speaking Saramaccan) and knocking the price from 900F to 700F. Why? Collected data on the artist, who was away in Paramaribo, for museum documentation. Turns out to be a recent invention by Basiá Kanêli from the village of Dan, who

JJ: Then what's it all for? What I mean is that, later on, perhaps we'll make the same judgment about the kind of anthropology that's being done today.

ML: I know. In terms of writing, which is the only activity that I indulge in these days, I've come to think that it's a kind of drug. Well, there's no sense to drugs. And yet one becomes incredibly dependent on them, and then it's not possible to do without them.

JJ: Wouldn't you say that with such a drug, if you will, one can have insights into reality?

ML: Do you mean literature?

JJ: Yes.

ML: Like any other drug. Just ask an addict. He'll tell you that when he's under the influence of his toxicant, he enjoys an extraordinary lucidity.

made the first one a couple of years ago in Paramaribo. Hot, boring ride through the savannahs back to Cayenne. We're both feeling draggy with wicked sore throats.

On the way in, we stop at Kalusé's. We've just missed him, his wife tells us, but he'll be back in an hour. Then on to AO's, who's also away from home, but shows up while we're writing him a note to say we've stopped by. Leisurely visit; we commiserate about his friend Michotte's death, discuss the museum, Saramaka-carved attaché cases and their possible commercialization, the current state of Aluku culture, and fine points of calabash cultivation, which AO engages in with seriousness. He invites us to dine with him on Friday at noon. On again to Kalusé's but he's still away; we promise to come by tomorrow night. Back to the apartment, made up some packaged soup and Chinese greens. More depressing war news on the radio. To bed, exhausted, at nine.

THURSDAY 23/VIII/90

Tea and bread, as usual. A couple of hours of intense writing. Sometimes we ask ourselves why we are forcing ourselves to write with such doggedness. What's the point?

Off to the BPE, bearing the several items of tourist art collected over the past few days. La Directrice is delighted at the varnished attaché case and admires the rest. All sweetness and light for a half-hour of chit-chat, while we wait for the appointment with the bureaucrat. Phone conversation with the secretary of LS — Regional Counselor, Committee-on-Culture President, and, as government veterinarian, Head Inspector of Guyanais Meat — who invites us to lunch tomorrow. Sally says we're to eat with AO, but the secretary knows this small world well enough to say she'll arrange for everyone to lunch together, including La Directrice. We instruct Mlle Z to load the whole collection into trunks so we can transport it at noon

JJ: But an addict takes drugs for himself. He doesn't exhibit himself, much less read.

ML: I grant that there's a very big difference. But then I ask myself whether, when one writes and publishes, one isn't simply an addict afflicted with vanity.

JJ: Leaving that aside, do you think you have a message to transmit?

ML: No, I don't think I do.

JJ: In that case, why do you write and who do you write for?

ML: I've already told you. It's like a drug.

JJ: But if, after all your writing and publishing, no one was responsive, if what you wrote left people indifferent—

ML: I would be very disappointed.

JJ: Would you continue to write?

ML: Yes, of course. And I would think of the possibility of receiving recognition later on. I might think about posterity.

SP: When I read *L'Afrique Fantôme*, I often found myself wondering who you were writing for. There were moments when I had the impression that you were doing it really for yourself, and then others—

ML: Essentially I wrote it for myself. I believe I've already mentioned that it was an experimental book. I'd had my fill of literature, especially surrealism; I'd had more than I could take of Western civilization. I wanted to see what would result when I forced myself to record virtually everything that happened around me and everything that went through my head. That was essentially the idea behind *L'Afrique Fantôme*.

SP: How did Marcel Griaule react? Did you show it to him?

ML: At one point I was going to show him the proofs, but I admit that I didn't do it—though I had said I would—because I could see, given the way he was behaving, that he was a completely different kind of person from me and that, being opposed to the spirit of the book in spite of our *camaraderie*, he would have asked me to cut it in ways that I wasn't willing to accept. So I decided not to show him the proofs. He was absolutely furious when the book came out; he felt that I had compromised future field studies, and so forth. . . .

JJ: What did Mauss think of this "travel log" approach?

ML: He reprimanded me, in a fatherly, good natured way; but he was not approving.

JJ: And Rivet?

ML: I think I've already told you about that. In order not to damage my image of him as a man of distinction and a perfect liberal, he quibbled

to the Annex. Off, with La Directrice, for the two-block walk to the bureaucrat's office at the Conseil Régional.

During last year's visit to Cayenne, some fifteen months ago, we were present at a wild and woolly meeting of the bureaucrat's committee, "Sur les traces de Boni," which had been convened to discuss the use of its publications budget. That meeting set the stage for today's encounter. Various of the participants had agitated for their own pet titles—by local amateur linguists, by European scholars who'd visited on lecture tours, by some of the people present at the meeting, and so on. Supporting documentation was passed out around the conference table—a diverse set of budgets, proposals, summaries of grouped proposals, and bibliographies of publications-to-be. We quickly understood that the correctness of details was not of primary concern; authors' names were garbled in the documents (Hoogbergen becoming Hoogreergem, etc.) and ethnic groups merged indiscriminately in the discussion. As various people put forward competing nominations for the generous budget available for translation and publication support, some of the debate had slipped beyond the bounds of collegial discussion and become quite heated. The plight of a locally-produced type-script dictionary giving lexical correspondences between French and a language it designated as "Taki-Taki" (for which the ethnic identity of the native speakers was the subject of confused debate), compiled with a maximum of devotion and something less than a minimum of linguistic competence, provided the dramatic climax of the meeting. One committee member, a close friend of the would-be lexicographer, got so hot under the collar that he stomped out of the meeting, shouting behind him in a voice halfway between a whine and a menace, that the shortcomings of this author's scholarship were no reason to treat the man with such blatant disrespect, and that the committee should be ashamed of its uncivil behavior toward a well-meaning and hard-working and supremely decent human being.

about questions of pure form, pointing out errors in French or bringing up that business I had mentioned in the course of reporting a
dream (completely forgetting that it came from a dream) about the
Hudson Bay being located in New York, and also my use of the
verb *recoller* instead of *récoler* ["to stick back together" and "to check
over," respectively]. I really wasn't pleased at all by that; I would
have preferred him to be straight with me, the way Mauss was. But
my relationship with Griaule was the only one that was spoiled by
L'Afrique Fantôme.

    — S. Price and Jamin, "A conversation with Michel Leiris," pp.
    170–71

As the discussion veered from one topic to another, varying degrees of formal approval for translation subsidies came and went for almost every proposition, including four of our own books, though no one present seemed clear about exactly which was which or what was what. Almost no mention was made of the actual contents of any of the books, and we saw no evidence that anyone had actually read any of the works being considered. Nor was there any sign of a person who had a realistic idea, even a rough one, of the time and cost involved in the publication of a book. The one project that did seem to receive unanimous approval was a request for 70,000F to translate a sixty-two-page typescript by a Dutch scholar who had visited Cayenne earlier in the year and had made friends with several members of the committee; somewhat taken aback by the page/price ratio, we later calculated that it worked out to $226 per typed double-spaced page, or, as the proposal itself specified, just under a dollar per word, counting every "if," "and," and "but."

In the subsequent months while at Stanford, we attempted to follow up on this surrealistic experience through several concise and cordial letters to the bureaucrat, inquiring about the committee's final decisions. We had not been successful in eliciting a response of any kind. And each of the several times we had attempted to speak with her by phone, she was said to be "away from the office," "traveling," "in a meeting," or "on another line." We began to entertain visions of the Wizard of Oz.

By the time we arrived in Cayenne for our collecting mission, more than a year had passed and we had essentially written off the whole idea. But here we are again, in the elegant, wood-panelled Meeting Room of the Conseil Régional, and the circus springs immediately back to life. The bureaucrat begins with a perfunctory apology for not having been in touch; it's been a busy year. In any case, all we need to know is that her committee has approved 100,000F for the publication of our books in French. Then she announces that the subject of today's meeting is the translation of

Fonctionnaires [bureaucrats]: Their number is incredible. . . . In place of action or accepting responsibility, they prefer "the rules." So it makes no sense to ask them to exercise their own judgment or will. They do not like to make decisions. They refuse to take any initiative. Something essential is missing: the human touch. They recoil from any problem that requires a quick resolution, since it means they would have to take some initiative. . . .

Guyanais public opinion, I would add, has to date ignored this state of affairs. . . . Yet nowhere has this epidemic of bureaucrats spread with such virulence and destruction as in this land of Guyane.

— Damas, *Retour de Guyane*, p. 113

Maroon Societies and *First-Time;* while we had proposed 80,000F and 60,000F, respectively, for the two books discussed a year ago, the Conseil, she tells us, voted instead 60,000F and 40,000F. She is, it turns out, oblivious to her committee's decision of recent months (communicated to us informally by two of its members) to translate our 1980 art book, and perhaps Stedman's *Narrative,* instead of the two titles originally under discussion. We mention this late-breaking development, citing the authority of DM (who seems to be the chairman of this committee); La Directrice confirms the news. The bureaucrat bats not an eyelash; she handles the shift with ease by changing the subject to say she's heard we made quite a collection for the museum. At which La Directrice smiles broadly with satisfaction.

Now that we're all focused conveniently on the same book (*Afro-American Arts of the Suriname Rain Forest*), the bureaucrat asks how much it will cost. We report that after consultation with Le Conseiller the other day, we've arrived at a price tag of 120,000F (80K for the translator, 40K for a subsidy to the publisher). She raises her eyebrows in alarm, commenting that it seems awfully high, given that "English is [classified by the French translating regulations as] an easy language, not like Dutch." But when we reinvoke Le Conseiller's authority, she quickly acquiesces and, rather than taking the time for calculating the rate or engaging in discussion, simply ups her budget with a flick of her pen, pointing out that they do have plenty of money to spend, but must be sure to spend it wisely. "But how long will it take?" she asks, perhaps realizing that she's lost a year by not answering our letters. We estimate a year for translation and another for publication. "It takes that long to make a book?" she gasps. We: "Yes indeed." "But we've got to have a publication in 1991," she and La Directrice reply, almost in unison. (So the committee will look like it's doing something, we both understand them to be saying.) "How about doing *First-Time* right away, then?" the bureaucrat queries, since she's been told that a translation has already been completed. Great, we say, but

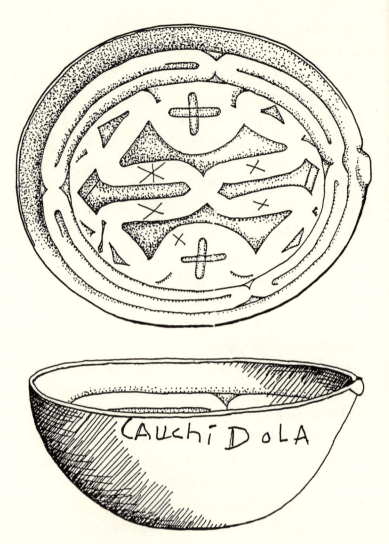

A calabash bowl carved by Ma Do (Couachi [sometimes Cauchi] Dola)
[See page 219]

it would still need a publication subsidy. She says the 40,000F voted earlier in the year could still be made available. In fact, she says, building enthusiasm, any publisher who could really bring it out in 1991 would be welcome to make the committee a proposition for, say, double that amount. They'll hold a meeting on September 10 with the whole committee to confirm all this and let us know before we set off for a projected trip to Europe in mid-October. We'll see.

The bureaucrat seems confused about which of our various books do or don't deal with matters Aluku, which is supposed to be the major criterion in her decision-making. We argue that the art book already treats Aluku in proportion to its population within the broader Maroon world (which is relatively minor) and that we're also willing to add a special Aluku chapter, illustrating the new museum collection, for this edition. We do not allude to the fact that *First-Time* never even mentions the Aluku. (Its passage through this committee depended on some remarks made by DM last year about the way it treats oral and written Maroon history.) In spite of all the confusion, we're pleased with the results (fingers crossed that they're not just another smokescreen), relieved not to have to worry about the complexities of seeing the multi-authored and multi-lingual texts of a *Maroon Societies* edition through the press, pleased that the art book can be used as part of the larger museum plan, and happy that the French version of *First-Time* (which we translated with a friend in Martinique before we went to Stanford) may yet see the light of Parisian/Guyanais day. The bureaucrat asks, by the by, if we have any copies of our art book she could buy as gifts for friends, and expresses amazement at the low (authors') price we quote. Indeed, she displays greater enthusiasm at the prospect of two or three low-priced art books for personal gift-giving than she had at working out publication commitments for the committee.

Back to the BPE to move the collection to the Annex. Mlle Z hasn't lifted a finger in our absence. La Directrice takes us all downstairs to load the trunks. Pulling out some wads of crumpled newspaper

Despite the multiple attempts since 1988 to arrive at a peaceful settlement, this has not yet happened. The civil war has had disastrous consequences, especially in the interior of the country. Hundreds of people have died, villages have been destroyed, and thousands have fled their home territories. Life among the Maroons has been thoroughly disrupted and traditional authority severely undermined. Furthermore, these societies have been saddled with a major drug problem among their youth.

— Scholtens, Wekker, et al., *Gaama Duumi, Buta Gaama*

to cushion the objects for their cross-town trip, we find a number of calabashes that had been overlooked in Mlle Z's unpacking of a previous collection. La Directrice looks distinctly displeased at the casualness of Mlle Z's reaction. La Directrice accompanies us as we transport everything to the Annex and unload it onto shelves. We agree with her that her storage space is going to run out quickly; in fact the Aluku collection alone will fill the space she's allowed for the whole Maroon collection. Before we leave, La Directrice hands a disgruntled Mlle Z the two-kilo bag of limes that she has purchased at the market that morning, with instructions to get busy cleaning the wood and calabashes we've collected. This is the second time that she has gone to Mme C, asked whether limes weren't 10F per kilo, formally received the amount from the petty cash box, driven to the market, made the purchase, and delivered the merchandise to a belligerent-looking Mlle Z for conservatorial use.

The two of us eat a quiet Chinese lunch and return to the apartment, where we write up notes all afternoon long. 7 PM visit to Kalusé's. Pleasant. He says he's about to go off to Paramaribo for a visit; there are still planes several times a week. We drink beer and watch the TV news about Kuwait-Iraq. First time we've seen pictures of the military buildup, the embassies being encircled by tanks, etc. Scary. The two videos he'd promised us of the Chiefs' funerals, which he said cost him 450F to have made, turned out to be faulty—sound but no picture, so we pay and ask him to have them redone for our return next year. Kalusé says the Suriname army has reached Djumu and that the Jungle Commandos have retreated into the forest. Saramakas have accompanied the soldiers upriver, "tying angúla" in support. Angúla, he reminds us, is a cloth tied around the waist when helping out with ritual work; here, it signals a readiness to join in and help out in a cause. Their idea, which Kalusé approves, is that the river belongs to Saramakas, not Ndjukas (who constitute the core of the JCs). Earlier, he and everyone else in Saramaka had supported Ronnie Brunswijk, but recently—since the Jungles have

Mandó's finished peanut-grinding board

beaten and stolen from Seemá (a storekeeper from the Pikílio) and pillaged elsewhere—they've withdrawn their support. "We helped them," he says, "and now in return they've been bullying the very people who fought on their side." Four bodies, he says, have been seen floating in the Suriname River, near Paramaribo, these past few days—all Saramakas, all men. Paramaribo itself is a disaster; even the telephones into Suriname no longer work, and to phone out, you have to go to one of the two working booths outside the post office between 1 AM and 4 AM, when there are only two possible destinations: the U.S. or Brazil. Otherwise, no outgoing long distance. And there's still nothing in the stores, no medicine in the hospitals. We say an affectionate goodbye, till next year.

We decide to try to talk to Boiko in Paramaribo, by calling his sister, but the phone lines to Suriname are in fact down—no one knows for how long. Take-out Chinese food, more war news, and to bed, both still feeling sick.

FRIDAY 24/VIII/90

Woke up to find hundreds of tiny ants in the croissants we'd bought last night as a treat for today's breakfast. Made do with tea. Off to see Mandó who was working on a peanut-grinding board that holds promise of real beauty. His co-worker Zivêti was carving a handsome round tray. We brought up the question of price. Lots of hesitation. Despite their extensive commercial experience, they're unsure how to price non-tourist carvings. After some discussion, we arrive at 800F for each. Then we talked about the canoe. We said we'd leave 1,000F as an advance but didn't know what the total should be. Discussion of current Suriname River prices, what we paid in Aluku, how canoe prices have changed over the years. Mandó finally suggested 5,000F and we let him know by a thoughtful silence it was on the high side. We played for a moment with the idea of taking

In these terms, are tourist Nikons worse than "Disappearing Worlds"? Is Riefenstahl [*The Last of the Nuba*] "worse" than Faris [*Nuba Personal Art*]? Is "60 Minutes" (or "20/20") "worse" than PBS and National Geographic? In the view here, all the parties listed have more in common than they have differences. Their differences are items of Western political disagreements, but their commonality *vis-a-vis* the subaltern is in fundamental ways uniform.

> — James C. Faris, "A Political Primer on Anthropology/
> Photography" (1992)

a bit off and then said we'd go ahead and pay what he asked. More conversation about the canoe—whether it would remain blackened from the fire used to "open" the dugout, like a standard Saramaka canoe (we said yes), whether it would have built-up gunwales, like some modern canoes (we said no)—and then Mandó, apparently still thinking about the price, announced that he was going to make a nice woman's paddle with it as well. After all, he said, when you make a boat for a wife, you always make a paddle to go with it. It was a nice gesture. We gave them careful instructions about how to get to the BPE to deliver the tray and peanut board next week, and get paid. As we were about to leave, they asked whether we still wanted the Ariane—which had slipped our minds. We said sure, and a youngster went to fetch it. A beauty—tall with its boosters attached and poised phallicly, dominating a wooden map of Guyane. Made by a nineteen-year old, it was 250F.

Then on to the BPE for our last business meeting with La Directrice. (It doesn't look as if there's going to be time to talk seriously about the fundamental form and mission of the future museum, at least this trip.) Deposited the final few fiches, left instructions for the two commissions, settled accounts with La Directrice (who liked the rocket), and went down our respective lists of business to discuss. La Directrice asked us about photographs and was understanding when we described Maroon reluctance at being photographed by strangers; we didn't discuss our ever-increasing intellectual and personal unease about field photography more generally (except, perhaps, in the context of long-term personal relations). She brought up the subject of a Mission Report and we told her we needed a better idea of what she wanted. Could she show us, for example, a copy of one of her other field collector's reports from last year? She did, but prefaced it by stressing that in her mind it didn't represent a model to be followed. Why?, we asked. She said she was interested less in mechanical lists of places visited and objects collected, which she herself could reconstruct from the fiches, than in

Which is the more poignant in this respect: Susan Sontag's notion that in *capturing* reality through photography, the thing thus represented is all the more irretrievably lost, or Michel Foucault's notion that the modern sciences of society and of the person depend upon a clinical way of seeing that comes close in order to distance itself in the orbit of control? These are the same eyes that put Huitoto baskets and blowpipes in museums and are taught to look at them as data in locked glass cases.

     — Taussig, *Shamanism, Colonialism, and the Wild Man*, p. 113

Peanut-grinding board carved by the late Da Malo, a Ndjuka, collected in Kotika

thoughtful reflections about the collecting process that might be helpful for future missions. She wanted something deeper, not just pages of formalities. We told her of the article we had been invited to write for a special issue of the *American Anthropologist* devoted to "cultural property" and suggested we could send her a draft in English, framed fore and aft in French by the more technical details of the Mission. She was supportive and emphasized that she wasn't posing a deadline because she'd rather have it done reflectively than simply done on time.

She then asked if we would contribute an article to *Version Guyane*, a glossy photo magazine. Rich used this opportunity as a way of raising the issue of our free-lance status, in contrast to the Grenands, etc. Le Conseiller had mentioned this to her in passing, she said, but she hadn't really understood our situation. So, we told her how we had left regular jobs and institutional affiliations several years ago and had since earned our livelihood through writing and short-term contracts—both by teaching, as at Stanford last year, and with museums or other research organizations. Our contribution to the project this year—our five weeks of time in Guyane plus preparation time and report-writing time, as well as the *petits matériaux* that she had asked us to contribute and which had been out-of-pocket expenses for Ken and us, were personal and uncompensated; we received no salary or institutional support for the project; our own expenses—including medical insurance, etc., etc.—were paid directly by us. She made clear she would try her best to see how things might be worked out differently in the future; she regretted not having known it earlier. "There's no problem that doesn't have some kind of solution," she mused, and we agreed. But she said she'd need time to think about it and we said that was fine. She mentioned her hopes for the Centre de Documentation that will be part of the Museum and especially asked for our help with that. We talked warmly about how we'd gotten to know each other during this stay, and extended an open invitation to visit us in Martinique

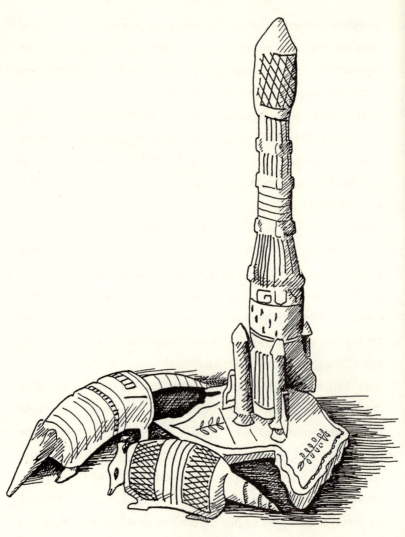

Tourist carvings: Ariane rocket made by Apindagoon and armadillos by Miseli and Elion, in Mandó's atelier

and consult our library. Back to our apartment to write notes, to meet again at 1:00 for lunch with LS and AO, in a restaurant described in Cayenne's Yellow Pages as "*ambiance feutré*" (read: quiet and classy, or: genteel and expensive).

3:50. Just back from a nearly-three-hour *déjeuner*. Even though the initiative was originally AO's, the rest of us (we, LS and his silent sidekick, plus La Directrice) had spent close to an hour *à table* before AO himself strolled in. A routine status play, reminiscent of La Directrice's delayed appearance to meet us when we first arrived at the airport.

LS, high-placed Chinese-Creole political figure, was clearly at home in the role of host, carefully seating the two ladies at the center of the table and taking responsibility for setting the tone of largesse. Cocktails were offered; LS quickly communicated to Sally the appropriateness of kir, while Rich was more or less assigned a gin-tonic and LS had scotch. LS tutoies men (Rich, AO), whom he treats as buddies, and vousvoies women (Sally, La Directrice), adopting with them the role of chivalrous patron; some of his comments about Alukus would sound about right to the Air Guyane lady in Maripasoula. LS is involved, as usual, in various development schemes. He felt out Rich about the idea of a large natural park (*réserve*) to the east of Aluku territory, a marriage of wild-life preservation and tourism. Rich didn't find it too awful an idea. LS then recounted his recent travels to Seattle, Miami, and San Francisco, expressing shock at the homeless he saw in this last.

An animated discussion about the possibility of hiring a designer to put the proper finishing touches on Saramaka-carved attaché cases, which AO and La Directrice were both enormously taken by, as a mini-development project for Guyane. LS, whose hobby, he tells us, is making scale models of things, had a plan involving plywood exteriors which Saramakas could carve. La Directrice marvels at the way Saramaka men can carve both for the market and for home use. We recount how Mandó told us this morning that as he was

A double-headed comb, carved pre-WW II, from Kotika

Here the ball continued till six o'clock in the morning, when we were all sent home to our lodgings in stately carriages, never once reflecting on the distressed situation of the poor soldier in the forest.

    — Stedman, *Narrative* (1790/1992), p. 166

The collecting ended very much in the same vein as it had begun. On the way back, our motor conked out between Apatou and Saint-Jean — a simple mechanical failure that could have easily been repaired on the spot had the BPE made sure that the boat was supplied with a few spare parts (such as spark plugs) — or better yet, a second motor for backup. With the entire remainder of the collection on board, we drifted around for a couple of hours, wondering whether any friendly boats (not to mention Jungles or government soldiers) might show up. Of course, no paddles had been provided (our original one had been removed in Maripasoula by an incensed *responsable* as the exclusive property of *La Commune*). So we

carving his peanut-grinding board for the BPE, he fantasized about the beautiful new wife it might be for, as a way of making it come out especially well. LS chimes in, "That makes perfect sense! When I buy a dress for 'Madame X,' it's always a lot nicer than the one I buy for my wife." AO ribs him a bit about the identity of "Madame X." Lots of joviality, culminating in questions about our year at Stanford, which we answered in part with a fanciful description of the liberated life of Californian hot-tubbers.

By that time enough wine had been poured so that everyone, including La Directrice, was much taken with the image of a nude woman—La Directrice, for example, suggests AO—being floated around a hot tub on her back (an image we'd plagiarized from a former Johns Hopkins colleague who'd been in California in the more free-wheeling seventies). "Frottée?" asks LS, thinking massage. "No! Flottée!" corrects La Directrice, restoring the hypothetical nude to her floating position. That's an image that's sure to come up again when next this slice of Cayenne society imbibes together.

We imagine that we're being presented now as La Directrice's people, and that this is figured in to her standing. It was an excellent, lavish meal à la française—easily $60 or $70 a head. (We feel very far away from Ken, who's still collecting in Maripasoula and, presumably, working away at the remaining stock of instant noodle soup.) At the conclusion, some jovial banter about sneaking out without paying, and then whether the men or the women were going to wash dishes to pay the bill. But LS slipped off to régler la note, and cordial good-byes were exchanged. In leaving, Sally asked LS, by the by, what had happened with the article that he had solicited from her over a year ago, and which she'd taken several days to write in French, for Nature Guyanaise, the ecology magazine edited by his faithful sidekick, who'd participated silently in the luncheon. He pleaded total ignorance of its reception in his office, and asked her to send off a new copy. Be sure it goes to me at the Service Vétérinaire, said he. What's the address? "Oh, LS, Service Vétérinaire,

paddled with enameled dishes to the nearest Ndjuka camp, which took another hour or two. That didn't help much, for all they had there was spark plugs that didn't work. We finally flagged down the first passing boat, which had only a 5 hp motor. I managed to bargain with the owner, and we towed him, using his motor, all the way to Saint-Jean at a snail's pace. You can imagine trying to find a ride from there to Saint-Laurent to go find Bwino and his station wagon.

     — Ken Bilby, letter of 14 May 1991

Thus, gentle reader, I have given thee a faithful history of my travels . . . wherein I have not been so studious of ornament as of truth. I could perhaps like others have astonished thee with strange improbable tales; but I rather chose to relate plain matter of fact in the simplest manner and style, because my principal design was to inform, and not to amuse thee. . . . I here take a final leave of my courteous readers, and return to enjoy my own speculations in my little garden.

     — Jonathan Swift, *Gulliver's Travels* (1726), Book IV, Chapter XII

Cayenne — That's more than sufficient." We'll see. Made a date half an hour later at AO's house to pick up calabash shoots to plant back in Martinique. All in all, a most convivial *déjeuner*.

5:30. Just back from AO's where we picked up not only calabash shoots he'd prepared, but baby *chataignes* (a chestnut-like sister of the breadfruit), and six varieties of Guyanese palms. La Directrice was there too; we spent an hour or so walking amidst AO's trees and chatting. We feel we've been partially accepted into a different and interesting Creole world. AO and La Directrice are like brother and sister in their interactions; they've grown up together in a very small social universe. We asked La Directrice to keep till next year two bottles of *rhum vieux* that we'd intended to take back to Martinique. That way there'll be room for the plants. La Directrice counsels us to hide them well, under newspaper, as they're illegal to import into Martinique. Warm goodbyes. Both AO and La Directrice promise they'll visit on their way through Martinique (to Paris, of course) in the coming months. Driving back to the apartment, we reflect again that our status as outsiders, more specifically non-*métropolitain* outsiders, is an asset as well as a drawback; not fitting automatically into ready-made, highly structured postcolonial roles permits certain degrees of freedom, some room to breathe.

Back at the apartment to pack and write these last notes for the manuscript that we're tentatively calling "Collecting Guyane." Or could it be, instead, in the end that Guyane has collected us?

References Cited

Andrade, Mário de. 1984. *Macunaíma*. New York: Random House (orig. 1928).

Anon. 1987. *Kourou: Ville en devenir*. Kourou: Le Point Hermes.

Asad, Talal. 1990. "Ethnography, Literature, and Politics: Some Readings and Uses of Salman Rushdie's *The Satanic Verses*." *Cultural Anthropology* 5:239–69.

Barthes, Roland. 1957. *Mythologies*. Paris: Éditions du Seuil.

Bettelheim, Judith, John Nunley, and Barbara Bridges. 1988. "Caribbean Festival Arts: An Introduction." In John W. Nunley and Judith Bettelheim, *Caribbean Festival Arts: Each and Every Bit of Difference*. Seattle: University of Washington Press, pp. 31–37.

Bilby, Kenneth M. 1990. "The Remaking of the Aluku: Culture, Politics, and Maroon Ethnicity in French South America." Unpublished Ph.D. dissertation, Johns Hopkins University.

Boon, James A. 1990. *Affinities and Extremes: Crisscrossing the Bittersweet Ethnology of East Indies History, Hindu-Balinese Culture, and Indo-European Allure*. Chicago: University of Chicago Press.

——. 1991. "Why Museums Make me Sad." In Ivan Karp and Steven D. Lavine (eds.), *Exhibiting Cultures: The Poetics and Politics of Museum Display*. Washington, D.C.: Smithsonian Institution Press, pp. 255–77.

Bourdieu, Pierre, and Alain Darbel. 1969. *L'Amour de l'art: Les musées d'art européens et leur publique*. Paris: Les Editions de Minuit.

Brana-Shute, Gary. 1991. "Suriname Tries Again." *Hemisphere* 4(1):33–35.

Buckley, Thomas, and Alma Gottlieb (eds.). 1988. *Blood Magic: The Anthropology of Menstruation*. Berkeley: University of California Press.

Carpenter, Edmund. 1972. *Oh, What a Blow that Phantom Gave Me!* New York: Holt, Rinehart and Winston.

——. 1976. "Collectors and Collections." *Natural History* 85(3):56–67.

Césaire, Aimé. 1955. *Discours sur le colonialisme*. Paris: Présence Africaine.

Chappell, Edward. 1989. "Museums." *The Nation*, 27 November, pp. 655–60.

Charrière, Henri. 1969. *Papillon*. Paris: Robert Laffont.

Chérubini, Bernard. 1988. *Cayenne: Ville créole et polyethnique*. Paris: Karthala.

Chatwin, Bruce. 1989. *Utz*. New York: Viking.

Clifford, James. 1988. *The Predicament of Culture: Twentieth-Century Ethnography, Literature, and Art*. Cambridge: Harvard University Press.

Cole, Douglas. 1985. *Captured Heritage: The Scramble for Northwest Coast Artifacts*. Seattle: University of Washington Press.

Collomb, Gérard. 1989. "La transmission d'un savoir anthropologique: Le Musée Régional de la Guyane." Unpublished manuscript.

Conrad, Joseph. 1902. "Heart of Darkness." In Morton Dauwen Zabel (ed.), *The Portable Conrad* (New York: Viking, 1965).

Contout, Auxence. 1987. *Langues et cultures guyanaises.* Cayenne: Imprimerie TRIMARG.

Conway, Sir Martin. 1914. *The Sport of Collecting.* London: Fisher Unwin.

Counter, S. Allen, Jr., and David L. Evans. 1981. *I Sought my Brother: An Afro-American Reunion.* Cambridge: MIT Press.

Damas, Léon-Gontran. 1938. *Retour de Guyane.* Paris: José Corti.

Davis, Hassoldt. 1952. *The Jungle and the Damned.* London: The Travel Book Club.

Dening, Greg. 1988. *History's Anthropology: The Death of William Gooch.* Lanham, MD: University Press of America.

Faris, James C. 1988. "'ART/artifact': On the Museum and Anthropology." *Current Anthropology* 29(5):775–79.

——. 1992. "A Political Primer on Anthropology/Photography." In Elizabeth Edwards (ed.), *Anthropology and Photography.* New Haven: Yale University Press.

Faust, Betty. 1991. "Collectors." *Anthropology Newsletter* 32(1):3.

Fischer, Michael M. J. 1989. "Museums and Festivals: Notes on the Poetics and Politics of Representation Conference, The Smithsonian Institution, September 26–28, 1988, Ivan Karp and Steven Levine (sic.), Organizers." *Cultural Anthropology* 4:204–21.

Franszoon, Adiante. 1989. "Crisis in the Backlands." *Hemisphere* 1(2):36–38.

French, Howard W. 1991. "Space Center or Not, Some Say It's Still a Jungle." *The New York Times,* 26 April, p. A4.

García Marquez, Gabriel. 1980. *In Evil Hour.* New York: Avon Books (orig. 1968).

Glissant, Edouard. 1980. *Le discours antillais.* Paris: Éditions du Seuil.

Greer, Germaine. 1971. *The Female Eunuch.* New York: McGraw-Hill.

Haraway, Donna. 1989. *Primate Visions: Gender, Race, and Nature in the World of Modern Science.* New York: Routledge.

Harriss, Joseph. 1976. *The Eiffel Tower.* London: Paul Elek.

Hearn, Lafcadio. 1923. *Two Years in the French West Indies.* New York: Harper & Bros. (orig. 1890).

Herskovits, Melville J., and Frances S. Herskovits. 1934. *Rebel Destiny: Among the Bush Negroes of Dutch Guiana.* New York: McGraw-Hill.

Hublin, A. 1987. "La proletarisation de l'habitat des Noirs Réfugiés Marrons de Guyane Française." Unpublished manuscript.

Hulme, Peter. 1990. "The Rhetoric of Description: The Amerindians of the Caribbean within Modern European Discourse." *Caribbean Studies* 23(3/4):35–49.

——. 1990. "Tales of distinction: European ethnography and the Caribbean." Unpublished manuscript.

Hurault, Jean. 1965. *La vie matérielle des Noirs Réfugiés Boni et des Indiens Wayana du Haut-Maroni (Guyane Française): Agriculture, économie et habitat.* Paris: ORSTOM.

——. 1972. *Français et Indiens en Guyane.* Paris: Union Générale d'Éditions.

——. 1980. "Analyse comparative d'ouvrages sur les Noirs Réfugiés de Guyane: Saramaka et Aluku (Boni)." *L'Homme* 20:119–27.

Instructions Sommaires. 1931. *Instructions sommaires pour les collecteurs d'objets ethnographiques.* Paris: Musée d'Ethnographie et Mission Scientifique Dakar-Djibouti. (Our copy of this pamphlet is marked in handwriting: "Conçue par Marcel Griaule, rédigée par Michel Leiris, à partir des notes de cours de Marcel Mauss.")

Jacknis, Ira. 1991. "George Hunt, Collector of Indian Specimens." In Aldona Jonaitis (ed.), *Chiefly Feasts: The Enduring Kwakiutl Potlatch.* New York: American Museum of Natural History; Seattle: University of Washington Press, pp. 177–224.

Jackson, Bruce. 1990. "The Perfect Informant." *Journal of American Folklore* 103:400–16.

Jolivet, Marie-José. 1982. *La question créole: Essai de sociologie sur la Guyane Française.* Paris: Editions de l'ORSTOM.

Kahn, Morton C. 1931. *Djuka: The Bush Negroes of Dutch Guiana.* New York: Viking.

Kamer, Henri. 1974. "The Authenticity of African Sculptures." *Arts d'Afrique Noire* 12:17–40.

Kesteloot, Lilyan. 1974. *Black Writers in French.* Philadelphia: Temple University Press.

Kirshenblatt-Gimblett, Barbara. 1991. "Objects of Ethnography." In Ivan Karp and Steven D. Lavine (eds.), *Exhibiting Cultures: The Poetics and Politics of Museum Display.* Washington, D.C.: Smithsonian Institution Press, pp. 386–443.

Kundera, Milan. 1981. *The Book of Laughter and Forgetting.* New York: Viking Penguin.

Larsen, Henry, and May Pellaton. 1958. *Behind the Lianas: Exploration in French Guiana.* Edinburgh: Oliver and Boyd.

Leclerc, Annie. 1974. *Parole de femme.* Paris: Grasset.

Leiris, Michel. 1981. *L'Afrique fantôme.* Paris: Éditions Gallimard (orig. 1934).

——. 1969. "Race et civilisation." In M. Leiris, *Cinq études d'ethnologie* (Paris: Éditions Gonthier) (orig. 1951).

Lévi-Strauss, Claude. 1955. *Tristes tropiques.* Paris: Plon.

——. 1966. "Anthropology: Its Achievement and Future." *Current Anthropology* 7:124–27

Lipset, David. 1980. *Gregory Bateson: The Legacy of a Scientist.* Englewood Cliffs: Prentice Hall.

Londres, Albert. 1923. *Au bagne.* Paris: Albin Michel.

MacCannell, Dean. 1990. "Cannibal Tours." *Society for Visual Anthropology Review* 6(2):14–24.

Mack, John. 1990. *Emil Torday and the Art of the Congo, 1900–1909.* Seattle: University of Washington Press.

Martin, Emily. 1987. *The Woman in the Body: A Cultural Analysis of Reproduction.* Boston: Beacon Press.

Métraux, Alfred. 1978. *Itinéraires 1 (1935–1953): Carnets de notes et journaux de voyage.* Paris: Payot.

Michelot, Jean-Claude. 1981. *La guillotine sèche: Histoire du bagne de Cayenne.* Paris: Fayard.

Miles, Alexander. 1988. *Devil's Island: Colony of the Damned.* Berkeley: Ten Speed Press.

Miller, Christopher L. 1985. *Blank Darkness: Africanist Discourse in French.* Chicago: University of Chicago Press.

Parépou, Alfred. 1885. *Atipa (roman guyanais).* Paris: A. Ghio. (reprint Paris: l'Harmattan, 1987).

Pierre, Michel. 1982. *La terre de la grande punition: Histoire des bagnes de Guyane.* Paris: Ramsay.

Polimé, Thomas. 1988. "Berichten van de Vluchtelingen." In T. S. Polimé and H. U. E. Thoden van Velzen, *Vluchtelingen, Opstandelingen en Andere Bosnegers van Oost-Suriname, 1986–1988.* Utrecht: Instituut voor Culturele Antropologie, pp. 32–73.

Price, Richard. 1983. *First-Time: The Historical Vision of An Afro-American People.* Baltimore: Johns Hopkins University Press.

——. 1990. *Alabi's World.* Baltimore: Johns Hopkins University Press.

Price, Richard, and Sally Price. 1989. "Working for the Man: A Saramaka Outlook on Kourou." *New West Indian Guide* 63:199–207.

——. 1991. *Two Evenings in Saramaka.* Chicago: University of Chicago Press.

Price, Sally. 1984. *Co-Wives and Calabashes.* Ann Arbor: University of Michigan Press.

——. 1989. *Primitive Art in Civilized Places.* Chicago: University of Chicago Press.

Price, Sally, and Jean Jamin. 1988. "A conversation with Michel Leiris." *Current Anthropology* 29:157–74.

Price, Sally, and Richard Price. 1980. *Afro-American Arts of the Suriname Rain Forest.* Berkeley: University of California Press.

Rabinow, Paul. 1977. *Reflections on Fieldwork in Morocco.* Berkeley: University of California Press.

Redfield, Peter. 1989. "The Natural Prison: French Guiana and the Penal Colony." Unpublished manuscript.

Resse, Alix. 1964. *Guyane française: Terre de l'espace.* Paris: Éditions Berger-Levrault.

Riemer, Johann Andreus. 1801. *Missions-Reise nach Suriname und Barbice.* Zittau and Leipzig.

Robbins, Warren M., and Nancy Ingram Nooter. 1989. *African Art in American Collections: Survey 1989.* Washington: Smithsonian Institution Press.

Rose, Dan. 1990. *Living the Ethnographic Life.* Newbury Park, CA: Sage Publications.

Rosenblum, Mort. 1979. *Coups and Earthquakes: Reporting the World for America.* New York: Harper and Row.

Royal Anthropological Institute of Great Britain and Ireland. 1951. *Notes and Queries on Anthropology.* London: Routledge & Kegan Paul. (1st edition 1874).

Rubin, William (ed.). 1984. *"Primitivism" in Twentieth Century Art: Affinity of the Tribal and the Modern*. New York: Museum of Modern Art.

Sanjek, Roger (ed.). 1990. *Fieldnotes: The Making of Anthropology*. Ithaca: Cornell University Press.

Sausse, André. 1951. *Populations primitives du Maroni (Guyane française)*. Paris: Institut Géographique National.

Schildkrout, Enid, and Curtis A. Keim. 1990. *African Reflections: Art from Northeastern Zaire*. Seattle: University of Washington Press.

Scholtens, Ben, Gloria Wekker, Laddy van Putten, and Stanley Dieko. 1992. *Gaama Duumi, Buta Gaama: Overlijden en Opvolging van Aboikoni, Grootopperhoofd van de Saramaka Bosnegers*. Paramaribo: Cultuurstudies/Vaco.

SEMAGU. 1988. "Musée des Arts et Traditions Populaires de Guyane: Programme technique détaillé." Unpublished manuscript.

Sokolov, Raymond A. 1974. "A Greenhorn's Tour of French Guiana's 'Green Hell.'" *The New York Times*, Sunday November 3, XX 1, 15.

Stedman, John Gabriel. 1790/1988. *Narrative of a Five Years Expedition Against the Revolted Negroes of Surinam*. Edited, with an introduction and notes, by Richard Price and Sally Price. Baltimore: Johns Hopkins University Press.

———. 1790/1992. *Stedman's Surinam: Life in an Eighteenth-Century Slave Society*. Edited by Richard Price and Sally Price. Baltimore: Johns Hopkins University Press.

Steiner, Christopher B. 1989. "Transnational Trajectories: The Circulation of African Art in the World Economy." Unpublished manuscript.

Swift, Jonathan. 1726. *Gulliver's Travels*. New York: Bantam Books (1962).

Taussig, Michael. 1987. *Shamanism, Colonialism, and the Wild Man: A Study in Terror and Healing*. Chicago: University of Chicago Press.

Thompson, Robert Farris. 1988. "Recapturing Heaven's Glamour: Afro-Caribbean Festivalizing Arts." In John W. Nunley and Judith Bettelheim, *Caribbean Festival Arts: Each and Every Bit of Difference*. Seattle: University of Washington Press, pp. 17–29.

Torgovnick, Marianna. 1990. *Gone Primitive: Savage Intellects, Modern Lives*. Chicago: University of Chicago Press.

Tripot, J. 1910. *La Guyane: Au pays de l'or, des forçats et des peaux-rouges*. Paris: Plon.

Vincent, Joan. 1991. "Engaging Historicism." In Richard G. Fox (ed.), *Recapturing Anthropology: Working in the Present*. Santa Fe: School of American Research Press.

Voltaire. 1963. *Candide ou l'optimisme*. Paris: Librairie Nizet (orig. 1759)